W9-DGH-670

THE ULTIMATE BOOK OF BUSINESS QUOTATIONS

THE
ULTIMATE
BOOK OF
BUSINESS
QUOTATIONS

Stuart Crainer

American Management Association

New York ● Atlanta ● Boston ● Chicago ● Kansas City ● San Francisco ● Washington, D.C.
● Brussels ● Mexico City ● Tokyo ● Toronto

This book is available at a special
discount when ordered in bulk quantities.
For information, contact Special Sales Department,
AMACOM, a division of American Management Association,
1601 Broadway, New York, NY 10019.

This publication is designed to provide accurate and authoritative
information in regard to the subject matter covered. It is sold with
the understanding that the publisher is not engaged in rendering legal, accounting, or other professional service. If legal advice or other
expert assistance is required, the services of a competent professional
person should be sought.

Library of Congress Cataloging-in-Publication Data

The ultimate book of business quotations / Stuart Crainer, editor.
    p.   cm.
  Includes index.
  ISBN 0-8144-0447-2
  1. Business—Quotations, maxims, etc. I. Crainer, Stuart.
PN6084.B87U58   1998
650—dc21   97-53258
                                               CIP

© 1998 Stuart Crainer
All rights reserved.
Printed in the United States of America.

Published in North America by arrangement with Capstone Publishing Limited, Oxford, United Kingdom.

This publication may not be reproduced,
stored in a retrieval system,
or transmitted in whole or in part,
in any form or by any means, electronic,
mechanical, photocopying, recording, or otherwise.
without the prior written permission of AMACOM,
a division of American Management Association,
1601 Broadway, New York, NY 10019.

Printing number

10 9 8 7 6 5 4 3 2 1

CONTENTS

*I*NTRODUCTION

The worlds of books and business are unlikely bedfellows. But, strangely, bedfellows they are. The business world is one where books still count – and not just the balancing of them. A best-selling business book can change the way millions of people do their jobs. It does not necessarily *improve* the way they do their jobs, but it does change it.

In the early 1990s, managers rushed to join the latest in a long line of fashionable bandwagons. This one was labelled 'reengineering.' Before long, companies in Idaho, India and Ipswich were reengineering themselves. And all because of a book. Of course, reengineering will not go down in history as a seismic event – unless you happened to live in Idaho where it was deemed to be hip and happening. It broke up companies rather than atoms. It was not important, but it was proof – yet again – that in business, books matter. In no other profession do the latest books and the ideas they contain change things so quickly. (Perhaps, cynics might say, no other profession has such a need to change.) Lawyers, clerics, engineers and doctors do not rush out to buy the latest outpourings of a California expert in their fields and then proceed to totally change the way they do their jobs. For that we can be thankful.

Books are influential in business, but that does not mean they are literary masterpieces. Indeed, stuffed with unpronounceable jargon and ludicrous acronyms, there is a lot of dross. For the optimist, the great thing about most mountains of rubbish is that somewhere, somehow, there are pearls of wisdom, classic phrases and wonders of wit. This book set out to discover the nuggets and to hold them up gleaming in the light. In this quest, I followed a few basic principles. First, quotes which include business jargon were gratuitously ignored. I thumbed my nose at strategic interfaces and cast a single digit in the air at the very mention of core competencies. This was highly satisfying.

My second rule was that businesspeople, consultants, academics and management gurus are not always the best sources of pithy, memorable phrases. The views of Groucho Marx, Jerry Garcia, Mark Twain and a ragbag of others with opinions were pored over. (Voltaire only just made it following a single ill-judged comment two hundred years ago – 'A witty saying proves nothing.')

The third rule was to keep the quotes short. The best lines are snappy. Lengthy dissertations on marketing are notable by their absence.

The end result proves, I hope, that though the business world may not be inhabited by great literary writers, it has other advantages. All life is there. The subjects covered in this book are diverse – everything from strategy to money, speeches to office politics. The range of people quoted is also vast. Business is something everyone has a view on or is involved in because, for better or worse, it touches the lives of everyone.

Stuart Crainer

Acknowledgments

A number of people have helped this book along the way from idea to finished product. Many of the quotes are drawn from interviews I have conducted over recent years, so thanks are due to those who were willing to talk. During my research I was helped by the ever quotable Gerry Griffin of London Business School. As usual, Mark Allin and Richard Burton of Capstone Publishing paid for lunch. Tom Fryer took the manuscript and turned it into a book. Ro, Dan, Ryan and Ceira helpfully ignored me when I was upstairs for a while.

I have tried to attribute quotes to the right people. My excuse comes from Fred Schwed's *Where Are the Customers' Yachts?* 'The information contained herein, while not guaranteed by us, has been obtained from sources which have not in the past proved particularly reliable.'

Action Heroes

Business is about action. 'People act in order to think,' says the American academic, Karl Weick. Survey after survey shows that managers spend little time in contemplation and a lot of time making phone calls, having impromptu meetings and rushing around in states of panic. As the moment is seized and squeezed, the sedentary manager is quickly an ex-manager.

'Some people make things happen, some watch while things happen, and some wonder what happened?'
   Anon

'We live in deeds, not years; in thoughts, not breaths;
In feelings, not in figures on a dial.
We should count time by heartthrobs. He most lives
Who thinks most – feels the noblest – acts the best.'
   PJ Bailey (1816–1902), American writer

'Ideas and strategies are important, of course, but execution is the real challenge.'
   Percy Barnevik (b. 1941), Swedish executive, former head of Asea Brown Boveri

'You can be very bold as a theoretician. Good theories are like good art. A practitioner has to compromise.'
   Warren Bennis (b. 1925), California-based academic and leadership guru

'Think like a man of action, act like a man of thought.'
   Henri-Louis Bergson (1859–1941), French philosopher

'Action springs not from thought, but from a readiness for responsibility.'
   Dietrich Bonhoeffer (1906–45), German pastor and theologian

'*Men of action* whose minds are too busy with the day's work to see beyond it. They are essential men, we cannot do without them, and yet we must not allow all our vision to be bound by the limitations of *men of action*.'
Pearl S. Buck (1892–1973), American writer

'In action, be primitive; in foresight, a strategist.'
René Char (b. 1907), French poet

'Action may not always be happiness, but there is no happiness without action.'
Benjamin Disraeli (1804–81), British politician and writer

'One starts an action
Simply because one must do *something*.'
TS Eliot (1888–1965), American-born poet

'An ounce of action is worth a ton of theory.'
Friedrich Engels (1820–95), communist theorist, fleetingly a Mancunian, Marx associate

'Do what's right. Do it right. Do it right now.'
BC Forbes (1880–1954), Scottish-born editor and founder of eponymous magazine

'*He that is everywhere is nowhere.*'
Thomas Fuller (1608–1661), British writer and doctor

'You must not be hampered by yesterday's myths in concentrating on today's needs.'
Harold Geneen (b. 1910), tough talking American executive

'My choice in everything is to say nothing and go do it.'
Lou Gerstner (b. 1942), American consultant and executive; CEO of IBM among others

'Knowing is not enough; we must apply. Willing is not enough; we must do.'
Johann Wolfgang von Goethe (1749–1832), German writer

'Act quickly, think slowly.'
Greek proverb

'Never confuse movement with action.'
Ernest Hemingway (1899–1961), American novelist and action addict

'The great end of life is not knowledge but action.'
TH Huxley (1825–95), British scientist, teacher and writer

'There is no kind of idleness by which we are so easily seduced as that which dignifies itself by the appearance of business.'
Dr. Samuel Johnson (1709–84), man of letters

'I have always though the actions of men the best interpreters of their thoughts.'
John Locke (1632–1704), British philosopher

'The manager works in an environment of stimulus-response, and he develops in his work a clear preference for live action.'
Henry Mintzberg (b. 1939), Canadian management academic and *agent provocateur* of the business school world

'Just do it.'
Nike advertisement

'Our nature consists in motion; complete rest is death.'
Blaise Pascal (1623–62), French writer and philosopher

'The invisible assumption of management is the focus on doing. People are selected because they get things done. But, while doing is variable, being is constant. The trouble is that the being of people and organizations is hard to move. As long as people's radar are tuned into doing, you have no place to get hold of the underlying issues.'
Richard Pascale (b. 1938), American management educator and author

'You can't think your way out of a box, you've got to act.'
Tom Peters (b. 1942), American author and consultant

'Do it, fix it, try it.'
Tom Peters and Robert Waterman (b. 1936), consultants and best-selling authors

'Even if you're on the right track, you'll get run over if you just sit there.'
Will Rogers (1879–1935), American humorist and showman

'Corporations, like individuals, need time out for reflection.'
Peter Senge (b. 1947), American academic, learning guru and fifth disciplinarian

'We know what a person thinks not when he tells us what he thinks, but by his actions.'
Isaac Bashevis Singer (1904–91), Polish-born Yiddish writer

'The mark of a good action is that it appears inevitable in retrospect.'
Robert Louis Stevenson (1850–94), British writer

'Where most of us end up there is no knowing, but the hellbent get where they are going.'
James Thurber (1894–1961), American humorist and satirist

'Try not. Do, or do not. There is no try.'
Yoda, from *The Empire Strikes Back*

'Ain't nothing to it but to do it.'
Zoot, Muppet Show sax maestro

A DS AND ADMEN

'An evil service' was how Aneurin Bevan labeled advertising. While the debate about the artistic and moral worth of advertising rumbles hopelessly on, no one has yet discovered the sure-fire route to successful advertising. If it works, so goes the famous phrase, you don't know which half of the advertising budget has done the trick. Mankind is more able to put a man on the moon than discover why the Marlboro cowboy works as an advertisement. An even greater mystery: If advertising is such guesswork, why do agencies make such huge amounts of money?

'Advertising is 85 percent confusion and 15 percent commission.'
Fred Allen (1894–1956), American comedian

'Advertising is the principal reason why the businessman has come to inherit the earth.'
Anon

'The number of agency people required to shoot a commercial on location is in direct proportion to the mean temperature of the location.'
Anon

'Doing business without advertising is like winking at a girl in the dark. You know what you are doing but nobody else does.'
Anon

'Advertising may be described as the science of arresting the human intelligence long enough to get money from it.'
Anon

'Advertising is what you do when you can't go see somebody.'
Anon

'Advertising is the very essence of democracy.'
Bruce Barton (1886–1957), American advertising executive and politician

'Advertising isn't a science. It's persuasion. And persuasion is an art.'
William Bernbach, advertising executive

'Word of mouth is the best medium of all.'
William Bernbach

'If your advertising goes unnoticed, everything else is academic.'
William Bernbach

'There is no such thing as soft sell and hard sell. There is only smart sell and stupid sell.'
Charles Browder, chairman of advertising agency BBDO

'I regard a great ad as the most beautiful thing in the world.'
Leo Burnett, advertising agency founder

'I have learned that it is far easier to write a speech about good advertising than it is to write a good ad.'
Leo Burnett

'Too many ads that try not to go over the reader's head end up beneath his notice.'
Leo Burnett

'It is pretty obvious that the debasement of the human mind caused by a constant flow of fraudulent advertising is no trivial thing. There is more than one way to conquer a country.'
Raymond Chandler (1888–1959), American novelist, creator of Philip Marlowe

'Advertising nourishes the consuming power of men. It sets up before man the goal of a better home, better clothing, better food for himself and his family. It spurs individual exertion and greater production.'
Sir Winston Churchill (1874–1965), politician, pithy, witty or statesmanlike on demand

'Being myself animated by feelings of affection toward my fellow men, I am saddened by the modern system of advertising. Whatever evidence it offers of enterprise, ingenuity, impudence and resource in certain individuals, it proves to my mind the wide prevalence of that form of mental degradation which is called gullibility.'
    Joseph Conrad (1857–1924), Polish-born novelist

'Mass demand has been created almost entirely through the development of advertising.'
    Calvin Coolidge (1872–1933), alliterative American President

'Advertising is the life of trade.'
    Calvin Coolidge

'I still believe that one can learn to play the piano by mail and that mud will give you a perfect complexion.'
    Zelda Fitzgerald (1900–48), American writer

'Advertising – a judicious mixture of flattery and threats.'
    Northrop Frye (1912–91), Canadian literary critic

'It is not necessary to advertise food to hungry people, fuel to cold people, or houses to the homeless.'
    JK Galbraith (b. 1908), Canadian-born economist and éminence grise of the business world

'Give them quality. That's the best kind of advertising.'
    Milton Snavely Hershey (1857–1945), American industrialist

'It is not the purpose of the advertisement or commercial to make the reader or listener say "My, what a clever ad." It is the purpose of advertising to make the reader or listener say, "I believe I'll buy one when I'm shopping tomorrow." '
    Morris Hite, advertising executive

'Advertising is salesmanship mass produced.'
    Morris Hite

'Advertisements are now so numerous that they are very negligently perused and it has therefore become necessary to gain attention by magnificence of promises and by eloquence sometimes sublime and sometimes pathetic.'
Dr. Samuel Johnson (1709–84), man of letters

'Promise, large promise, is the soul of an advertisement.'
Samuel Johnson

'Advertising is a valuable economic factor because it is the cheapest way of selling goods, particularly if the goods are worthless.'
Sinclair Lewis (1885–1951), American novelist

'What kills a skunk is the publicity it gives itself.'
Abraham Lincoln (1809–65), highly quotable American President

'Advertising is the greatest art form of the twentieth century.'
Marshall McLuhan (1911–80), Canadian sociologist and commentator

'Ads are the cave art of the twentieth century.'
Marshall McLuhan

'The modern Little Red Riding Hood, reared on singing commercials, has no objection to being eaten by the wolf.'
Marshall McLunhan

'Advertising is an environmental striptease for a world of abundance.'
Marshall McLuhan

'All advertising advertises advertising.'
Marshall McLuhan

'Advertising in the final analysis should be news. If it is not news it is worthless.'
Adolph S. Ochs (1858–1935), publisher and editor

'Every advertisement should be thought of as a contribution to the complex symbol which is the brand image.'
David Ogilvy (b. 1911), advertising practitioner turned guru

'Advertising is only evil when it advertises evil things.'
David Ogilvy

'Ninety-nine percent of advertising doesn't sell much of anything.'
David Ogilvy

'When you advertise fire extinguishers, open with the fire.'
David Ogilvy

'I do not regard advertising as entertainment or an art form, but as a medium of information.'
David Ogilvy

'What you say in advertising is more important than how you say it.'
David Ogilvy

'Advertising is the rattling of a stick inside a swill bucket.'
George Orwell (1903–50), British novelist

'One ad is worth more to a paper than 40 editorials.'
Will Rogers (1879–1935), American humorist and showman

'Advertising is the modern substitute for argument. Its function is to make the worse appear the better.'
George Santayana (1863–1952), Spanish-born writer and philosopher

'With the supermarket as our temple and the singing commercial as our litany, are we likely to fire the world with an irresistible vision of America's exalted purpose and inspiring way of life?'
Adlai Stevenson (1900–65), American Republican politician and presidential candidate

'Many a small thing has been made large by the right kind of advertising.'
Mark Twain (1835–1910), literary genius

'I know half the money I spend on advertising is wasted, but I can never find out which half.'
Variously attributed (to John Wanamaker and Viscount Lever-hulme among others)

'Advertising is legalized lying.'
HG Wells (1866–1946), British writer

'The people who flood our living rooms with a smorgasbord of commercial messages about fetid breath, moist underarms and troubled intestines know this: an appropriate time, place and manner to sell a product is any that sells the product.'
George Will (b. 1941), American writer and columnist

Advice and Advisers

'We give advice by the bucket, but take it by the grain', noted one anonymous sage. There is a strange and eerie consensus when it comes to advice. The message is that it is rarely useful and advisers should be tiptoed around as delicately as if they were carriers of a highly infectious disease. Those who genuinely and supportively proffer advice are invariably wrong; and the remainder may be right, but their advice is tainted by their motives. And yet, despite such observations, one of the great modern industries – management consultancy – is advice with invoices attached.

'There is nothing we receive with so much reluctance as advice.'
Joseph Addison (1672–1719), British writer

'Never trust the advice of a man in difficulties.'
Aesop (c. 620–560 BC), Greek writer of timeless fables

'He that gives good advice, builds with one hand; he that gives good counsel and example, builds with both; he that gives good admonition and bad example, builds with one hand and pulls down with the other.'
Francis Bacon (1561–1626), Elizabethan all-rounder

'The worst men often give the best advice.'
PJ Bailey (1816–1902), American writer

'Advice is like castor oil; easy to give, but dreadful to take.'
Josh Billings (1818–85), pen name of Henry Wheeler Shaw

'Good but rarely comes from good advice.'
Lord Byron (1788–1824), carefree romantic poet

'Advice is seldom welcome; and those who want it the most always like it the least.'
Lord Chesterfield (1694–1773), British statesman

'Whenever a man seeks your advice he generally seeks your praise.'
Lord Chesterfield

'Advice is like snow; the softer it falls, the longer it dwells upon, and the deeper in sinks into the mind.'
Samuel Taylor Coleridge (1772–1834), romantic poet

'The contribution I make to a client is basically to be very stupid and very dense; ask simple, fundamental questions; demand that he be thoughtful with the answers; and demand that he makes decisions on what is important. I feel very strongly that a client who leaves my office feeling that he has learned a lot that he didn't know before is a stupid client; either that, or I haven't done my job. He should leave the office saying: 'I know all this – but why haven't I done anything about it?' "
Peter Drucker (b. 1909), father of modern management thinking

'A consultant solves other people's problems. I could never do that. I want to help other people solve their own problems.'
Charles Handy (b. 1932), only British management guru

'Well-found consultants can stay in a company forever; moving from one divisional trouble spot to another like Arabs wandering from oasis to oasis.'
Robert Heller, British management writer

'Whatever advice you give, be brief.'
Horace (65–8 BC), Roman poet

'Of the few innocent pleasures left to men past middle life, the jamming of common sense down the throats of fools is perhaps the keenest.'
TH Huxley (1825–95), scientist and writer

'All my life, I've known better than to depend on the experts. How could I have been so stupid as to let them go ahead?'
John F. Kennedy (1917–63), 35th American President

'I don't like to hire consultants. They're like castrated bulls; all they can do is advise.'
Victor Kiam (b. 1926), entrepreneur who famously liked Remington so much he bought the company

'I give myself sometimes admirable advice, but I am incapable of taking it.'
Lady Mary Montagu (1689–1762), woman of letters

'Consultants have strong professional values, a very strong sense of independence but they don't like being responsible for lots of people. Being a consultant is the next best thing to being self-employed.'
Archie Norman (b. 1954), executive and politician

'You don't need to take a person's advice to make him feel good – just ask for it.'
Laurence J. Peter (1919–90), Canadian creator of The Peter Principle

'One gives nothing so freely as advice.'
Duc de la Rochefoucauld (1613–80), French writer

'No enemy is worse than bad advice.'
Sophocles (496–406 BC), Athenian tragedian

'No one wants advice, only corroboration.'
John Steinbeck (1902–68), American novelist

'I have lived over 30 years on this planet, and I have yet to hear the first syllable of valuable or even earnest advice from my seniors.'
Henry David Thoreau (1817–62), American naturalist and writer

'They [consultants] are the people who borrow your watch to tell you what time it is and then walk off with it.'
Robert Townsend (b. 1920), author of *Up the Organization*

'McKinsey thinks it sells grand strategies and big ideas when really its role is to keep management from doing a lot of dumb things. They do great analysis, but it won't get your company to the top.'
Robert Waterman (b. 1936), consultant and author

'The only thing to do with good advice is pass it on; it is never of any use to oneself.'
Oscar Wilde (1854–1900), wit

'My advice to you is not to inquire why or whither, but just enjoy the ice cream while it's on your plate.'
Thornton Wilder (1897–1975), American novelist and playwright

AMBITION: NAKED INTENT

Whether a train driver or astronaut, we all want to be something or some-one. But, some want a little bit more. They are consumed by an obsessive desire to control the marketing department or to run their own business empire. Of course, it would be wrong to condemn all ambitious people as blinkered obsessives who should be speedily dispatched to their nearest psychoanalyst, but only a little.

'A man's worth is no greater than the worth of his ambitions.'
Marcus Aurelius Antonius (121–80), Roman Emperor and part-time philosopher

'Ah, but a man's reach should exceed his grasp,
Or what's a heaven for?'
Robert Browning (1812–89), British poet

'There are only two ways by which to rise in this world, either by one's own industry or by the stupidity of others.'
Jean de La Bruyère (1812–89), poet

'I don't try to jump over seven-foot bars. I look around for one-foot bars that I can step over.'
Warren Buffet (b. 1930), American investment guru

'When you reach for the stars you may not quite get one, but you won't come up with a handful of mud either.'
Leo Burnett, advertising agency founder

'Like dogs in a wheel, birds in a cage, or squirrels in a chain, ambitious men still climb and climb with great labor and incessant anxiety, but never reach the top.'
Robert Burton (1576–1640), British clergyman and writer

'A man should have any number of little aims about which he should be conscious and for which he should have names, but he should have neither name for, nor consciousness concerning, the main aim of his life.'
Samuel Butler (1612–80), British poet and satirist

'All ambitions are lawful except those which climb upward on the miseries or credulities of mankind.'
Joseph Conrad (1857–1924), Polish-born novelist

'No one rises so high as he who knows not whither he is going.'
__Oliver Cromwell (1599–1658), British soldier and statesman__

'Without ambition one starts nothing. Without work one finishes nothing. The prize will not be sent to you. You have to win it. The man who knows how will always have a job. The man who also knows why will always be his boss. As to methods there may be a million and then some, but principles are few. The man who grasps principles can successfully select his own methods. The man who tries methods, ignoring principles, is sure to have trouble.'
Ralph Waldo Emerson (1803–82), American poet

'The way up and the way down are one and the same.'
Heracleitus (c. 500 BC), Greek philosopher

'Ambition is only vanity ennobled.'
Jerome K. Jerome (1859–1927), Thames-inspired writer

'Ambition makes more trusty slaves than need.'
Ben Jonson (1572–1637), Elizabethan playwright

'He who stands on tiptoe does not stand firm.'
Lao-tzu (604–531 BC), Chinese philosopher and founder of Taoism

'The people who get on in this world are the people who get up and look for the circumstances they want, and, if they can't find them, make them.'
George Bernard Shaw (1856–1950), Irish playwright

'Ambition often puts men upon doing the meanest offices; so climbing is performed in the same posture with creeping.'
Jonathan Swift (1667–1745), British writer of *Gulliver's Travels*

'In private enterprises men may advance or recede, whereas they who aim at empire have no alternative between the highest success and utter downfall.'
Cornelius Tacitus (55–117?), Roman historian

'People think that at the top there isn't much room. They tend to think of it as an Everest. My message is that there is tons of room at the top.'
Margaret Thatcher (b. 1925), former British Prime Minister

'This is the posture of fortune's slave: one foot in the gravy, one foot in the grave.'
James Thurber (1894–1961), American humorist and satirist

'There is always room at the top.'
Daniel Webster (1782–1852), American statesman

ANGER AND ARGUMENTS

As motivational tools go, anger is neither the most subtle nor the most controllable. But it is highly entertaining, and unlike many other motivational tools, often works. Forget the sophisticated motivational temptation of a carrot; lose your temper, rage and bawl. The trick is to be able to use anger rather than have anger use you.

'No one can make you jealous, angry, vengeful, or greedy – unless you let him.'
Anon

'How much more grievous are the consequences of anger than the causes of it.'
Marcus Aurelius Antonius (121–80), Roman emperor and part-time philosopher

'Anyone can become angry. That is easy. But to be angry with the right person, to the right degree, at the right time, for the right purpose and in the right way – that is not easy.'
Aristotle (384–322 BC), Greek philosopher

'Anger makes dull men witty, but it keeps them poor.'
Francis Bacon (1561–1626), Elizabethan jack-of-all-trades

'The only way to get the best of an argument is to avoid it.'
Dale Carnegie (1888–1955), motivational trainer and author of *How to Make Friends and Influence People*

'I enjoy discord. I must say, I enjoy slam dancing. I enjoy putting it up in your face without a clear protagonist or antagonist. I'm attracted to ambivalence because that's what I see around us.'
Michael Douglas (b. 1944), actor

'Why is there no conflict at this meeting? Something's wrong when there's no conflict.'
Michael Eisner (b. 1942), Disney chief

'Whatever is begun in anger ends in shame.'
Benjamin Franklin (1706–90), American inventor, statesman, writer, etc.

'Honest differences are often a healthy sign of progress.'
Mahatma Gandhi (1869–1948), Hindhu nationalist leader

'Convincing yourself doesn't win an argument.'
Robert Half (b. 1918), American executive

'No matter what side of the argument you are on, you always find people on your side that you wish were on the other.'
Jascha Heifetz (1901–87), Russian-born violinist

'Opposition brings concord. Out of discord comes the fairest harmony.'
Heracleitus (c. 500 BC), Greek philosopher

'The sounder your argument, the more satisfaction you get out of it.'
Edgar Watson Howe (1853–1937), American writer

'If you cannot answer a man's argument, all is not lost; you can still call him vile names.'
Elbert Hubbard (1856–1915), American author who died on the *Lusitania*

'When angry, count ten before you speak; if very angry, a hundred.'
Thomas Jefferson (1743–1826), third American President

'If two men agree on everything, you may be sure that one of them is doing the thinking.'
Lyndon B. Johnson (1908–73), 36th American President

'Sir, I have found you an argument. I am not obliged to find you an understanding.'
Dr. Samuel Johnson (1709–84), great man of letters

'The aim of argument, or of discussion, should not be victory, but progress.'
Joseph Joubert (1754–1824), French writer

'There's a whiff of the lynch mob or the lemming migration about any over-large concentration of like-thinking individuals, no matter how virtuous their cause.'
PJ O'Rourke (b. 1947), Toledo-born right-wing humorist

'Never argue; repeat your assertion.'
Robert Owen (1771–1858), farsighted British industrialist

'Most executives are uneasy with conflict and things that seem contradictory. They seek the middle ground, and inevitably the result is mediocrity: organizations without distinction and lacking creative tension. Too little constructive disagreement lulls an organization into complacency.'
Richard Pascale (b. 1938), management thinker, writer and educator

'A threat that everyone perceives but no one talks about is far more debilitating than a threat that is clearly revealed and resources mobilized to address it. Companies, like people, tend to be as sick as their secrets.'
Richard Pascale

'Argument, as usually managed, is the worst sport of conversation, as in books it is generally the worst sort of reading.'
Jonathan Swift (1667–1745), British writer of *Gulliver's Travels*

'Arguments only confirm people in their own opinions.'
Booth Tarkington (1869–1946), American novelist

'When angry, count to four; when very angry, swear.'
Mark Twain (1835–1910), literary leader not renowned for his numerical skills

'A sovereign should not start a war out of anger, nor should a general give battle out of rage. For while anger can revert to happiness and rage to delight, a nation that has been destroyed cannot be restored, nor can the dead be brought back to life.'

Sun Tzu (500 BC), author of contemporary best-seller, *The Art of War*

'To fight and conquer in all your battles is not supreme excellence; supreme excellence consists in breaking the enemy's resistance without fighting.'

Sun Tzu

'Keep cool; anger is not an argument.'

Daniel Webster (1782–1852), American statesman and cool orator

'Arguments are to be avoided; they are always vulgar and often convincing.'

Oscar Wilde (1854–1900), playwright, wit and prisoner

BALANCING THE BOOKS

'Neither a borrower nor a lender be; for loan oft loses both itself and friend,' wrote Shakespeare in *Hamlet*. The world of corporate finance is not one guaranteed to nurture friendship. It is inhabited by accountants – "An accountant is a person hired to explain that you didn't make the money you thought you did," noted one particularly caustic observer – as well as banks and a legion of others anxious to lend you money. Dismiss them at your peril.

'Over a long weekend, I could teach my dog to be an investment banker.'
Herbert A. Allen (b. 1940), president of Allen & Company

'There are four things that hold back human progress: ignorance, stupidity, committees and accountants.'
Anon

'Interest works night and day, in fair weather and in foul. It gnaws at a man's substance with invisible teeth.'
Henry Ward Beecher (1813–87), abolitionist and clergyman

'Acquaintance: a person whom we know well enough to borrow from but not well enough to lend to.'
Ambrose Bierce (1842–1914), journalist and writer

'Never run into debt, not if you can find anything else to run into.'
Josh Billings (1818–85), American writer

'Capitalism without bankruptcy is like Christianity without hell.'
Frank Borman (b. 1928), astronaut and airline executive

'There are but two ways of paying debt: increase of industry in raising income, increase of thrift in laying out.'
Thomas Carlyle (1795–1881), essayist

'Nothing so cements and holds together all the parts of a society as faith or credit, which can never be kept up unless men are under some force or necessity of honestly paying what they owe to one another.'
Marcus Tullius Cicero (106–43 BC), Roman writer and statesman

'Annual income twenty pounds, annual expenditure nineteen nineteen six, result happiness. Annual income twenty pounds, annual expenditure twenty pounds nought and six, result misery.'
Charles Dickens (1812–70), Victorian novelist

'A person who can't pay, gets another person who can't pay, to guarantee that he can pay.'
Charles Dickens

'Our expense is almost all for conformity. It is for cake that we all run in debt.'
Ralph Waldo Emerson (1803–82), poet and writer

'Remember that credit is money.'
Benjamin Franklin (1706–90), writer, inventor, philosopher, etc.

'Creditors are a superstitious sect, great observers of set days and times.'
Benjamin Franklin

'Never of money spent
Where the spender thinks it went.
Nobody was ever meant
To remember or invent
What he did with every cent.'
Robert Frost (1874–1963), American poet

'Business is many things, the least of which is the balance sheet. It is a fluid, ever changing, living thing, sometimes building to great peaks, sometimes falling to crumbled lumps. The soul of a business is a curious alchemy of needs, desires, greed and gratifications mixed together with selflessness, sacrifices and personal contributions far beyond material rewards.'
Harold Geneen (b. 1910), head of ITT, famed for his dedication to the balance sheet

'If you owe the bank $100, that's your problem. If you owe the bank $100 million, that's the bank's problem.'
John Paul Getty (1892–1976), oil tycoon

'No man's credit is as good as his money.'
Edgar Watson Howe (1853–1937), American writer

'An accountant is a man who puts his head in the past and backs his ass into the future.'
Ross Johnson, American executive and former Nabisco CEO

'Do not accustom yourself to consider debt only as an inconvenience. You will find it a calamity.'
Samuel Johnson (1709–84), man of letters

'I was borrowing money from 30 leading banks. How could they all be wrong? I'm only a simple businessman.'
Sir Freddie Laker (b. 1922), simple businessman

'The human species, according to the best theory I can form of it, is composed of two distinct races, the men who borrow, and the men who lend.'
Charles Lamb (1775–1834), essayist

'It's easier to teach a poet how to read a balance sheet than it is to teach an accountant how to write.'
Henry R. Luce (1898–1967), founder of *Fortune* and *Time* magazines

'The debt is like a crazy aunt we keep down in the basement. All the neighbors know she's there, but nobody wants to talk about her.'
H. Ross Perot (b. 1930), American executive and would-be politician

'Credit is like a looking glass, which when once sullied by a breath, may be wiped clear again; but if once cracked can never be repaired.'
Sir Walter Scott (1771–1832), Scottish novelist

'The banks are made of marble,
With a guard at every door,
And the vaults are stuffed with silver
That the worker sweated for.'
     Song from the 1950s

'A pig bought on credit is forever grunting.'
     Spanish proverb

'The private control of credit is the modern form of slavery.'
     Upton Sinclair (1878–1968), American writer

'The person whom you favored with a loan, if he be a good man, will think himself in your debt after he has paid you.'
     Richard Steele (1672–1729), writer and politician

'A small loan makes a debtor; a great one, an enemy.'
     Publilius Syrus (c. 42 BC), Latin writer

'Men ... are sent into the world with bills of credit, and seldom draw to their full extent.'
     Horace Walpole (1717–97), writer and historian

'Most people become bankrupt through having invested too heavily in the prose of life.'
     Oscar Wilde (1854–1900), poet of life

Belief and Believers

Though the ultimate business book would be *How to Make a Million and Go to Heaven,* the spirituality of commerce is usually as difficult to find as a coin in a cloud of incense. Recent years, however, have seen a resurgence in interest in matters spiritual. Belief is all. 'I'll see it when I believe it,' quips Karl Weick. The new age executive is as likely to refer to Zen Buddhism as to re-engineering while practicing neither.

'If only God would give me some clear sign! Like making a large deposit in my name at a Swiss bank.'
Woody Allen (b. 1935), American filmmaker

'When the praying does no good, insurance does help.'
Bertolt Brecht (1898–1956), German playwright

'The three most important things a man has are, briefly, his private parts, his money and his religious opinions.'
Samuel Butler (1612–80), poet and satirist

'The physical world, including our bodies, is a response of the observer. We create our bodies as we create the experience of our world.'
Deepak Chopra (b. 1947?), author and self-improvement guru

'The majority of mankind is lazy-minded, incurious, absorbed in vanities, and tepid in emotion, and is therefore incapable of either much doubt or much faith.
TS Eliot (1888–1965), American-born modern poet

'To accomplish great things, we must not only act, but also dream; not only plan, but also believe.'
Anatole France (1844–1924), French writer

'Mythology distracts us everywhere – in government as in business, in politics as in economics, in foreign affairs as in domestic policy.'
John F. Kennedy (1917–63), 35th American President

'The bottom line? The bottom line is in heaven!'
Edwin Land (1909–91), inventor of the Polaroid

'Let us have faith that might makes right, and let us do our duty as we understand it.'
Abraham Lincoln (1809–65), American President

'Disbelief in magic can force a poor soul into believing in government and business.'
Tom Robbins (b. 1936), American author of *Even Cowgirls Get the Blues* among others

'I want to work for a company that contributes to and is part of the community. I want something not just to invest in. I want something to believe in.
Anita Roddick (b. 1943), founder of The Body Shop

'This is the true joy of life, the being used for a purpose recognized by yourself as a mighty one; the one being a force of nature instead of a feverish, selfish little clod of ailments and grievances complaining that the world will not devote itself to making you happy.'
George Bernard Shaw (1856–1950), dramatist

'No man or woman is an island. To exist just for yourself is meaningless. You can achieve the most satisfaction when you feel related to some greater purpose in life, something greater than yourself.'
Denis Waitley, writer

'You are not here merely to make a living. You are here in order to enable the world to live more amply, with greater vision, with a finer spirit of hope and achievement. You are here to enrich the world, and you impoverish yourself if you forget the errand.'
Woodrow Wilson (1856–1924), 28th American President

Big business

Big is best would serve as a three-word summary of business thinking in the twentieth century. Unfortunately it is often expanded into eulogies to corporate might. In an era of downsizing and corporate shrinkage, big is increasingly questioned. This, however, does not automatically mean that small is the answer.

'If a company gets too large, break it into smaller parts. Once people start not knowing the people in the building and it starts to become impersonal, it's time to break up a company.'
   Richard Branson (b. 1950), British entrepreneur

'Less is more.'
   Robert Browning (1812–89), English poet

'Large organization is loose organization. Nay, it would be almost as true to say that organization is always disorganization.'
   GK Chesterton (1874–1936), writer

'The Fortune 500 is over.'
   Peter Drucker (b. 1909), management thinker and writer

'The only big companies that succeed will be those that obsolete their own products before somebody else does.'
   Bill Gates (b. 1955), co-founder of Microsoft

'Size works against excellence.'
   Bill Gates

'Economy, stability, and absence of friction are striking characteristics of large corporations.'
   King Gillette (1855–1937), friends called him King

'If you believe that 10 guys in pin-striped suits are back in kindergarten class playing with building blocks, you'll get a rough picture of what life in a corporation is like.'
Lee Iacocca (b. 1924), former Chrysler chief, turned best-selling author

'One of the nicest things about being big is the luxury of thinking little.'
Marshall McLuhan (1911–80), Canadian sociologist and commentator

'In big industry new ideas are invited to rear their heads so they can be clobbered at once. The idea department of a big firm is a sort of lab for isolating dangerous viruses.'
Marshall McLuhan

'Why anybody thinks they will produce a gazelle by mating two dinosaurs is beyond me.'
Tom Peters (b. 1942), management guru and best-selling author

'If you can build a business up big enough, it's respectable.'
Will Rogers (1879–1935), American humorist and showman

'In practically all our activities we seem to suffer from the inertia resulting from our great size. There are so many people involved and it requires such a tremendous effort to put something new into effect that a new idea is likely to be considered insignificant in comparison with the effort that it take to put it across....Sometimes I am almost forced to the conclusion that General Motors is so large and its inertia so great that it is impossible for us to be leaders.'
Alfred P. Sloan (1875–1966), legendary General Motors chief

'I think that big organizations just make big mistakes and a big mess.'
Martin Taylor (b. 1952), British executive and political adviser

'Big companies are small companies that succeeded.'
Robert Townsend (b. 1920), former Avis chief and author of *Up the Organization*

'It's not the size of the dog in the fight, it's the size of the fight in the dog.'
Mark Twain (1835–1910), American novelist and canine commentator

'Big business is not dangerous because it is big, but because its bigness is an unwholesome inflation created by privileges and exemptions which it ought not to enjoy.'
Woodrow Wilson (1856–1924), 28th American President

Books and bookmen

Literary masterpieces they are not. Hugely successful they certainly are. The business book market was a fairly humdrum niche until, in 1982, *In Search of Excellence* was published. Almost single-handedly, this book by two American consultants turned a niche into a mainstream market. Businesspeople ventured into bookshops and found that they had an uncontrollable urge to buy books. Quantity should not be mistaken for quality. Alison Lurie, an American writer, observed that business books are 'equal parts of commonsense and nonsense – that is, of the already obvious and the probably false.'

'Any survey of what businessmen are reading runs smack into the open secret that most businessmen aren't.'
   Anon

'Either write something worth reading or do something worth writing about.'
   Benjamin Franklin (1706–90), American Renaissance man

'The most technologically efficient machine that man has ever invented is the book.'
   Northrop Frye (1912–91), literary critic

'My aim is to put down on paper what I see and what I feel in the best and simplest way.'
   Ernest Hemingway (1899–1961), novelist

'I can write better than anybody who can write faster, and I can write faster than anybody who can write better.'
   AJ Liebling (1904–63), journalist

'The future of the book is the blurb.'
   Marshall McLuhan (1911–80), Canadian sociologist and commentator

'I would be delighted to know that everybody read everything. And dismayed to find that nobody read anything.'

Henry Mintzberg (b. 1939), Canadian management thinker, realist and author

'In his heart everyone knows that the only people who get rich from the *get rich quick* books are those who write them.'

Richard M. Nixon (1913–94), American President

'Heaven forbid that students should cease to read a book on the science of public or business administration provided that these works are classified as fiction.'

C. Northcote Parkinson (1909–93), creator of the timeless Parkinson's Law

'A couple of hours in a hot kitchen can teach you as much about business and management as the latest books on reengineering or total quality management.'

Tom Peters (b. 1942), consultant and author

'Read more novels and fewer business books.'
Tom Peters

Bosses and Bastards

In the era of empowerment, the word 'boss' is clearly outdated. Yet it remains the most reliable shorthand to describe the overweight middle-aged man in the next room who signs your monthly paycheck. Another thing which can be relied on is that bosses are generally viewed in a negative light – little wonder when you meet targets only for them to be increased yet again. If you don't think you couldn't do your boss's job better than he or she does, you are pathetically unambitious and probably very happy in your work.

'Never work for a boss who opens the company mail.'
   Anon

'A throne is only a bench covered with velvet.'
   Napoléon Bonaparte (1769–1821), French velvet lover

'I have found some of the best reasons I ever had for remaining at the bottom simply by looking at the men at the top.'
   Frank Moore Colby (1865–1925), American writer and humorist

'The basic cause of sickness in American industry and resulting unemployment is failure of top management to manage. He that sells not can buy not.'
   W. Edwards Deming (1900–93), quality guru first discovered in Japan but made in America

'The greatest monarch on the proudest throne
is obliged to sit upon his own arse.'
   Benjamin Franklin (1706–90), inventor and blunt stater of home truths

'By working faithfully eight hours a day you may eventually get to be boss and work twelve hours a day.'
Robert Frost (1874–1963), American poet

'Where are you likely to find people with the least diversity of experience, the largest investment in the past, and the greatest reverence for industry dogma? At the top.'
Gary Hamel (b. 1954), consultant, educator and co-author of *Competing for the Future*

'The boss is no longer the supervisor responsible for overseeing the detail of your work, but is the coach, back-up, mentor and friend.'
Sir John Harvey-Jones (b. 1924), former ICI chief turned troubleshooter

'You are fair, compassionate and intelligent, but you are perceived to be biased, callous and dumb.'
New Yorker **cartoon**

'Unless you are willing to drench yourself in your work beyond the capacity of the average person, you are just not cut out for positions at the top.'
JC Penney, former chairman of JC Penney

'Bosses are clearly the chief source of our troubles....I attack bosses for a living!'
Tom Peters (b. 1942) consultant and author

'Top management (the board of directors) is supposed to be a tree full of owls – hooting when management heads into the wrong part of the forest. I'm still unpersuaded they even know where the forest is.'
Robert Townsend (b. 1920), American executive and author of *Up the Organization!*

BRANDS

In the beginning the brand was little more than a manufacturer's mark. Today, the brand is an omnipresent reminder of the corporate world at work. Nothing, it seems, is beyond branding. Sports teams are brands; management gurus are brands; bananas are brands; pop groups are brands as well as bands. The potential for branding is limitless. And the effort is sometimes worth it – 'It's just like Pepsi Cola!' noted Eduard Shevardnadze at the opening of the new Coke bottling plant in Tblisi, Georgia.

'Brand loyalty is very much like an onion. It has layers and a core. The core is the user who will stick with you until the very end.'
Edwin Artzt, chief executive of Procter & Gamble

'Your premium brand better be delivering something special or it's not going to get the business.'
Warren Buffet (b. 1930), American investment genius

'Well-managed brands live on, only bad brand managers die.'
George Bull (b. 1936), British executive and brand champion

'I am irresistible, I say, as I put on my designer fragrance. I am a merchant banker, I say, as I climb out of my BMW. I am a juvenile lout, I say, as I down a glass of extra strong lager. I am handsome, I say, as I don my Levi's jeans.'
John Kay, British economist and educator

'[A brand name is] a name, term, sign, symbol or design, or a combination of these, which is intended to identify the goods or services of one group of sellers and differentiate them from those of competitors.'
Philip Kotler, marketing guru

'Any damn fool can put on a deal, but it takes genius, faith, and perseverance to create a brand.'
David Ogilvy (b. 1911), advertising practitioner and thinker

'Today brands are everything, and all kinds of products and services – from accounting firms to sneaker makers to restaurants – are figuring out how to transcend the narrow boundaries of their categories and become a brand surrounded by a Tommy Hilfiger-like buzz.'
Tom Peters (b. 1942), the ultimate guru brand

'We are CEOs of our own companies: Me Inc. To be in business today, our most important job is to be head marketer for the brand called You.'
Tom Peters

'A brand is a promise, and in the end, you have to keep your promises. A product is the artifact of the truth of a promise. Coke promises refreshment; Gateway Computer promises to be your wagon master across the Silicon prairie. There is no difference between what you sell and what you believe.'
Watts Wacker, futurist

BUREAUCRACY AND BUREAUCRATS

Managers have long thrown off the unwanted title of administrator. Administration is bureaucracy, paper shuffling by another name. It is the weary art of dotting the i's and crossing the t's, not the grand world of strategy. Little wonder that managers remain uncomfortable with the fact that their premier qualification, the MBA, stands for Master of Business Administration. Any one for filing?

'A memorandum is written not to inform the reader but to protect the writer.'
Dean Acheson (1893–1971), American lawyer and politician

'What the world really needs is more love and less paperwork.'
Pearl Bailey (1918–90), singer

'You will find my last words in the blue folder.'
Sir Max Beerbohm (1872–1956), well-organized last words of the essayist and caricaturist

'An efficiency regime cannot be run without a few heroes stuck about it to carry off the dullness – much as plums have to be put into a bad pudding to make it palatable.'
EM Forster (1879–1970), novelist

'The only thing that saves us from bureaucracy is its inefficiency.'
Eugene McCarthy (b. 1916), American politician and presidential candidate

'The person who is devoted to paperwork has lost the initiative. He is dealing with things that are brought to his notice, having ceased to notice anything for himself. He has been essentially defeated in his job.'
C. Northcote Parkinson (1909–93), academic and author

'The man who is denied the opportunity of taking decisions of importance begins to regard as important the decisions he is allowed to take. He becomes fussy about filing, keen on seeing pencils are sharpened, eager to ensure that the windows are opened (or shut) and apt to use two or three different colored pencils.'
   C. Northcote Parkinson

'People think the president has to be the main organizer. No, the president is the main disorganizer. Everybody *manages* quite well; whenever anything goes wrong, they take immediate action to make sure nothing'll go wrong again. The problem is, nothing new will ever happen, either.'
   Harry Quadracci, American executive

'An administration, like a machine, does not create. It carries on.'
   Antoine de Saint-Exupéry (1900–44), French flier and writer

'Most managers were trained to be the thing they most despise – bureaucrats.'
   Alvin Toffler (b. 1928), best-selling American futurist

'There is something about a bureaucrat that does not like a poem.'
   Gore Vidal (b. 1929), American author and occasional would-be politician

'Bureaucracy is basically just machinery for mistake avoidance. The whole emphasis is negative. And of course you can always figure out why something shouldn't be done. But before the fact, it's very hard to figure out why something should be done.'
   Robert Waterman (b. 1936), consultant and author

'Experience tends universally to show that the purely bureaucratic type of administrative organization – that is, the monocratic variety of bureaucracy – is, from a purely technical point of view, capable of attaining the highest degree of efficiency and is in this sense formally the most rational known means of carrying our imperative control over human beings. It is superior to any other form in precision, in stability, in the stringency of its discipline, and in its reliability.'
   Max Weber (1864–1920), German sociologist

'Boundaryless behavior is a way of life here. People really do take ideas from A to B. And if you take an idea and share it, you are rewarded. In the old culture, if you had an idea you'd keep it. Sharing it with someone else would have been stupid, because the bureaucracy would have made him the hero, not you.'
Jack Welch (b. 1935), General Electric chief

'It is not necessary to imagine the world ending in fire or ice. There are two other possibilities: one is paper work, and the other is nostalgia.'
Frank Zappa (1940–93), iconoclastic American musician

CAPITAL AND MARKETS

Money makes the world go round. Money, itself, rotates endlessly in markets, as mysterious to most as the value of a groat. But, amid the feeding frenzy of the city, lies the fragile, bloated and ever-hungry heartbeat of capitalism. 'Markets are pitiless. They reward whatever creates value and ignore or punish whatever does not. It's nothing personal,' says *Fortune's* Thomas Stewart. The trouble is, it still feels personal.

'Capitalism arose and took off its pajamas. Another day, another dollar. Each man is valued at what he will bring in the marketplace. Meaning has been drained from work and assigned instead to remuneration.'
Donald Barthelme (1931–89), American short story master

'The highest use of capital is not to make more money, but to make money do more for the betterment of life.'
Henry Ford (1863–1947), American industrialist

'Economic freedom is an essential prerequisite for political freedom.'
Milton Friedman (b. 1912), American economist

'Under capitalism, man exploits man. Under communism, it's just the opposite.'
JK Galbraith (b. 1908), Canadian-born economist

'The market is a mechanism for sorting the efficient from the inefficient, it is not a substitute for responsibility.'
Charles Handy (b. 1932), Irish-born corporate seer and author

'The cement in our whole democracy today is the worker who makes $15 an hour. He's the guy who will buy a house and a car and a refrigerator. He's the oil in the engine.'
Lee Iacocca (b. 1924), savior of Chrysler who has been telling the world ever since

'When the operations of capitalism come to resemble those of the casino, ill fortune will be the lot of the many.'
John Maynard Keynes (1883–1946), economist

'Modern capitalism is absolutely irreligious, without internal union, without much public spirit, often, though not always, mere congeries of possessors and pursuers. Such a system has to be immensely successful if it is to succeed. Today, it is only moderately successful.'
John Maynard Keynes (in 1923)

'A market consists of all the potential customers sharing a particular need or want who might be willing and able to engage in exchange to satisfy that need or want.'
Philip Kotler, marketing guru

'If you want a really dynamic, effective economy, the only damn thing you can do is pursue the market logic completely, whole hog, not halfway.'
Michael Manley (1924), Jamaican politician

'Capital is dead labor that, vampire-like, lives only by sucking living labor, and lives the more, the more labor it sucks.'
Karl Marx (1818–83), the original Marxist

'I create markets.'
Akio Morita (b. 1921), co-founder of Sony

'A businessman is someone who buys at ten and is happy to get out at twelve. The other kind of man buys at ten, sees it rise to eighteen and does nothing. He is waiting for it to rise to twenty. When it drops to two he waits for it to get back to ten.'
VS Naipaul (b. 1932), novelist

'The success or failure of a company is determined as much by the fortunes of the marketplace as by the management. You can have an extremely good CEO of a failing company.'
Archie Norman (b. 1954), retailing chief and politician

'Capitalism and altruism are incompatible; they are philosophical opposites; they cannot co-exist in the same man or in he same society.'
   Ayn Rand (1905–82), Russian-born writer and champion of right-wing causes

'Capital is that part of the wealth of a country which is employed in production and consists of food, clothing, tools, raw materials, etc., necessary to give effect to labor.'
   David Ricardo (1772–1823), British economist

'Free trade holds much of the blame for continued international conflict. Markets are said to possess wisdom that is somehow superior to man. Those of us in business who travel in the developing world see the results of such western wisdom and have a rumbling disquiet about much of what our economic institutions have bought into.'
   Anita Roddick (b. 1943), founder of The Body Shop

CAREER SNAKES AND LADDERS

There was once a time when you didn't have to think about a career. If you were a manager, you had a job and that tended to stretch endlessly ahead through life. You could have called it a career but that would have seemed presumptuous. Nowadays, everyone has a career. Bright graduates don't discuss job possibilities, but think anxiously about which career to pursue. The beauty of a career is that it can include many different jobs for many different organizations. It gives structure are and logic where there are none – you could pursue a career in manufacturing industry by operating a machine in a cat food factory or by becoming chef executive of ICI. Now there are a multitude of careers including portfolio careers (definitely presumptuous).

'Always be nice to people on the way up; because you'll meet the same people on the way down.'
   Anon

'In the past we said to employees, do as you're told and you have a job for life. Then we betrayed them.'
   AT&T manager

'You cannot leave your career development solely to your employer – he just is not good enough to manage this for you!'
   Neville Bain (b. 1940), New Zealand-born executive

'Even if you sit at the same desk for the rest of your life, you'd better get a lot of new skills.'
   Larry Bossidy (b. 1935), Allied Signal chief

'There are two ways of rising in the world, either by your own industry or by the folly of others.'
   Jean de La Bruyère (1812–89), poet

'Career opportunities are ones that never knock.'
The Clash, British rock group

'Ambitious young people should be reasonably patient and hold the success of the company as more important than their own success.'
Sir John Egan (b. 1939), British executive

'Ability will never catch up with the demand for it.'
Malcolm S. Forbes (1919–90), publisher and *bon vivant*

'One of the great discoveries man makes, one of his great surprises, is to find he can do what he was afraid he couldn't do. Most of the bars we beat against are in ourselves – we put them there, and we can take them down.'
Henry Ford (1863–1947), automobile manufacturer

'The first mistake in public business is the going into it.'
Benjamin Franklin (1706–90), American inventor and writer

'No longer can one expect to sell 100,000 hours of one's life to an organization.'
Charles Handy (b. 1932), new forms of work thinker

'It's wrong to say you fill somebody's shoes. You should never do that. You bring your own shoes along and make them march around the job in the way that they should do.'
Lord Hanson (b. 1922), conglomerate chief

'Men of genius do not excel in any profession because they labor in it, but they labor in it because they excel.'
William Hazlitt (1778–1830), essayist

'One shining quality lends a luster to another, or hides some glaring defect.'
William Hazlitt

'Life is to be lived. If you have to support yourself, you had bloody well better find some way that is going to be interesting. And you don't do that by sitting around.'
Katharine Hepburn (b. 1907), actress

'There are no shortcuts to the top. There is one thing that is worse than not getting to where you want go and that is not being equipped once you get there.'
Sir Christopher Hogg (b. 1936), British executive

'The way to rise is to obey and please.'
Ben Jonson (1572–1637), subservient Elizabethan playwright

'Anyone in an environment that is not preparing him or her for a tougher future should move out fast.'
John Kotter (b. 1947), Harvard Business School guru

'Unless a man believes in himself and makes a total commitment to his career and puts everything he has into it – his mind, his body, his heart – what's life worth to him?'
Vince Lombardi (1913–70), American football coach

'If I have seen further it is by standing on the shoulder of giants.'
Sir Isaac Newton (1642–1727), physicist and mathematician

'Business life is a game of snakes and ladders, and I've had to come up two or three fast ladders. I accept that my approach carries with it career risk. My approach is to make explicit the risks we are facing and invite people to support me.'
Archie Norman (b. 1954), British executive and politician

'The employee who proves himself good at obeying orders will get promotion to the rank where his job is to give orders.'
Laurence J. Peter (1919–90), Canadian academic and writer

'For each individual, for you, for me, the final promotion is from a level of competence to a level of incompetence.'
Laurence J. Peter

'The higher a monkey climbs the more you see its arse.'
Proverb

'Doing it means figuring out how to do it yourself. If your way works most of the time, you'll get promoted.'
Burt Reinhardt, former CNN president

'The man who is a pessimist before forty-eight knows too much; if he is an optimist after it, he knows too little.'
Mark Twain (1835–1910), novelist and career adviser

'There is probably no man living, though ever so great a fool, that cannot do *something* or other well.'
Samuel Warren (1807–77), optimist

CHANGE

Change is the managerial mantra of the nineties. But, it was ever thus. Management and business resolutely refuse to stand still. 'We stand at the gates of an important epoch, a time of ferment,' warned Hegel in 1806. Managing change successfully is repeatedly identified as the true business challenge. Change makes people edgy – little wonder that David Bowie stuttered his way through the chorus of his song 'Changes.' After centuries of effort, few are nearer finding a solution to the perennial challenge of change. Today's victors are virtually always tomorrow's failures and lessons are as liable to come from Machiavelli as contemporary gurus.

'Metamorphosis in a world of change.'
   Andersen Consulting mission statement

'Change starts when someone sees the next step.'
   Anon

'Change in all things is sweet.'
   Aristotle (384–322 BC), Greek philosopher

'Not everything that is faced can be changed. But nothing can be changed until it is faced.'
   James Baldwin (1924–87), American novelist

'The absurd man is he who never changes.'
   Auguste Barthélemy (1796–1867), poet and satirist

'Great cultural changes begin in affectation and end in routine.'
   Jacques Barzun (b. 1907), French educator and critic

'Radical changes require adequate authority. A man must have inner strength as well as influential position. What he does must correspond with a higher truth.'
Confucius (551–479 BC), Chinese philosopher

'If anything is certain, it is that change is certain. the world we are planning for today will not exist in this form tomorrow.'
Philip Crosby, quality guru and former executive

'All is change; all yields its place and goes.'
Euripides (484–406 BC), Greek tragedian

'We must become the change we want to see.'
Mahatma Gandhi (1869–1948), Indian leader

'Every new change forces all the companies in an industry to adapt their strategies to that change.'
Bill Gates (b. 1955), co-founder of Microsoft

'Who wants to be part of the establishment? Jeez, they're there to be overthrown, that's how the world works. You're young and establish a new way of looking at things.'
Bill Gates

'To change and change for the better are two different things.'
German proverb

'I'm a mover and a shaker. The movers and shakers are all about change. Not doing things the way they've always been done, or keeping your head below the parapet.'
Sir Ralph Halpern (b. 1938), British retailer

'We are all prisoners of our past. It is hard to think of things except in the way we have always thought of them. But that solves no problems and seldom changes anything.'
Charles Handy (b. 1932), author of *The Age of Unreason* and *The Empty Raincoat* among others

'It is impossible to change organizations which do not accept the danger of their present way of doing things...organizations only change when the people in them change, and people will only change when they accept in their hearts that change must occur.'
Sir John Harvey-Jones (b. 1924), British executive, submariner and television troubleshooter

'Management...is not about the preservation of the status quo, it is about maintaining the highest rate of change that the organization and the people within it can stand.'
Sir John Harvey-Jones

'Nothing is permanent but change.'
Heracleitus (c. 500 BC), Greek philosopher

'Change masters are – literally – the right people in the right place at the right time. The right people are the ones with the ideas that move beyond the organization's established practice, ideas they can form into visions. The right places are the integrative environments that support innovation, encourage the building of coalitions and teams to support and implement visions. The right times are those moments in the flow of organizational history when it is possible to reconstruct reality on the basis on accumulated innovations to shape a more productive and successful future.'
Rosabeth Moss Kanter (b. 1943), former editor of the *Harvard Business Review* and author of *The Change Masters* and *When Giants Learn to Dance*

'Change is the law of life. And those who look only to the past or the present are certain to miss the future.'
John F. Kennedy (1917–63), American President

'Progress is a nice word. But change is its motivator. And change has its enemies.'
Robert F. Kennedy (1925–68), American politician

'Producing major change in an organization is not just about signing up one charismatic leader. You need a group – a team – to be able to drive the change. One person, even a terrific charismatic leader, is never strong enough to make all this happen.'
John Kotter (b. 1947), Harvard-based business commentator

'Transformation is impossible unless hundreds or thousands of people are willing to help, often to the point of making short term sacrifices. Employees will not make sacrifices, even if they are unhappy with the status quo, unless they believe useful change is possible. Without credible communication, and a lot of it, the hearts and minds of the troops are never captured.'
   John Kotter

'If you want truly to understand something, try to change it.'
Kurt Lewin (1890–1947), American psychologist

'There is nothing more difficult to take in hand, more perilous to conduct, or more uncertain in its success, than to take the lead in the introduction of a new order of things.'
   Nicolò Machiavelli (1469–1527), Florentine diplomat and writer

'Whoever desires constant success must change his conduct with the times.'
   Nicolò Machiavelli

'Where there are changes, there are always business opportunities.'
   Minoru Makihara (b. 1930), Japanese executive

'To achieve genuine culture change takes time, effort and the overriding concern to get at the values involved. The reason so many companies seem to achieve a useful culture and then slowly disintegrate over the passage of even short spans of time is that one suspects they confuse the appearance of culture change, the presence of the symbols, with the needed solid change in values and their acceptance.'
   Sir Colin Marshall (b. 1933), masterminded change program at British Airways

'The new always carries with it the sense of violation, of sacrilege. What is dead is sacred; what is new, that is, *different*, is evil, dangerous, or subversive.'
   Henry Miller (1891–1980), American writer

'Why does every generation have to think that it lives in the period with the greatest turbulence?'
   Henry Mintzberg (b. 1939), Canadian management thinker and collector of aphorisms

'If it ain't broke, break it.'
Richard Pascale (b. 1938), former Stanford academic turned best-selling guru

'The incremental approach to change is effective when what you want is more of what you've already got.'
Richard Pascale

'Incremental change is not enough. The traditional models of how to govern organizations no longer do what is now necessary. The whole command and control tradition is being tipped on its head.'
Richard Pascale

'The manager, in today's world, doesn't get paid to be a *steward of resources,* a favored term not so many years ago. He or she gets paid for one and only one thing – to make things better (incrementally and dramatically), to change things, to act – today.'
Tom Peters (b. 1942), co-author of *In Search of Excellence*

'We cannot become what we need to be, by remaining what we are.'
Max De Pree, American executive and leadership guru

'*Change* is scientific, *progress* is ethical; change is indubitable, whereas progress is a matter of controversy.'
Bertrand Russell (1872–1970), philosopher and mathematician

'There are companies which are prepared to change the way they work. They realize that nothing can be based on what used to be, that there is a better way. But, 99 percent of companies are not ready, caught in an industrial *Jurassic Park.*'
Ricardo Semler (b. 1957), Brazilian executive and author of the best-selling *Maverick!*

'Change Management: The process of paying outsiders to create the pain that will motivate insiders to change, thereby transferring the change from the company's coffers into those of the consultants.'
Eileen Shapiro, management consultant and author

'We are watching the dinosaurs die, but we don't know what will take their place.'
Lester Thurow (b. 1938), economist and educator

'If an organization is to meet the challenges of a changing world, it must be prepared to change everything about itself except beliefs as it moves through corporate life ... The only sacred cow in an organization should be its basic philosophy of doing business.'
Thomas Watson, Jr. (1914–93), businessman and diplomat

COMMITTEES AND TEAMS

A committee was once described as a group of the unwilling, picked from the unfit, to do the unnecessary. Experience provides a great deal of justification for such skepticism. Traditionally, committees have been a favored means of delaying decision making. Now, they are more likely to be labeled teams, though the effect is often identical.

'A conference is a gathering of important people who singly can do nothing, but together can decide that nothing can be done.'
Fred Allen (1894–1956), American comedian

'Team – Together everyone achieves more.'
Anon

'None of us is as smart as all of us.'
Anon

'We are born for cooperation, as are the feet, the hands, the eyelids, and the upper and lower jaws.'
Marcus Aurelius Antonius (121–80), Roman emperor and philosopher

'A committee is a group that keeps the minutes and loses hours.'
Milton Berle (b. 1908), American actor and comedian

'The inevitable end of multiple chiefs is that they fade and disappear for lack of unity.'
Napoléon Bonaparte (1769–1821), not renowned for his team play

'The good ideas are all hammered out in agony by individuals, not spewed out by groups.'
Charles Browder, advertising agency head

'A committee is an animal with four back legs.'
John Le Carré (b. 1931), novelist

'We always carry out by committee anything in which any one of us alone would be too reasonable to persist.'
Frank Moore Colby (1865–1925), American writer and humorist

'Coming together is a beginning, staying together is progress and working together is success.'
Henry Ford (1863–1947), American car manufacturer

'Whatever you do will be insignificant, but it is very important that you do it.'
Mahatma Gandhi (1869–1948), Indian statesman

'Our blend of youth and experience worked well. The experienced players stood around watching the youngsters do all the work.'
Graham Gooch (b. 1953), English cricketer

'A committee is a thing which takes a week to do what one good man can do in an hour.'
Elbert Hubbard (1856–1915), American author who died in the sinking of the *Lusitania*

'Committees are to get everybody together and homogenize their thinking.'
Art Linkletter (b. 1912), American television personality

'There are no passengers on spaceship earth. We are all crew.'
Marshall McLuhan (1911–80), Canadian sociologist and commentator

'All the world's ills stem from the fact that a man cannot sit in a room alone.'
Blaise Pascal (1623–62), French writer and philosopher

'We trained hard to meet our challenges but it seemed as if every time we were beginning to form into teams we would be reorganized. I was to learn later in life that we tend to meet any new situation by reorganizing; and a wonderful method it can be for creating the illusion of progress while producing confusion, ineffectiveness and demoralization.'

Gaius Petronius (first century AD), Latin writer at the court of Nero

'The ultimate power of a successful general staff lies not in the brilliance of its individual members, but in the cross-fertilization of its collective abilities.'

Reg Revans (b. 1907), Olympic athlete and champion of action learning

'The way a team plays as a whole determines its success. You may have the greatest bunch of individual stars in the world, but if they don't play together, the club won't be worth a dime.'

Babe Ruth (1895–1948), baseball player

'We're all in this alone.'
Lily Tomlin (b. 1939), actress and comedienne

COMMON SENSE

It is a cliché to observe that business is all common sense. It is undoubtedly true that there are a handful of basic principles on which companies can be run. But, quantum physics is guided by a few simple rules, too, yet understanding the rules does not make us experts in quantum physics. Business is common sense and a lot more.

'Success is more a function of consistent common sense than it is of genius.'
   Anon

'Common sense is instinct, and enough of it is genius.'
   Josh Billings (1818–85), perennially quotable

'Common sense is the knack of seeing things as they are, and doing things as they ought to be done.'
   Josh Billings

'The voice of the Lord is the voice of common sense, which is shared by all that is.'
   Samuel Butler (1612–80), poet and satirist

'Common sense always speaks too late. Common sense is the guy who tells you ought to have had your brakes relined last week before you smashed a front end this week. Common sense is the Monday morning quarterback who could have won the ball game if he had been on the team, but he never is. He's high up in the stands with a flask in his hip. Common sense is the little man in a gray suit who never makes a mistake in addition. But it's always somebody else's money he's adding up.'
   Raymond Chandler (1888–1959), novelist

'The great discoveries are usually obvious.'
   Philip Crosby, author of *Quality Is Free*

'Of all things, good sense is the most fairly distributed: everyone thinks he is so well supplied with it that even those who are the hardest to satisfy in every other respect never desire more of it than they already have.'
> **René Descartes (1596–1650), French philosopher and mathematician**

'Common sense is the collection of prejudices acquired by age eighteen.'
Albert Einstein (1879–1955), physicist

'Common sense is the wick of the candle.'
> **Ralph Waldo Emerson (1803–82), poet and writer**

'Common sense is very uncommon.'
> **Horace Greeley (1811–72), American politician, writer and campaigner**

'Common sense is compelled to make its way without the enthusiasm of anyone.'
> **Edgar Watson Howe (1853–1937), American writer**

'Common sense is in spite, not as the result of education.'
> **Victor Hugo (1802–85), French writer**

'All truth, in the long run, is only common sense clarified.'
> **TH Huxley (1825–95), biologist, teacher and writer**

'Common sense and nature will do a lot to make the pilgrimage of life not too difficult.'
> **W. Somerset Maugham (1874–1965), British author**

'That rarest gift
To beauty, common sense!'
> **George Meredith (1828–1909), British author**

'To see what is in front of one's nose requires a constant struggle.'
> **George Orwell (1903–50), author of *1984* among others**

'One ounce of learning requires ten pounds of common sense to apply it.'
> **Persian proverb**

'To make *sense* is the hallmark of nonsense. Nature does not make sense. Nothing makes sense.'

Ayn Rand (1905–82), Russian-born writer and champion of right-wing causes

'We seldom attribute common sense except to those who agree with us.'

Duc de la Rochefoucauld (1613–80), French writer

'Common sense is not so common.'
Voltaire (1694–1778), French philosopher and writer

'Nowadays most people die of a sort of creeping common sense, and discover when it is too late that the only things one never regrets are one's mistakes.'

Oscar Wilde (1854–1900), wit and dandy

COMMUNICATION

The art of communication has always lain at the heart of effective management. On that all are agreed. But, the question is, Communication with whom? Traditionally, managers were more than willing to talk to each other, but regarded it as demeaning to talk to humble employees. The man operating a machine doffed his cap to management – or raised a finger – as managers made their way to their elevated offices. Times change. Now the job of management is to communicate with everyone – shareholders, the media, colleagues, superiors, customers, suppliers and even the people doing the work on the factory floor. The measure of managers in the late twentieth century is how well they communicate – not so much what they communicate.

'We got the mushroom treatment. Right after the acquisition we were kept in the dark, then they covered us with manure, then they cultivated us. After that they let us stew for awhile and, finally, they canned us.'
   Anon

'Well-timed silence hath more eloquence than speech.'
   Anon

'In communications, familiarity breeds apathy.'
   William Bernbach, advertising executive

'It is insight into human nature that is the key to the communicator's skill. For whereas the writer is concerned with what he puts into his writings, the communicator is concerned with what the reader gets out of it. He therefore becomes a student of how people read or listen.'
   William Bernbach

'Never express yourself more clearly than you are able to think.'
   Niels Bohrs (1885–1962), Danish physicist

' "When I use a word," said Humpty Dumpty in a rather scornful tone, "it means just what I choose it to mean – neither more nor less." '
Lewis Carroll (1832–98), creator of Alice

'If you have an important point to make, don't try to be subtle or clever. Use a pile driver. Hit the point once. Then come back and hit it again. Then hit it a third time with a tremendous whack.'
Sir Winston Churchill (1874–1965), statesman

'Seek first to understand, then to be understood.'
Stephen Covey (b. 1932), motivational guru

'The most important thing in communication is to hear what isn't being said.'
Peter Drucker (b. 1909), management author and perennially perceptive commentator

'It is not necessary for any one department to know what any other department is doing. It is the business of those who plan the entire work to see that all of the departments are working ... towards the same end.'
Henry Ford (1863–1947), American car manufacturer

'How can I know what I think till I see what I say?'
EM Forster (1879–1970), novelist

'Tell them the truth, first because it is the right thing to do and second they'll find out anyway.'
Paul Galvin, American business executive

'You can't communicate your way out of reality.'
Gerry Griffin (b. 1966), communications director

'Unless one is a genius, it is best to aim at being intelligible.'
Sir Anthony Hope Hawkins (1863–1933), novelist

'Never explain. Your friends do not need it and your enemies will not believe you anyway.'
Elbert Hubbard (1856–1915), American writer and businessman

'Words are, of course, the most powerful drug used by mankind.'
   Rudyard Kipling (1865–1936), writer

'If a person feels he can't communicate, the least he can do is shut up about it.'
   Tom Lehrer (b. 1928), American humorist, singer and song-writer

'He can compress the most words into the smallest idea of any man I know.'
   Abraham Lincoln (1809–65), American President

'You can fool all the people some of the time, and some of the people all the time, but you cannot fool all the people all the time.'
   Abraham Lincoln

'Better to remain silent and be thought a fool than to speak out and remove all doubt.'
   Abraham Lincoln

'Good communication is as stimulating as black coffee, and just as hard to sleep after.'
   Anne Morrow Lindbergh (b. 1906), writer

'Don't write anything you can phone, don't phone anything you can talk face to face, don't talk anything you can smile, don't smile anything you can wink, and don't wink anything you can nod.'
   Earl Long (1895–1960), American politician

'Sincerity is the key to success. If you can fake that, you got it made.'
   Groucho Marx (1890–1977), comedian

'Put it before them briefly so they will read it, clearly so they will appreciate it, picturesquely so they will remember it and above all accurately so they will be guided by its light.'
   Joseph Pulitzer (1847–1911), newspaper publisher

'Verbosity leads to unclear, inarticulate things.'
   Dan Quayle (b. 1947), American politician and gifted orator

'We are in great haste to construct a magnetic telegraph from Maine to Texas; but Maine and Texas, it may be, have nothing important to communicate.'
Henry David Thoreau (1817–62), American naturalist

'You can fool too many of the people too much of the time.'
James Thurber (1894–1961), American humorist and satirist

'Precision of communication is important, more important than ever, in our era of hair-trigger balances, when a false, or misunderstood word may create as much disaster as a sudden thoughtless act.'
James Thurber

'Where misunderstanding serves others as an advantage, one is helpless to make oneself understood.'
Lionel Trilling (1905–75), critic and writer

'If you can't convince them, confuse them.'
Harry S Truman (1884–1972), 33rd American President

COMPANIES AND COMPANY MEN

There was a time when companies assumed god-like status in the eyes of their employees. Enticed by jobs for life and security, managers became the embodiment of corporate values. The corporate man of the fifties and sixties, wore a regulation staid suit, progressed gently up the hierarchy, and watched impassively as the corporate juggernaut rolled surely on. It was dull, but in those days, dullness paid. 'The premise is simply that the goals of the individual and the goals of the organization will work out to be one and the same,' wrote William Whyte in his 1956 classic *The Organization Man.* 'The young men have no cynicism about the system and very little scepticism – they don't see it as something to be bucked but something to be conformed to.'

'There are five types of companies: those who make things happen; those who think they make things happen; those who watch things happen; those who wonder what happened; and those that did not know anything had happened.'
   Anon

'You ask me what it is I do. Well actually, you know,
I'm partly a liaison man and partly PRO
Essentially I integrate the current export drive
And basically I'm viable from ten o'clock till five.'
   Sir John Betjeman (1906–84), poet

'A man is known by the company he organizes.'
   ***Ambrose Bierce (1842–1914), writer and journalist**†

'Corporation, *n.* An ingenious device for obtaining individual profit without individual responsibility.'
   Ambrose Bierce

'The company is the hero. I am simply a tool to try to help it, if the company is the hero, then it lives on, and I can then go and play golf, which is what I really want to get on and do.'
  George Bull (b. 1936), British executive

'An empowered organization is one in which individuals have the knowledge, skill, desire and opportunity to personally succeed in a way that leads to collective organizational success.'
  Stephen Covey (b. 1932), self-improvement guru and bestselling author

'Organization is not an end in itself, but a means to an end of business performance and business results. Organization structure is an indispensable means, and the wrong structure will seriously impair business performance and may even destroy it ... The first question in discussing organization structure must be: What is our business and what should it be? Organization structure must be designed so as to make possible the attainment of the objectives of the business for five, ten, fifteen years hence.'
  Peter Drucker (b. 1909), author, sage and consultant

'Organization is not an end in itself, but a means to an end of business performance and business results.'
  Peter Drucker

'The riskiness of modern corporate life is in fact the harmless conceit of the modern corporate executive, and it is vigorously proclaimed. Precisely because he lives an orderly and careful life the executive is moved to identify himself with the dashing entrepreneur of economic literature.'
  JK Galbraith (b. 1908), economist

'The bigger the headquarters the more decadent the company.'
  Sir James Goldsmith (1933–97), multimillionaire businessman and politician

'It was once the case that unless you were caught with your hand in the till, or publicly slandered your boss, you could count on a job for life in many large companies. Loyalty was valued more than capability, and there was always a musty corner where mediocrity could hide. Entitlement produced a reasonably malleable workforce, and dependency enforced a begrudging kind of loyalty. That was then, this is now.'

Gary Hamel (b. 1954), co-author of *Competing for the Future*

'Corporations are not things, they are the people who run them.'
Charles Handy (b. 1932), Irish-born management guru

'Organization should always be a function of the task which you wish to achieve, and should change constantly.'

Sir John Harvey-Jones (b. 1924), former ICI chief

'It is clearly necessary to invent organizational structures appropriate to the multicultural age.'

Václav Havel (b. 1936), Czech President

'The great modern corporations are so similar to independent or semi-independent states of the past that they can only be fully understood in terms of political and constitutional history, and management can only be properly studied as a branch of government.'

Sir Antony Jay (b. 1930), writer

'Companies have to throw away the sheet music. You want improvisation, but you can't improvise on nothing. You have to have a tune.'

John Kao, Harvard Business School academic

'The achievements of an organization are the results of the combined effort of each individual.'

Vince Lombardi (1913–70), American football coach

'He got a corporation mind. He don't believe in nature; he puts his trust and distrust in man.'

Norman Mailer (b. 1923), novelist

'A group of people get together and exist as an institution that we call a company so they are able to accomplish something collectively that they could not accomplish separately.'
David Packard (1912–96), computer company founder

'Organizations are, in the last analysis, interactions among people.'
Richard Pascale (b. 1938), author of best-selling *Managing on the Edge*

'Most organizations bore me stiff. I can't imagine working in one of them. I'd be sad if my children chose to. Most organizations, large and even small, are bland as bean curd.'
Tom Peters (b. 1942), consultant and author

'Crazy times call for crazy organizations.'
Tom Peters

'We're all in Milan's *haute couture* business and Hollywood's movie business.'
Tom Peters

'The day of combination is here to stay. Individualism has gone, never to return.'
John D. Rockefeller (1839–1937), oil tycoon

'The company is an economic vehicle invented by society. It has no rights to survive. But value systems and philosophies survive. People take it with them.'
Edgar H. Schein (b. 1928), MIT-based corporate culture guru

'Our dream for the 1990s is a boundaryless company ... where we knock down the walls that separate us from each other on the inside and from our key constituents on the outside.'
Jack Welch (b. 1935), General Electric chief

'What is good for the country is good for General Motors, and vice versa.'
Charles E. Wilson (1886–1972), American businessman

COMPETITION AND COMPETITORS

'Competition as we know it is dead. Not that competition is vanishing. In fact it is intensifying. But we need to think about it differently,' says management author James Moore. The new competition is built around innovation, adapting quickly to change and shaping the future with dramatic leaps into the unknown. Motorola chief Gary Tooker asserts: 'Gaining and maintaining competitive advantage depends upon the ability of individuals at all levels of the organization to learn and adapt quickly to changing business realities.'

'People are not dumb. They know that if their company is not competitive, there is no job security.'
Percy Barnevik (b. 1941), Swedish executive

'An opponent is our helper.'
Edmund Burke (1729–97), statesman and writer

'Thou shalt not covet; but tradition approves all forms of competition.'
AH Clough (1819–61), poet

'Let the strongest live and the weakest die.'
Charles Darwin (1809–82), evolutionist

'The danger in today's environment is that the competition may not attack you head on, but eat away at growth opportunities over time until they've made you irrelevant.'
Gary Hamel (b. 1954), author and consultant

'A company surrenders today's businesses when it gets smaller faster than it gets better. A company surrenders tomorrow's businesses when it gets better without getting different.'
Gary Hamel

'Competition generates energy, rewards winners and punishes losers. It is therefore the fuel for the economy.'
   Charles Handy (b. 1932), author and thinker

'Competitive advantage is based not on doing what others already do well, but on doing what others cannot do as well.'
   John Kay, economist and educator

'You can duplicate the airplanes. You can duplicate the gate facilities. You can duplicate all the hard things, the tangible things you can put your hands on. But it's the intangibles that determine success. They're the hardest to duplicate, if you can do it at all. We've got the right intangibles.'
   Herb Kelleher, airline executive

'In truth, there is no such thing as a growth industry.'
   Theodore Levitt (b. 1925), marketing academic

'A horse never runs so fast as when he has other horses to catch up and outpace.'
   Ovid (43 BC–17 AD), Roman poet

'In any industry, whether it is domestic or international or produces a product or a service, the rules of competition are embodied in five competitive forces: the entry of new competitors, the threat of substitutes, the bargaining power of buyers, the bargaining power of suppliers, and the rivalry among the existing competitors.'
   Michael Porter (b. 1947), Harvard Business School competitiveness guru

'Competition brings out the best in products and the worst in people.'
   David Sarnoff (1891–1971), picked up first distress signals from the Titanic and became president of RCA

'Knowing where to fight, where to sit tight, and when and where to withdraw requires one to know one's competitor better than he knows himself.'
   David Stout (b. 1932), London Business School professor

'Histories will look back on the 20th century as a century of niche competition and the 21st century as a century of head-to-head competition.'
   Lester Thurow (b. 1938), economist and educator based at MIT

COMPUTERS CRASH

The world was once divided into those who used computers and those who did not. No more. The new world is divided into those who watch helplessly as their computers crash and those who are waiting for it to happen. Computers are fixtures in our offices, in our homes and in our cars. There is no escape. The only consolation is that PCs don't yet eat and drink.

'A computer terminal is not some clunky old television with a typewriter in front of it. It is an interface where the mind and body can connect with the universe and move bits of it about.'
   Douglas Adams (b. 1952), author of *The Hitchhiker's Guide to the Galaxy*

'In the old days it was important to be able to run down an antelope and kill it with a single blow to the forehead. But that skill is becoming less important every year. Now all that matters is if you can install your own Ethernet card without having to call tech support and confess your inadequacies to a stranger whose best career option is to work in tech support.'
   Scott Adams (b. 1957), creator of *Dilbert*

'Henry Kissinger said power is the ultimate aphrodisiac. And Bill Clinton said that knowledge is power. Therefore, logically, according to the U.S. Government, knowledge of computers is the ultimate aphrodisiac.'
   Scott Adams

'The most likely way for the world to be destroyed, most experts agree, is by accident. That's where we come in; we're computer professionals. We cause accidents.'
   Anon

'One computer manufacturer was so successful he had to move to smaller premises.'
   Anon

'If you lie to the computer, it will get you.'
Anon

'I do not fear computers. I fear the lack of them.'
Isaac Asimov (1920-92), science fiction writer

'Computer users soon learn that the miraculous power of personal computers are based on avoidance of error.'
Robert Burchfield (b. 1923), language scholar

'Twenty years ago, a conference called *The CEO in a Wired World* would not have been possible. Twenty years from now it will not be necessary.'
Peter Drucker (b. 1909), wired management writer

'The best software writer is the one who can make the program small, make it clever.'
Bill Gates (b. 1955), Microsoft co-founder

'Man is still the most extraordinary computer of all.'
John F. Kennedy (1917–63), American President

'A distributed system is one in which the failure of a computer you didn't even know existed can render your own computer unusable.'
Leslie Lamport (b. 1941), computer scientist

'There is no reason anyone would want a computer in their home.'
Ken Olsen (b. 1926), computer designer and founder of DEC

'The nerds have won!'
Tom Peters (b. 1942), management guru

'Computers are useless. They can only give you answers.'
Pablo Picasso (1881–1973), artist

'Computers make it easier to do a lot of things, but most of the things they make it easier to do don't need to be done.'
Andrew S. Rooney (b. 1919), journalist

'The business value of a computer is its *management*. The productivity of management is the decisive element that makes the difference of whether a computer hurts or helps.'

Paul A. Strassmann (b. 1929), American executive and educator

CORPORATE CLASSROOMS

Not everyone likes masters of business administration. The media features regular reports and articles proving that possession of the premier business qualification of our times is little guarantee of business success. This is undoubtedly true – there is always going to be a pimply software enthusiast from Delaware who accumulated billions by the age of twenty. But what then explains the amazing growth of MBA programs throughout the world? Is it a massive act of self-delusion?

'The business schools in the U.S., set up less than a century ago, have been preparing well-trained clerks.'
Peter Drucker (b. 1909), writer and educator (but not at a business school)

'Classrooms construct wonderful models of a non-world.'
Peter Drucker

'The worst thing in the world is to take an MBA direct from Harvard or London.'
Lord Hanson (b. 1922), British executive

'I am not impressed by diplomas. They don't do the work. My marks were not as good as those of others, and I didn't take the final examination. The principal called me in and said I have to leave. I told him that I didn't want a diploma. They had less value than a cinema ticket. A ticket at least guaranteed that you would get in. A diploma guaranteed nothing.'
Soichiro Honda (1906–91), founder of Honda

'Formal learning can teach you a great deal, but many of the essential skills in life are the ones you have to develop on your own.'
Lee Iacocca (b. 1924), American executive

'While we teach many of the right things in our MBA programs, we don't teach some critical things we ought to teach...like leadership, vision, imagination and values...the major reasons we don't is because if we teach those untaught things it will become more difficult to teach and to justify what we design for MBA-level education. We then lay it upon well-proportioned young men and women, distorting them (when we are lucky enough to succeed) into critters with lopsided brains, icy hearts, and shrunken souls.'
Harold Leavitt, management educator

'The idea that you can take smart but inexperienced 25–year olds who have never managed anything or anybody and turn them into effective managers via two years of classroom training is ludicrous.'
Henry Mintzberg (b. 1939), MBA sceptic based at McGill University and INSEAD

'Business schools train people to sit in their offices and look for case studies. The more Harvard succeeds, the more business fails.'
Henry Mintzberg

'MBAs develop a can-do mentality and you set out to achieve things. The technical knowledge you pick up from Harvard Business School is peripheral.'
Archie Norman (b. 1954), MBA, consultant, executive and politician

'Though MBA students may take a few specialized courses in their second year, the fact is that these so-called citadels of professional learning, turn out dilettantes (would the degree better be called PBA, for Pastiche of Business Administration?) who walk away with an acceptable technical vocabulary but little in-depth knowledge and, worse, because of the abiding focus on finding jobs, little taste for perpetual learning and true mastery.'
Tom Peters (b. 1942), consultant and author

'Sometime during the two-year curriculum, every MBA student ought to hear it clearly stated that numbers, techniques and analysis are all side matters. What is central to business is the joy of creating.'
Peter Robinson (b. 1957), author of *Snapshots from Hell*, the inside story of acquiring an MBA

'A great advantage I had when I started the Body Shop was that I had never been to business school.'

Anita Roddick (b. 1943), founder of The Body Shop

'Don't hire Harvard Business School graduates. This elite, in my opinion, is missing some pretty fundamental requirements for success: humility; respect for people on the firing line; deep understanding of the nature of the business and the kind of people who can enjoy themselves making it prosper; respect from way down the line; a demonstrated record of guts, industry, loyalty down, judgment, fairness, and honesty under pressure.'

Robert Townsend (b. 1920), author of *Up the Organization*

'A man can seldom – very, very, seldom – fight a winning fight against his training: the odds are too heavy.'

Mark Twain (1835–1910), novelist

CREATIVITY AT WORK

'Imagination is a good horse to carry you over the ground – not a flying carpet to set you free from probability,' writes the novelist Robertson Davies. Creativity is the essence of many business activities but it can never be allowed to cloud commercial reality. Traditionally, reality has suffocated creativity or dispatched it to corporate obscurity. Little wonder. Creativity thrives on disorder, disturbance, and relentless questioning – anathema to bureaucrats, fuel for creatives.

'Creativity is allowing yourself to make mistakes. Art is knowing which ones to keep.'
    Scott Adams (b. 1957), best-selling cartoonist

'The thing that makes a creative person is to be creative and that is all there is to it.'
    Edward Albee (b. 1928), playwright

'Whatever creativity is, it is in part a solution to a problem.'
    Brian Aldiss (b. 1925), writer

'The man who has no imagination has no wings.'
    Muhammad Ali (b. 1942), The Greatest

'Imagination is intelligence having fun.'
    Anon

'Don't let the facts get in the way of your imagination.'
    Anon

'Imagination is the one weapon in the war against reality.'
    Anon

'Imagination is the highest kite that one can fly.'
    Lauren Bacall (b. 1924), actress

'There are lots of people who mistake their imagination for their memory.'
Josh Billings (1818–85), writer

'I must create a system or be enslaved by another man's
I will not reason and compare: my business is to create.'
William Blake (1757–1827), poet and artist

'Imagination with substance, execution with style.'
Burson-Marsteller mission statement

'Curiosity about life in all of its aspects, I think, is still the secret of great creative people.'
Leo Burnett, advertising agency founder

'Imagination offers people consolation for what they cannot be, and humor for what they actually are.'
Albert Camus (1913–60), French writer

'I love fools' experiments. I am always making them.'
Charles Darwin (1809–82), naturalist

'If anybody wants to keep creating they have to be about change.'
Miles Davis (1926–91), master of change as well as the trumpet

'Don't play what's there, play what's not there.'
Miles Davis

'Disneyland will never be completed, as long as there is imagination left in the world.'
Walt Disney (1901–66), founder of entertainment empire

'It's like driving a car at night. you never see further than your headlights, but you can make the whole trip that way.'
EL Doctorow (b. 1931), novelist and short story writer

'To invent, you need a good imagination and a pile of junk.'
Thomas Alva Edison (1847–1931), inventor and industrialist

'The secret to creativity is knowing how to hide your sources.'
Albert Einstein (1879–1955), physicist

'Imagination is more important than knowledge.'
   Albert Einstein

'Creative minds have always been known survive any kind of bad training.'
   Anna Freud (b. 1895), psychoanalyst

'Companies should throw out the old ideas and let their imaginations flow.'
   Gary Hamel (b. 1954), best-selling author and consultant

'The most gifted member of the human species are at their creative best when they cannot have their way.'
   Erik Hoffer (b. 1902), philosopher

'An essential aspect of creativity is not being afraid to fail.'
   Edwin Land (1909–91), inventor of the Polaroid camera

'Creation is a drug I can't do without.'
   Cecil B. de Mille (1881–1959), filmmaker

'The mind uses its faculty for creativity only when experience forces it to do so.'
   Jules-Henri Poincaré (1854–1912), mathematician and physicist

'You can't depend on your judgement when your imagination is out of focus.'
   Mark Twain (1835–1910), focused novelist

'If people never did silly things, nothing intelligent would ever get done.'
   Ludwig Wittgenstein (1889–1951), philosopher

CRISES AND DRAMAS

Crisis, what crisis? Crises and dramas are as inevitable in business as in life. The consensus from the great and the good is that instead of being desperately avoided and denied, they should be faced. Crises can present opportunities to seize the initiative and move forward rather than standing transfixed as your whole life passes in front of you. Mere mortals usually find the latter approach irresistible. Creation is preferable to crisis. 'It's more fun building a bridge than putting sandbags on a levy,' said an unhappy departing IBM executive

'*Don't panic.* It's the first helpful or intelligible thing anybody's said to me all day.'
Douglas Adams (b. 1952), writer and producer

'Calamities are of two kinds: misfortune to ourselves, and good fortune to others.'
Ambrose Bierce (1842–1914), journalist and author

'Public calamity is a mighty leveller.'
Edmund Burke (1729–97), statesman and writer

'Adversity is the first path to Truth.'
Lord Byron (1788–1824), romantic poet

'It is the fashion to style the present moment an extraordinary crises.'
Benjamin Disraeli (1804–81), statesman and novelist

'When things are bad, we take comfort in the thought that they could always be worse. And when they are, we find hope in the thought that things are so bad they have to get better.'
Malcolm S. Forbes (1919–90), optimistic publisher

'As you go through life, there are thousands of little forks in the road, and there are a few really big forks – those moments of reckoning, moments of truth.'
Lee Iacocca (b. 1924), executive and author

'In times of great stress or adversity, it's always best to keep busy, to plow your anger and your energy into something positive.'
Lee Iacocca

'When written in Chinese, the word crisis is compounded of two characters – one represents danger, and the other represents opportunity.'
John F. Kennedy (1917–63), 35th American President

'Great crises produce great men and great deeds of courage.'
John F. Kennedy

'There cannot be a crisis next week. My schedule is already full.'
Henry Kissinger (b. 1923), politician

'If I can't fire people – and I never would want to – how can I instil a sense of crisis? How can I persuade people that if nothing changes, the company will slowly die?'
Minoru Makihara, Japanese chief of Mitsubishi

'Crises and deadlocks when they occur have at least this advantage, that they force us to think.'
Jawaharlal Nehru (1889–1964), first Indian Prime Minister

'Every little thing counts in a crisis.'
Jawaharlal Nehru

'These are the times that try men's souls.'
Thomas Paine (1737–1809), political thinker

'I believe that crisis really tends to help develop the character of an organization.'
John Sculley (b. 1939), Pepsi marketer and Apple boss

'Necessity is the theme and the inventress, the eternal curb and law of nature.'
Leonardo da Vinci (1452–1519), the Renaissance man

Customer Delight

The business world rediscovered customers in the 1980s. Companies proclaimed themselves *customer focused*. The more emotional confessed to loving their customers. Often this involved sending a receptionist on a customercare course, promising to answer the telephone within five rings and smiling a lot. It was hoped, the end result would be customer delight, legions of happy customers who would return time and time again. A small number of companies got it right. But these were largely the companies who had never forgotten their customers in the first place. The rest were left with a smile on their face.

'I am sick and tired of visiting plants to hear nothing but great things about quality and cycle time only then to visit customers who tell me of problems.'
John Akers (b. 1934), former head of IBM

'Never underestimate the power of the irate customer.'
Anon

'There's a sucker born every minute.'
Phineas T. Barnum (1810–91), cynical businessman

'To serve is beautiful, but only if it is done with a whole heart and a free mind.'
Pearl S. Buck (1892–1973), American writer

'To all our nit-picky – overdemanding – ask-awkward-questions customers: Thank you, and keep up the good work.'
Dell Computers advertisement

'The consumer is the most important part of the production line.'
W. Edwards Deming (1990–93), quality guru, creator of the 14 points

'Profit in business comes from repeat customers, customers that boast about your product and service, and that bring friends with them.'
W. Edwards Deming

'The customer does not know what he will need in one, three, five years from now. If you, as just one of his potential suppliers, wait until then to find out, you will hardly be ready to serve him.'
W. Edwards Deming

'To satisfy the customer is the mission and purpose of every business.'
Peter Drucker (b. 1909), author and commentator

'The customer only wants to know what the product or service will do for him tomorrow. All he is interested in are his own values, his own wants, his own reality. For this reason alone, any serious attempt to state what our business is must start with the customer, his realities, his situation, his behavior, his expectations, and his values.'
Peter Drucker

'You pounce in here expecting to be waited on hand and foot. Well I'm trying to run a hotel here. Have you any idea of how much there is to do? Do you ever think of that? Of course not, you're all too busy sticking your noses into every corner, poking around for things to complain about, aren't you?'
Basil Fawlty, aka John Cleese (b. 1939), actor and comedian

'Those who enter to buy, support me. Those who come to flatter, please me. Those who complain, teach me how I may please others so that more will come. Only those hurt me who are displeased but don't complain. They refuse me permission to correct my errors and thus improve my service.'
Marshall Field (1834–1906), department store merchant

'The customer is an object to be manipulated, not a concrete person whose aims the businessman is interested to satisfy.'
Erich Fromm (1900–80), German-born psychoanalyst

'The customer is frequently wrong. We don't carry those sorts of customers. We write them and say, *Fly somebody else. Don't abuse our people.*'
Herb Kelleher, airline executive

'If you are not thinking customer, you are not thinking.'
Theodore Levitt (b. 1925), marketing guru

'An industry begins with the customer and his needs, not with a patent, a raw material, or a selling skill.'
Theodore Levitt

'There are no such things as service industries. There are only industries whose service components are greater or less than those of other industries. Everybody is in service.'
Theodore Levitt

'No organization can achieve greatness without a vigorous leader who is driven onward by his own pulsating will to succeed. He has to have a vision of grandeur, a vision that can produce eager followers in vast numbers. In business, the followers are the customers.'
Theodore Levitt

'Be everywhere, do everything, and never fail to astonish the customer.'
Macy's motto

'About 40 percent of the population really never smiles, and if they never smile then forget it. They shouldn't be in our business.'
Archie Norman (b. 1954), retailer and politician

'The consumer is not a moron; she is your wife.'
David Ogilvy (b. 1911), advertising guru

'Treat the customer as an appreciating asset.'
Tom Peters (b. 1942), champion of customer service

'You can automate the production of cars but you cannot automate the production of customers.'
Walter Reuther (1907–70), United Auto Workers president

'Our people are my first line of customers.'
Anita Roddick (b. 1943), founder of The Body Shop

'The pretense that corporations are necessary for the better government of the trade is without any foundation. The real and effectual discipline which is exercised over a workman is not that of his corporation, but that of his customers.'

Adam Smith (1723–90), the original free marketer

'Our goal as a company is to have customer service that is not just the best, but legendary.'

Sam Walton (1918–92), founder of Wal-Mart retail chain

'From this day forward, I solemnly promise and declare that every time a customer comes within ten feet of me, I will smile, look him in the eye, and greet him, so help me Sam.'

Sam Walton

'If we provide real satisfaction to real customers – we will be profitable.'

John Young (b. 1932), former Hewlett-Packard chief

Decision time

The decision is the crunch. You have collected a mound of information. The computer has whirred through every regression analysis in existence. The room is full of expectant faces staring at you. Yes or no? Stop or go? There is no easy answer and no easy means of reaching an answer.

'A decision is the action an executive must take when he has information so incomplete that the answer does not suggest itself.'
Anon

'Decide promptly, but never give your reasons. Your decisions may be right, but your reasons are sure to be wrong.'
Anon

'No sensible decision can be made any longer without taking into account not only the world as it is, but the world as it will be.'
Isaac Asimov (1920–92), science fiction writer

'Nothing is more difficult, and therefore more precious than to be able to decide.'
Napoléon Bonaparte (1769–1821), French General

'It is the characteristic excellence of the strong man that he can bring momentous issues to the fore and make a decision about them. The weak are always forced to decide between alternatives they have not chosen themselves.'
Dietrich Bonhoeffer (1906–45), German pastor and theologian

'The importance of decision making in management is generally recognized. But a good deal of the discussion tends to center on problem-solving, that is, on giving answers. And that is the wrong focus. Indeed, the most common source of mistakes in management decisions is the emphasis on finding the right answer, rather than the right question.'
   Peter Drucker (b. 1909), management writer, educator and consultant

'Wherever you see a successful business, someone once made a courageous decision.'
   Peter Drucker

'The books and articles on leadership are full of advice on how to make fast, forceful and incisive decisions. But there is no more foolish – and no more wasting – advice that to decide quickly what a problem really is.'
   Peter Drucker

'I believe every decision is stronger when a group of people argue about it, debate it, try to figure out how to make it better.'
   Lou Gerstner (b. 1942), former consultant now IBM chief

'The most decisive actions of our life – I mean those that are most likely to decide the whole course of our future – are, more often than not, unconsidered.'
   André Gide (1869–1951), French novelist and Nobel prize winner

'No one can be right all of the time, but it helps to be right most of the time.'
Robert Half (b. 1918), American personnel agency executive

'There are one-storey intellects, two-storey intellects, and three-storey intellects with skylights. All fact-collectors, who have no aim beyond their facts, are one-storey men. Two-storey men compare, reason, generalize, using the labors of fact-collectors as well as their own. Three-storey men idealize, imagine, predict; their best illumination comes from above, through the skylight.'
   Oliver Wendell Holmes, Jr. (1841–1935), American writer

'If I had to sum up in one word what makes a good manager, I'd say decisiveness. You can use the fanciest computers to gather the numbers, but in the end you have to set a timetable and act.'
Lee Iacocca (b. 1924), former Chrysler chief

'Exercising judgment and making decisions is what you pay people (everyone) for.'
Elliott Jaques (b. 1917), management researcher

'A lot of companies I deal with seem incapable of making a decision. It doesn't matter if the decision you make is right or wrong. What matters is that you make it and don't waste your company's time. If you make the decision, you begin to distinguish the good from the bad.'
Peter Kindersley (b. 1941), publisher

'When important decisions have to be taken, the natural anxiety to come to a right decision will often keep you awake. Nothing, however, is more conducive to healthful sleep than plenty of open air.'
Sir John Lubbock (1834–1913), British author and financier

'Ever notice that what the hell is always the right decision?'
__Marilyn Monroe (1926–62), American actress__

'Businessmen don't have all the information. This idea that decisions are made based on lots of rational facts is wrong – you take decisions based on 25 percent of available facts.'
Martin Taylor (b. 1952), journalist and businessman

'Never flinch – make up your own mind and do it.'
Margaret Thatcher (b. 1925), politician

DELEGATION

'Here lies a man who knew how to bring into his service men better than he was himself,' is the epitaph the industrialist Andrew Carnegie chose for himself. Business greats are also usually great delegators. They know, as one wit pointed out, that there are three ways of ensuring that something gets done: do it yourself, pay someone else to do it or tell your children not to do it.

'What is worth doing is worth the trouble of asking somebody to do it.'
  Ambrose Bierce (1842–1914), journalist and writer

'If you want a thing done well, do it yourself.'
  Napoléon Bonaparte (1769–1821), French DIY enthusiast

'Some great men owe most of their greatness to the ability of detecting in those they destine for their tools the exact quality of strength that matters for their work.'
  Joseph Conrad (1857–1924), Polish-born novelist

'It's easy to decide what you're going to do. The hard thing is figuring out what you're not going to do.'
  Michael Dell (b. 1964), computer boss

'Often you find out you're abdicating not delegating. That is wrong, because you abdicate, give the situation to people, and it causes all sorts of problems. Then you learn that abdication is not the right thing to do either. The real art of delegation is to be able to give people responsibility, give them authority, but also make them accountable, and ensure there is a very good report-back system to you.'
  Tom Farmer (b. 1940), Kwik-Fit founder

'According to the experience of all but the most accomplished jugglers, it is easier to keep one ball in the air than many.'
  JK Galbraith (b. 1908), economist

'Big things and little things are my job. Middle-level arrangements can be delegated.'
Konosuke Matsushita (1894–1989), Japanese businessman

'I try to keep in touch with the details – you can't keep in touch with them all, but you've got to have a feel for what's going on. I also look at the product daily. That doesn't mean you interfere, but it's important occasionally to show the ability to be involved. It shows you understand what's happening.'
Rupert Murdoch (b. 1931), Australian media mogul

'Never tell people how to do things. Tell them what you want them to achieve and they will surprise you with their ingenuity.'
General George S. Patton (1885–1945), American soldier

'Surround yourself with the best people you can find, delegate authority, and don't interfere.'
Ronald Reagan (b. 1911), American President

'Anyone who is any good has to be given space to get on with it.'
Gerry Robinson (b. 1948), laid-back Granada boss

'If you want good service, serve yourself.'
Spanish Proverb

'A burden in the bush is worth two on your hands.'
James Thurber (1894–1961), humorist and satirist

'It is amazing what you can accomplish if you do not care who gets the credit.'
Harry S Truman (1884–1972), 33rd American President

'We can't all do everything.'
Virgil (70–19 BC), Roman poet and delegator

DREAMS AND DREAMERS

'A personal computer on every desk and in every home,' dreamed Bill Gates and Paul Allen. It seemed complete nonsense at the time. But, instead of being speedily certified, Gates and Allen set about making their fortunes. You don't have to be in Disneyland for dreams to come true and behind every desk there is a dreamer.

'When your dreams turn to dust, vacuum.'
  Anon

'But a man who doesn't dream is like a man who doesn't sweat. He stores up a lot of poison.'
  Truman Capote (1924–84), novelist

'A man must have his dreams – memory dreams of the past and eager dreams of the future. I never want to stop reaching for new goals.'
  Maurice Chevalier (1888–1972), French entertainer

'To fulfill a dream, to be allowed to sweat over lonely labor, to be given a chance to create, is the meat and potatoes of life. The money is the gravy.'
  Bette Davis (1908–89), actress

'If you can dream it, you can do it.'
  Walt Disney (1901–66), corporate dreamer on a large scale

'When I examine myself and my methods of thought, I come to the conclusion that the gift of fantasy has meant more to me than any talent for abstract, positive thinking.'
  Albert Einstein (1879–1955), physicist

'Dreaming is zero-value. I mean anyone can dream.'
  Bill Gates (b. 1955), computer boffin

'It may be that those who do most, dream most.'
Stephen Butler Leacock (1869–1944), Canadian economist and humorist

'A salesman has got to dream, boy. It comes with the territory.'
Arthur Miller (b. 1915), American dramatist

'Those who dream by day are cognizant of many things that escape those who dream only at night.'
Edgar Allan Poe (1809–49), American writer

'If a little dreaming is dangerous, the cure for it is not to dream less but to dream more, to dream all the time.'
Marcel Proust (1871–1922), French novelist

'The future belongs to those who believe in the beauty of their dreams.'
Eleanor Roosevelt (1884–1962), first lady

'Nothing happens unless first a dream.'
Carl Sandburg (1878–1967), American poet

'You see things; and you say *why?* But I dream things that never were; and I say "why not?" '
George Bernard Shaw (1856–1950), playwright

'If you have built castles in the air, your work need not be lost; that is where they should be. Now put the foundations under them.'
Henry David Thoreau (1817–62), naturalist and writer

'Go confidently in the direction of your dreams! Live the life you've imagined. As you simplify your life, the laws of the universe will be simpler; solitude will not be solitude, poverty will not be poverty, nor weakness weakness.'
Henry David Thoreau

'If the world's population had the productivity of the Swiss, the consumption habits of the Chinese, the egalitarian instincts of the Swedes and the social discipline of the Japanese, then the planet could support many times its current population without privation for anyone. On the other hand, if the world's population had the productivity of Chad, the consumption habits of the United States, the inegalitarian instincts of India, and the social discipline of Argentina, then the planet could not support anywhere near its current numbers.'

Lester Thurow (b. 1938), economist and educator, based at MIT's Sloan School

'Society often forgives the criminal; it never forgives the dreamer.'
Oscar Wilde (1854–1900), wit

'Dreams never hurt anybody if you keep working right behind the dreams to make as much of them become real as you can.'

Frank W. Woolworth (1852–1919), retailer who opened first Woolworth's store in 1879

Economics and Economists

Thomas Carlyle labeled economics the 'dismal science.' A century later, things haven't improved. With their macro models and ability to provide detailed explanations of why they weren't really wrong, economists are perennial scapegoats.

'Take care to be an economist in prosperity. There is no fear of your being one in adversity.'
Anon

'Economists have been insulated from industrial and commercial problems, and encouraged to apply themselves to those fascinating conundrums in which pure theory is rich.'
Sir Alec Cairncross (b. 1911), British economist

'Economics is extremely useful as a form of employment for economists.'
JK Galbraith (b. 1908), Canadian-born economist and more

'The fully planned economy, so far from being unpopular, is warmly regarded by those who know it best.'
JK Galbraith

'If economists could manage to get themselves thought of as humble, competent people, on a level with dentists, that would be splendid.'
John Maynard Keynes (1883–1946), economist

'In most circles, the idea of economic planning has been in disrepute most of the time and, particularly in America, has almost carried connotations of intellectual and moral perversion and even political subversion.'
Gunnar Myrdal (1898–1987), Swedish economist and sociologist

'Economics is fate.'
Walter Rathenau (1867–1922), German industrialist

'An economist's guess is liable to be just as good as anybody else's.'
Will Rogers (1879–1935), American comedian and showman

'Economists are about as useful as astrologers in predicting the future (and, like astrologers, they never let failure on one occasion diminish certitude on the next).'

Arthur Schlesinger, Jr. (b. 1917), historian

'If all economists were laid end to end, they would not reach a conclusion.'
George Bernard Shaw (1856–1950), playwright

Ego, Esteem and Self

The American sage Ambrose Bierce noted that an egotist was 'a person more interested in himself than in me.' The business world is notoriously egotistical. Corporate success is all well and good but it is inextricably linked to the success of the individuals it employs. Business is nothing if not personal and personal improvement is an increasing obsession.

'None will improve your lot
If you yourselves do not.'
  Bertolt Brecht (1898–1956), German playwright

'Self-confidence is the most important thing, and this comes from identifying your goals, knowing your limits and roping in all the help you can get.'
  Shirley Conran (b. 1932), Superwoman

'To know all is not to forgive all. It is to despise everybody.'
  Quentin Crisp (b. 1908), writer

'Being convinced one knows the whole story is the surest way to fail.'
  Philip Crosby, quality guru

'I gotta be me.'
  Sammy Davis, Jr. (1925–90), entertainer

'Respect your efforts, respect yourself. Self-respect leads to self-discipline. When you have both firmly under your belt, that's real power.'
  Clint Eastwood (b. 1930), actor

'Don't bother just to be better than your contemporaries or predecessors. Try to be better than yourself.'
  William Faulkner (1897–1962), American novelist and night-watchman

'Modesty is a vastly overrated virtue.'
JK Galbraith (b. 1908), a humble economist

'All these ego-feeding activities – the long hours in the limousine, the sky-larking in the corporate jet, the collection of press clippings, the unnecessary speeches – feed the corporate sickness and one way or another make a corporate problem out of what had been an otherwise perfectly competent, even brilliant executive.'
Harold Geneen (b. 1910), Bournemouth-born former ITT chief

'It is extremely difficult to teach grown-up people anything. It is, however, relatively easy to create conditions under which people will train themselves.'
Sir John Harvey-Jones (b. 1924), British executive

'There's a world of difference between a strong ego, which is essential, and a large ego, which can be destructive.'
Lee Iacocca (b. 1924), American executive and best-selling author

'Those who are well assured of their own standing are least apt to trespass on that of others.'
Washington Irving (1783–1859), *Rip van Winkle* author

'Individualism if it can be purged of its defects and abuses, is the best safeguard of individual liberty.'
John Maynard Keynes (1883–1946), author

'But enough of me. Let's talk about you. What do you think of me?'
Ed Koch (b. 1924), former mayor of New York

'Egotism is the anesthetic that dulls the pain of stupidity.'
Frank Leahy (b. 1908), American football coach

'We are not in a position in which we have nothing to work with. We already have capacities, talents, direction, missions, callings.'
Abraham Maslow (1908–70), motivational expert

'Don't be so humble – you are not that great.'
Golda Meir (1898–1978), Israeli Prime Minister

'The only one who can tell you "you can't" is you. And you don't have to listen.'
Nike advertisement

'You don't have to believe in all the hype, just in yourself, that's all.'
Bruce Oldfield (b. 1950), British clothes designer

'Any effort that has self-glorification as its final endpoint is bound to end in disaster.'
Robert M. Pirsig (b. 1928) author of *Zen and the Art of Motorcycle Maintenance*

'Avoid having your ego so close to your position that when your position falls, your ego goes with it.'
General Colin Powell (b. 1937), American soldier

'There is no relationship between the process of succeeding and any genuine desire to get to know yourself and to understand the roots of whatever it is that makes you strive.'
Gerry Robinson (b. 1948), Granada chief

'One of the symptoms of an approaching nervous breakdown is the belief that one's work is terribly important.'
Bertrand Russell (1872–1970), mathematician and philosopher

'All men who have turned out worth anything have had the chief hand in their own education.'
Sir Walter Scott (1771–1832), novelist

'Nothing makes a man so selfish as work.'
George Bernard Shaw (1856–1950), playwright

'If you see a company where the ego rules the brain you'd better sell the shares.'
Martin Taylor (b. 1952), journalist and businessman

'The sin of Hubris is inevitably and inexorably followed by Nemesis.'
Robert Townsend (b. 1920), former Avis chief and author

ENTHUSIASTS AND ENTREPRENEURS

'A self-made man is one who believes in lunch and sends his sons to Oxford,' wrote the novelist Christine Stead in 1938. Sixty years later, entrepreneurs probably miss lunch and may well have missed out on Oxford as well. Entrepreneurial achievers of today combines ambition with attitude. They are commercial fanatics and fantasists, some of whom make good.

'A positive attitude may not solve all your problems, but it will annoy enough people to make it worth the effort.'
   Anon

'If you can give your son or daughter only one gift, let it be enthusiasm.'
   Bruce Barton (1886–1967), American ad man and politician

'When small men attempt great enterprises, they always end by reducing them to the level of their mediocrity.'
   Napoléon Bonaparte (1769–1821), small but perfectly formed

'There is no place in a fanatic's head where reason can enter.'
   Napoleon Bonaparte

'A fanatic is one who can't change his mind and won't change the subject.'
   Sir Winston Churchill (1874–1965), statesman

'Zeal without knowledge is the sister of folly.'
   Sir John Davies (1569–1626), knowledgeable observer

'He is a self-made man, very much in love with his creator.'
   __Benjamin Disraeli (1804–81), statesman__

'Nothing great was ever achieved without enthusiasm.'
   Ralph Waldo Emerson (1803–82), poet

'Zeal will do more than knowledge.'
William Hazlitt (1778–1830), essayist

'If you start off with a view to just making money, you'll probably make some, but you won't make a lot – you have to have a passion to succeed.'
Howard Hodgson (b. 1950), British businessman

'An enterprise culture is one in which every individual understands that the world does not owe him or her a living.'
Peter Morgan (b. 1936), British executive

'You cannot be successful at anything doing it for 90 percent of the time.'
Arne Naess, shipping magnate

'We are shifting from a managerial society to an entrepreneurial society.'
John Naisbitt, futurist

'I reckon one entrepreneur can recognize another at 300 yards on a misty day.'
Sir Peter Parker (b. 1924), British executive

'Without fanaticism we cannot accomplish anything.'
__Eva Perón (1919–52), Argentinean politician__

[Entrepreneurship is] 'unreasonable conviction based on inadequate evidence.'
Tom Peters (b. 1942), the original management guru

'Obsession does not guarantee success. On the other hand a lack of obsession does guarantee failure.'
Tom Peters

'A friendship founded on business is better than a business founded on friendship.'
John D. Rockefeller Jr. (1839–1937), oil tycoon

'There is a fine line between the delinquent mind of an entrepreneur and that of a crazy person. The entrepreneur's dream is almost a kind of madness, and it is almost as isolating. When you see something new, your vision usually isn't shared by others, the difference between a crazy person and the successful entrepreneur is that the latter can convince others to share the vision. That force of will is fundamental to entrepreneurship.'
   Anita Roddick (b. 1943), founder of The Body Shop

'Whenever you are asked if you can do a job, tell 'em, "Certainly, I can!" Then get busy and find out how to do it.'
   Theodore Roosevelt (1858–1919), 26th American President

'Fanaticism consists in redoubling your effort when you have forgotten your aim.'
   George Santayana (1863–1952), Spanish-born philosopher and writer

'Real commitment is rare in today's organizations. It is our experience that 90 percent of the time what passes for commitment is compliance.'
   Peter Senge (b. 1947), academic and author

'Perpetual devotion to what a man calls his business is only to be sustained by perpetual neglect of many other things.'
   Robert Louis Stevenson (1850–94), novelist

'The best lack all conviction, while the worst are full of passionate intensity.'
   WB Yeats (1865–1939), Irish poet

Ethics and values

Day in, day out, managers face ethical decisions. Should they buy from a supplier which employs children in India? Should they spend more money on safety? Has everything been thoroughly tested? Yet, despite having to continually make ethical judgements, managers usually receive precious little training or instruction on business ethics. Their ethics and values are more likely to have been learned in the school playground than at a business school.

'A man should be upright, not be kept upright.'
Marcus Aurelius Antonius (121–80), Roman Emperor and philosopher

'If it is not right do not do it; if it is not true do not do it.'
Marcus Aurelius Antonius

'The distinguishing mark of the executive responsibility is that it requires not merely conformance to a complex code of morals but also the creation of moral codes for others.'
Chester Barnard (1886–1961), executive and author

'For the merchant, even honesty is a financial speculation.'
Charles Baudelaire (1821–67), French poet

'When a man sells eleven ounces for twelve, he makes a compact with the devil, and sells himself for the value of an ounce.'
Henry Ward Beecher (1813–87), clergyman abolitionist

'Alliance, *n.* In international politics, the union of two thieves who have their hands so deeply inserted in each other's pocket that they cannot separately plunder a third.'
Ambrose Bierce (1842–1914), American Dr. Johnson

'Occident, *n.* The part of the world lying west (or east) of the Orient. It is largely inhabited by Christians, a powerful subtribe of the Hypocrites, whose principal industries are murder and cheating, which they are pleased to call "war" and "commerce". These, also are the principal industries of the Orient.'
Ambrose Bierce

'We speak of being anchored to our principles. But if the weather turns nasty you up with an anchor and let it down where there's less wind, and the fishing's better.'
Robert Bolt (b. 1924), dramatist

'The surest way to remain poor is to be an honest man.'
Napoléon Bonaparte (1769–1821), French soldier

'The best way to keep one's word is not to give it.'
Napoléon Bonaparte

'A show of a certain amount of honesty is in any profession or business the surest way of growing rich.'
Jean de La Bruyère (1812–89), poet

'Integrity has no need of rules.'
Albert Camus (1913–60), poet and goalkeeper

'Prefer a loss to a dishonest gain; the one brings pain at the moment, the other for all time.'
Chilon (c. 6th century BC), Greek sage

'To know what is right and not to do it is the worst cowardice.'
Confucius (551–479 BC), Chinese philosopher

'Just being honest is not enough. The essential ingredient is executive integrity.'
Philip Crosby, author of *Quality Is Free*

'Honor sinks where commerce long prevails.'
Oliver Goldsmith (1730?–74), Irish-born writer

'A company's values – what it stands for, what its people believe in – are crucial to its competitive success. Indeed, values drive the business.'
Robert Haas, consultant and Levi Strauss chief

'If we think of the future – a central part of the obligation to rising generations – we must adopt the cyclical approach on which the whole of nature is based.'
Carl Hahn (b. 1926), chairman of Volkswagen

'It horrifies me that ethics is only an optional extra at Harvard Business School.'
Sir John Harvey-Jones (b. 1924), straight talking former ICI chief

'The value system that makes your firm work is exactly the same as the value system that makes your family work.'
Will Hutton, newspaper editor and author of *The State We're In*

'A good man should and must
Sit rather down with loss than rise unjust.'
Ben Jonson (1572–1637), Elizabethan dramatist

'A man's word
Is believed just to the extent of the wealth in his covers stored.'
Juvenal (60–140), Roman satirist

'Go ahead and be inconsistent. You're not a wind-up toy. If they are consistent in values, which they are, then we have nothing to worry about.'
Herb Kelleher, airline executive

'Moral principle is a looser bond than pecuniary interest.'
__Abraham Lincoln (1809–65), American President__

'In the end, managers are loyal not to a particular boss or even to a company but to a set of values they believe in and find satisfying.'
Goran Lindahl, Asea Brown Boveri chief executive

'The best way to tell if a man is honest is to ask him. If he says he is, you know he's a crook.'
Groucho Marx (1890–1977), comic genius

> *'Those are my principles, if you don't like them I have others.'*
> **Groucho Marx**

'A man may be a tough, concentrated, successful money-maker and never contribute to his country anything more than a horrible example. A manager may be tough and practical, squeezing out, while the going is good, the last ounce of profit and dividend, and may leave behind him an exhausted industry and a legacy of industrial hatred. A tough manager may never look outside his own factory walls or be conscious of his partnership in a wider world. I often wonder what strange cud such men sit chewing when their working days are over, and the accumulating riches of the mind have eluded them.'
> **Sir Robert Gordon Menzies (1894–1978), Australian Prime Miniseter**

'If we face a recession, we should not lay off employees; the company should sacrifice a profit. It's management's risk and management's responsibility. Employees are not guilty; why should they suffer?'
> **Akio Morita (b. 1921), co-founder of Sony**

'Honesty is for the most part less profitable than dishonesty.'
> **Plato (c. 428–348 BC)**

'Being good is good business.'
> **Anita Roddick (b. 1943), founder of The Body Shop**

'If you do things well, do them better. Be daring, be first, be different, be just.'
> **Anita Roddick**

'The truth of the matter is that you always know the right thing to do. The hard part is doing it.'
> **General H. Norman Schwarzkopf (b. 1934), American soldier**

'More men come to doom / through dirty profits than are kept by them.'
> **Sophocles (496–406 BC), Athenian tragedian**

'Integrity can be neither lost nor concealed nor faked nor quenched nor artificially come by nor outlived, nor, I believe, in the long run denied.'
> **Eudora Welty (b. 1909), American writer**

EXPERIENCE

Experience is history. But what can we remember and what do we do with what we can recall? If we do nothing with experience we run the risk of repeating a single year's experience throughout our careers. Who knows, after thirty or so attempts, we might just get it right.

'Human beings, who are almost unique in having the ability to learn from the experience of others, are also remarkable for their apparent disinclination to do so.'
Douglas Adams (b. 1952), British writer and producer

'You should make a point of trying every experience once, excepting incest and folk-dancing.'
Anon

'Good judgement comes from experience ... experiences comes from poor judgement.'
Anon

'Experience is what you got by not having it when you need it.'
Anon

'Experience is what causes a person to make new mistakes instead of old ones.'
Anon

'Experience is often what you get when you were expecting something else.'
Anon

'Experience is something you don't get until just after you need it.'
Anon

'To a great experience one thing is essential, an experiencing nature.'
Walter Bagehot (1826–1877), writer

'Age is only a number, a cipher for the records. A man can't retire his experience. He must use it. Experience achieves more with less energy and time.'
Bernard Baruch (1870–1965), American financier and economic adviser

'You cannot create experience. You must undergo it.'
Albert Camus (1913–60), French writer

'The knowledge of the world is only to be acquired in the world, and not in a closet.'
Lord Chesterfield (1694–1773), statesman

'Experience is a great advantage. The problem is that when you get the experience, you're too damned old to do anything about it.'
Jimmy Connors (b. 1952), tennis player

'A sturdy lad ... who in turn tries all the professions, who teams it, farms it, peddles, keeps a school, preaches, edits a newspaper, goes to Congress, buys a township, and so forth, in successive years, and always like a cat falls on his feet, is worth a hundred of these city dolls ... he has not one chance, but a hundred chances.'
Ralph Waldo Emerson (1803–82), poet

'The only history that is worth a tinker's damn is the history we make today.'
Henry Ford (1863–1947), auto manufacturer

'Experience is valuable only to the extent that the future is like the past. In industry after industry the terrain is changing so fast that experience is becoming irrelevant and even dangerous.'
Gary Hamel (b. 1954), consultant and author

'Measurement of life should be proportioned rather to the intensity of the experience than to its actual length.'
Thomas Hardy (1840–1928), novelist and poet

'Experience is not what happens to a man. It's what a man does with what happens to him.'
Aldous Huxley (1894–1963), author of *Brave New World*

'One thorn of experience is worth a whole wilderness of warning.'
James Russell Lowell (1819–91), writer and diplomat

'Everybody experiences far more than he understands. Yet it is experience rather than understanding, that influences behavior.'
Marshall McLuhan (1911–80), media commentator and critic

'A optimist is a guy
that has never had
much experience.'
Donald Marquis (1878–1937), journalist and humorist

'Nothing is a waste of time if you use the experience wisely.'
Auguste Rodin (1840–1917), artist

'Those who cannot remember the past are condemned to repeat it.'
George Santayana (1863–1952), Spanish-born philosopher and writer

'We learn from experience that men never learn anything from experience.'
George Bernard Shaw (1856–1950), playwright

'The past, at least, is secure.'
Daniel Webster (1782–1852), statesman

'Experience is the name everyone gives to their mistakes.'
*** Oscar Wilde (1854–1900), wit***

'Good judgement is the result of experience, and experience is the result of bad judgement.'
Walter Wriston, former chairman of Citibank

Eyes and ears

'The art of listening is most important,' said James Allen, founder of the consultants Booz, Allen & Hamilton. Observing and listening are arts in which consultants undoubtedly excel. The rest of humanity lags far behind. Most executives – despite protestations to the contrary – prefer the sound of their own voice to those of others. They regard listening as an inert activity rather than a means of information gathering.

'Practical observation commonly consists of collecting a few facts and loading them with guesses.'
   Anon

'The reason why we have two ears and only one mouth is that we may listen the more and talk the less.'
   Anon

'To listen acutely is to be powerless, even if you sit on a throne.'
   Anon

'You can observe a lot just by watching.'
   Yogi Berra (b. 1925), baseball player, coach and manager

'You must look into people, as well as at them.'
   Lord Chesterfield (1694–1773), English statesman

'Listening to other companies' customers is the best way to gain market share, while listening to the visionaries is the best way to create new markets.'
   Esther Dyson (b. 1951), computer businesswoman and commentator

'When people talk, listen completely. Most people never listen.'
   Ernest Hemingway (1899–1961), novelist

'The mark of real genius is simply the facility to see the world in unhabitual ways.'
William James (1842–1910), philosopher and psychologist

'One eye sees, the other feels.'
Paul Klee (1879–1940), Swiss artist

'The only real voyage of discovery consists not in seeking new landscapes but in having new eyes.'
Marcel Proust (1871–1922), French writer

'When doctors listen to nurses, patients recover more quickly; if mining engineers pay more attention to their men than to their machinery, the pits are more efficient. As in athletics and nuclear research, it is neither books nor seminars from which managers learn much, but from here-and-now exchanges about the operational job in hand.'
Reg Revans (b. 1907), Olympic athlete, educator and author

'One of the best ways to persuade others is with your ears – by listening to them.'
Dean Rusk (1909–94), diplomat and politician

'Hundreds of people can talk for one who can think, but thousands can think for one who can see. To see clearly is poetry, prophecy, and religion – all in one.'
John Ruskin (1819–1900), writer and critic

'Give every man thine ear, but few thy voice.'
William Shakespeare (1564–1616), bard

'The power of accurate observation is commonly called cynicism by those who haven't got it.'
George Bernard Shaw (1856–1950), playwright

'I well believe it, to unwilling ears; none love the messenger who brings bad news.'
Sophocles (496–406 BC), Athenian tragedian

'The first step in getting ahead is to listen.'
Liam Strong (b. 1945), British executive

'My job is to see things differently; to spot what others haven't picked up.'
Liam Strong

'A stander-by may sometimes, perhaps, see more of the game than he that plays it.'
Jonathan Swift (1667–1745), author of *Gulliver's Travels*

FACTS, FICTIONS AND STATISTICS

'One can't say that figures lie. But figures, as used in financial arguments, seem to have the bad habit of expressing a small part of the truth forcible, and neglecting the other part, as do some people we know,' noted Fred Schwed in *Where Are the Customers' Yachts?* It is amazing how suspicious the human race is of figures and statistics. This is carried over into the business world where statistics are used and misused every day without breaking down our skepticism about their worth. Only an outbreak of total honesty could achieve that and statistics were never designed with honesty in mind.

'Just try explaining the value of statistical summaries to the widow of the man who drowned crossing a stream, with an average depth of four feet.'
Anon

'Basic research is what I am doing when I don't know what I am doing.'
Anon

'Statistics: the mathematical theory of ignorance.'
Anon

'Where facts are few, experts are many.'
Anon

'The weaker the data available upon which to base one's conclusion, the greater the precision which should be quoted in order to give the data authenticity.'
Norman R. Augustine (b. 1935), author and executive

'Errors using inadequate data are much less than those using no data at all.'
Charles Babbage (1792–1871), scientist and computer pioneer

'Every man has a right to be wrong in his opinions. But no man has a right to be wrong in his facts.'
Bernard Baruch (1870–1965), American financier and economic adviser

'If you get all the facts, your judgment can be right; if you don't get all the facts, it can't be right.'
Bernard Baruch

'Statistics are the triumph of the quantitative method, and the quantitative method is the victory of sterility and death.'
Hillaire Belloc (1870–1953), writer

'The construction of life is at present in the power of facts more than convictions.'
Walter Benjamin (1892–1940), German writer

'A fact in itself is nothing. It is valuable only for the idea attached to it or for the proof which it furnishes.'
Claude Bernard (1813–78), French physiologist

'It is the nature of all greatness not to be exact.'
Edmund Burke (1729–97), statesman and writer

'A witty statesman said, you might prove anything by figures.'
__Thomas Carlyle (1795–1881), essayist__

'I grow daily to honor facts more and more, and theory less and less. Fact, it seems to me, is a great thing – a sentence printed, if not by God then at least by the devil.'
Thomas Carlyle

'Now, what I want is facts. Teach these boys and girls nothing but facts. Facts alone are wanted in life. Plant nothing else, and root out everything else. You can only form the minds of reasoning animals upon facts: nothing else will ever be of any service to them. This is the principle on which I bring up my own children, and this is the principle on which I bring up these children. Stick to the facts, sir!'
Charles Dickens (1812–70), novelist

'There are three kinds of lies: lies, damned lies and statistics.'
Benjamin Disraeli (1804–81), British statesman

'Facts are the images of history just as images are the facts of fiction.'
EL Doctorow (b. 1931), author

'If the facts don't fit the theory, change the facts.'
Albert Einstein (1879–1955), physicist

'To write it, it took three months; to conceive it – three minutes; to collect the data in it – all my life.'
F. Scott Fitzgerald (1896–1940), American novelist

'Anyone who says businessmen deal in facts, not fiction, has never read old five-year projections.'
Malcolm S. Forbes (1919–90), publisher

'Get the facts, or the facts will get you. And when you get 'em, get 'em right, or they will get you wrong.'
Thomas Fuller (1608–1661), doctor and writer

'Facts are power.'
Harold Geneen (b. 1910), former ITT chief

'When you have mastered numbers, you will in fact no longer be reading numbers, any more than you read words when reading books. You will be reading meanings.'
Harold Geneen

'It has been said that figures rule the world. Maybe. But I am sure that figures show us whether it is being ruled well or badly.'
Johann Wofgang von Goethe (1749–1832), German writer

'A wise man recognises the convenience of a general statement, but he bows to the authority of a particular fact.'
Oliver Wendell Holmes, Jr. (1841–1935), long-lived American jurist

'Facts are ventriloquists' dummies. Sitting on a wise man's knee, they may be made to utter words of wisdom; elsewhere, they say nothing, or talk nonsense, or indulge in sheer diabolism.'
   Aldous Huxley (1894–1963), author

'A world of facts lies outside and beyond the world of words.'
   TH Huxley (1825–95), scientist and teacher

'Statistics show that of those who contract the habit of eating, very few survive.'
   Wallace Irwin (1873–1948), writer and humorist

'He uses statistics as a drunken man uses lampposts – for support rather than for illumination.'
   Andrew Lang (1844–1912), author

'Facts become impregnated with value when they consistently line up behind a single set of goals. In Vietnam they supported the military goals; the humanitarian goals, supported only by soft data, were driven out of the analysis. We see the same thing in corporations when the hard data line up behind the economic goals – cost reduction, profit increase, growth in market share – leaving the social goals – product quality, employee satisfaction, protection of the environment – to fend for themselves.'
   Henry Mintzberg (b. 1939), researcher and author

'There are no facts, only interpretations.'
   Friedrich Nietzsche (1844–1900), philosopher

'The facts are to blame, my friend. We are all imprisoned by facts: I was born, I exist.'
   Luigi Pirandello (1867–1936), Italian playwright and author

'For every fact there is an *infinity* of hypotheses. The more you *look* the more you *see*.'
   Robert M. Pirsig (b. 1928), Zen engineer

'Comment is free but facts are sacred.'
   Charles P. Scott, *Manchester Guardian* editor

'Facts are stubborn things.'
Tobias G. Smollett (1721–71), novelist

'A single death is a tragedy. A million deaths is a statistic.'
Joseph Stalin (1879–1953), dictator

'Get your facts first and then you can distort them as much as you wish.'
Mark Twain (1835–1910), imaginative writer

'Facts are generally over-esteemed. For most practical purposes, a thing is what men think it is. When they judged the earth flat, it was flat. As long as men thought slavery tolerable, tolerable it was. We live down here among shadows, shadows among shadows.'
John Updike (b. 1932), prolific novelist and part-time golfer

'It is the spirit of the age to believe that any fact, no matter how suspect, is superior to any imaginative exercise, no matter how true.'
Gore Vidal (b. 1925), novelist

'Fools make researches and wise men exploit them.'
HG Wells (1866–1946), writer

'Prayers for the condemned man will be offered on an adding machine. Numbers constitute the only universal language.'
Nathanael West (1903–40), short-lived American writer

*F*AIR SHARES

Ever since Tony Blair introduced the word *stakeholder* into the popular vocabulary, corporate ownership has attracted greater attention. The debate
about how best to allow employees participation in the companies they
work for slowly moves on – though best practice remains rooted in companies which have been doing much the same for decades. 'If people have
total control over their business, they will have the best possible emotional
involvement,' says American CEO Pat McGovern.

'The average IBM'er has lost sight of the reasons for his company's existence. IBM exists to provide a return on invested capital to the stockholders.'
 John Akers (b. 1934), former head of IBM

'The commerce of the world is conducted by the strong, and usually it op-
erates against the weak.'
 Henry Ward Beecher (1813–87), clergyman abolitionist

'No matter who reigns, the merchant reigns.'
 Henry Ward Beecher

'Soldiers win battles and generals get the credit.'
 Napoléon Bonaparte (1769–1881), French General

'The progress of human society consists in the better and better apportion-
ing of wages to work.'
 Thomas Carlyle (1795–1881), essayist

'[A manager] must be at least part owner of the enterprise which he manages and to which he gives his attention, and chiefly dependent for his rev-
enues not upon salary but upon profit.'
 Andrew Carnegie (1835–1919), industrialist and philanthropist

'There is no right to strike against the public safety by anybody, anywhere, any time.'
Calvin Coolidge (1872–1933), 30th American President

'O let us love our occupations,
Bless the squire and his relations,
Live upon our daily rations,
And always know our proper stations.'
Charles Dickens (1812–70), novelist

'The idea of making workers share in profits is a very attractive one and it would seem that it is from there that harmony between capital and labor should come. But the practical formula for such sharing has not yet been found.'
Henri Fayol (1841–1925), French manager and business thinker

'Any business arrangement that is not profitable to the other fellow will in the end prove unprofitable for you. The bargain that yields mutual satisfaction is the only one that is apt to be repeated.'
BC Forbes (1880–1954), publisher

'Who will argue that only public men and corporation heads are entitled to have their names emblazoned on the scroll of honor? ... Workers are made of exactly the same stuff as generals or presidents or governors or industrial leaders.'
BC Forbes

'You own the company, that's right, you, the stockholders, and you are being royally screwed by these bureaucrats with their stock lunches, their hunting and fishing trips, their corporate jets and their golden parachutes.'
Gordon Gekko, fictional exemplar of the 1980s featured in the movie *Wall Street*

'There is nothing more short-term than a sixty-year-old CEO holding a fistful of share options.'
Gary Hamel (b. 1954), consultant and educator

'I am aware of the need to watch the shareholders' interests and that is all that matters when it's a public company. You can't have your own private thoughts on whether it is going to affect your livelihood, or anything like that.'
Lord Hanson (b. 1922), stalwart of shareholders

'Good business should contain something for both parties.'
Sir John Harvey-Jones (b. 1924), author and businessman

'If you find a way of working so that people are cared for, they will give of their best, strive for excellence, or at least do better than the competition. That way round you cannot lose. Yes it is about good staff canteens, cloakrooms, pay and pensions. But in the end it is about caring.'
Sir Hector Lang, United Biscuits chief

'What I am trying to do is communicate harmony of interest between the company and the staff. We are not adversaries. We are partners.'
Sir Hector Lang

'We have created an industrial order geared to automatism, where feeblemindedness, native or acquired, is necessary for docile productivity in the factory; and where a pervasive neurosis is the final gift of the meaningless life that issues forth at the other end.'
Lewis Mumford (1895–1990), writer and philosopher

'I've always believed industrial democracy starts in the lavatory.'
Sir Peter Parker (b. 1924), British manager of British Rail, among others

'Workers in the United States – and even more so in England – have been treated like dog food for the past 150 years. In fact, such treatment forms the bedrock logic of the Industrial Revolution: Forget craft. Specialize jobs to the point any idiot can perform them.'
Tom Peters (b. 1942), outspoken guru

'We all differ in what we know, but in our infinite ignorance we are all equal.'
Sir Karl Popper (1902–89), Austrian-born philosopher

'When men are rightly occupied, their amusement grows out of their work, as the color-petals out of a fruitful flower.'
John Ruskin (1819–1900), critic and writer

'The great companies take all their stakeholders seriously. They value customers, employees and stockholders. Saying the customer is king is as stupid as saying the stockholder is king. The great executives understand it is a complex game.'
Edgar H. Schein (b. 1928), MIT-based writer and researcher

'Democracy has yet to penetrate the workplace. Dictators and despots are alive and well in offices and factories all over the world.'
Ricardo Semler (b. 1957), Brazilian champion of industrial democracy

'Our experience proves that a policy of good human relations results in self-discipline, staff stability, good service to the customer, high productivity and good profits in which we all share: employees, shareholders, pensioners and the community.'
Lord Sieff (1889–1972), Marks & Spencer leader

'Top management must know how good or bad employees' working conditions are. They must eat in the employees' restaurants, see whether the food is well cooked, visit the washroom and lavatories—if they are not good enough for those in charge they are not good enough for anyone.'
Lord Sieff

'Every man is rich or poor according to the degree in which he can afford to enjoy the necessaries, conveniences, and amusements of human life.'
Adam Smith (1723–90), writer adopted by the right

FAME AND FORTUNE

It is hard being famous. Almost as hard as being rich. Being rich and famous would be too much to bear. Even worse would be to have the money handed to you on a salver – 'Inherited wealth is a real handicap to happiness. It is as certain a death to ambition as cocaine is to morality,' said William K. Vanderbilt. But who needs ambition when you've got the fortune?

'The rich man has his motor car,
His country and his town estate.
He smokes a fifty-cent cigar
And jeers at fate.'
> **Franklin P. Adams (1881–1960), American journalist and humorist**

'I feel that being a microcelebrity is the best of both worlds. I get enough recognition to feel good, but I can go to stores and still be treated rudely by the sales staff.'
> **Scott Adams (b. 1957), creator of *Dilbert***

'A celebrity is a person who works hard all his life to become known, then wears dark glasses to avoid being recognized.'
> **Fred Allen (1894–1956), American comedian**

'The real measure of your wealth is how much you'd be worth if you lost all your money.'
> **Anon**

'Getting rich is easy. It just takes a lot of work.'
> ***Anon***

'Anybody with money to burn will easily find someone to tend the fire.'
> **Anon**

'A man who has a million dollars is as well off as if he were rich.'
> **John Jacob Astor III (b. 1918), affluent and in touch**

'The only thing I like about rich people is their money.'
   Lady Nancy Astor (1879–1964), first woman to sit in the House of Commons

'Riches are for spending.'
   Francis Bacon (1561–1626), Elizabethan writer

'Seek not proud riches, but such as thou mayest get justly, not soberly, distribute cheerfully, and leave contentedly.'
   Francis Bacon

'Riches are a good handmaiden, but the worst mistress.'
   Francis Bacon

'Prosperity is not without many fears and distastes; and adversity is not without comforts and hopes.'
   Francis Bacon

'Prosperity doth best discover vice, but adversity doth best discover virtue.'
   Francis Bacon

'Behind every great fortune there is a crime.'
   Honoré de Balzac (1799–1850), writer

'Glory is fleeting, but obscurity is forever.'
   Napoléon Bonaparte (1769–1821), French General, now obscure

'No one can earn a million dollars honestly.'
   William Jennings Bryan (1860–1925), politician and orator

'If we command our wealth, we shall be rich and free; if our wealth commands us, we are poor indeed.'
   Edmund Burke (1729–97), statesman and writer

'The millionaire should be ashamed to die rich.'
   Andrew Carnegie (1835–1919), Scottish-born industrialist

'Prosperity is only an instrument to be used, not a deity to be worshipped.'
   Calvin Coolidge (1872–1933), American President

'Fame is a bee.
It has a song –
It has a sting –
Ah, too, it has a wing.'
      Emily Dickinson (1830–86), American poet

'Fame is proof that people are gullible.'
      Ralph Waldo Emerson (1803–82), poet

'Wealth is not his that has it, but his who enjoys it.'
      Benjamin Franklin (1706–90), writer, inventor, etc.

'If you can actually count your money then you are not a really rich man.'
      J. Paul Getty (1892–1976), oil tycoon

'What is fame? an empty bubble;
Gold? a transient, shining trouble.'
      James Grainger (1721?–66), rhymester

'Fame is vapour, popularity an accident, riches take wings. Only one thing endures and that is character.'
      Horace Greeley (1811–72), politician and writer

'Recognition is a sort of Frankenstein monster. It can easily persuade you that you are something special and the moment that you think you are something special, you've had it.'
      Sir John Harvey-Jones (b. 1924), former ICI chief

'Prosperity is a great teacher; adversity is a greater.'
      William Hazlitt (1778–1830), essayist

'It is easy to get everything you want, provided you first learn to do without the things you cannot get.'
      Elbert Hubbard (1856–1915), writer and businessman

'I glory
More in the cunning purchase of my wealth
Than in the glad possession.'
Ben Jonson (1572–1637), Elizabethan dramatist

'Affluence means influence.'
Jack London (1876–1916), novelist

'Fortune is the rod of the weak, and the staff of the brave.'
James Russell Lowell (1819–91), American writer and diplomat

'What's a thousand dollars? Mere chicken feed. A poultry matter.'
Groucho Marx (1895–1977), comedian

'The only incurable troubles of the rich are
the troubles that money can't cure,
Which is a kind of trouble that is even more troublesome if you are poor.'
Ogden Nash (1902–71), light verse writer

'A very quiet and tasteful way to be famous is to have a famous relative.
Then you can not only be nothing, you can do nothing, too.'
PJ O'Rourke (b. 1947), right-wing commentator

'There is no wealth but life.'
John Ruskin (1819–1900), critic and writer

'There is no real wealth but the labor of man.'
PB Shelley (1792–1822), short-lived Romantic poet

'I've been rich and I've been poor. Rich is better.'
Frank Sinatra (b. 1915), crooner

'Fame is the perfume of heroic deeds.'
Socrates (469–399 BC), teacher of Plato

'The only wealth is life.'
Henry David Thoreau (1817–62), naturalist and writer

'I have concentrated all along on building the finest retailing company that we possibly could. Period. Creating a huge personal fortune was never particularly a goal of mine.'

Sam Walton (1918–92), founder of Wal-Mart

'You can't have money like that and not swell out.'

HG Wells (1866–1946), writer

'Give me the luxuries of life and I will willingly do without the necessities.'
Frank Lloyd Wright (1869–1959), architect

'The information revolution has changed wealth. Intellectual capital is far more important than money.'

Walter Wriston, banker

*F*EAR AND FAILURE

'Failure is our most important product,' observed Johnson & Johnson's chief executive raising a few eyebrows along the way. In a success-oriented world managers live in fear of failure. Or, at least, they can do. Some, brave souls, have learned that you cannot have the success without the failures. Learning from failure marks the leaders of tomorrow apart from yesterday's men.

'If at first you don't succeed, you'll get a lot of free advice from people who didn't succeed either.'
  Anon

'Because many professionals are almost always successful at what they do, they rarely experience failure. And because they have rarely failed, they have never learned how to learn from failure.'
  Chris Argyris (b. 1923), Harvard Business School professor

'Prosperity is not without many fears and distastes; adversity not without many comforts and hopes.'
  Francis Bacon (1561–1626), optimistic Elizabethan

'It's not companies that fail; it's their leaders who fail.'
  Warren Bennis (b. 1925), leadership guru

'We may stop ourselves when going up, never when coming down.'
  Napoléon Bonaparte (1769–1821), French soldier

'People are much more interested in the guy that sits next to them than in people outside. You've got to drive them outside the walls of their company—to make sure they're contemporary. Most of the failures you've seen in corporate business are basically isolated companies. They don't understand what's going on around them.'
  Larry Bossidy (b. 1935), American executive

'Difficulty, my brethren, is the nurse of greatness – a harsh nurse, who roughly rocks her foster children into strength and athletic proportion.'
William C. Bryant (1794–1878), American writer, critic and educator

'I'd rather be a failure at something I enjoy than be a success at something I hate.'
George Burns (1896–1996), cigar-chewing American comedian

'Failure is the condiment that gives success its flavor.'
Truman Capote (1924–84), novelist

'Adversity is sometimes hard upon a man; but for one man who can stand prosperity, there are a hundred that will stand adversity.'
Thomas Carlyle (1795–1881), essayist

'99 percent of failures come from people who have the habit of making excuses.'
George Washington Carver (1864?-1943), the man who invented peanut butter

'Doing is overrated, and success undesirable, but the bitterness of failure even more so.'
Cyril Connolly (1903–74), critic and novelist

'We can spend our whole lives underachieving.'
Philip Crosby, quality guru

'Very few of the great leaders ever get through their careers without failing, sometimes dramatically.'
Philip Crosby

'I have not failed. I've just found 10,000 ways that don't work.'
Thomas Alva Edison (1847–1931), inventor and optimist

'Results! Why man, I have gotten a lot of results, I know several thousand things that don't work.'
Thomas Alva Edison

'To try something you can't do, to try and fail, then try it again. That to me is success. My generation will be judged by the splendor of our failures.'
William Faulkner (1897–1962), novelist

'Life is a series of experiences each one of which makes us bigger, even though sometimes it is hard to realize this. For the world was built to develop character, and we must learn that the setbacks and griefs which we endure help us in our marching onward.'
Henry Ford (1863–1947), automobile manufacturer

'If all else fails, immortality can always be assured by spectacular error.'
JK Galbraith (b. 1908), economist

'The more successful I am the more vulnerable I feel.'
Bill Gates (b. 1955), computer enthusiast

'In Britain the quickest way to get rich is to fail at the top. Sign a three-year contract and then fail in the first six months, walk away with a million pounds for six months' work.'
Charles Handy (b. 1932), management thinker and commentator

'Most of the things I have learned were not learned formally but through accidents and failure. I learned from small catastrophes.'
Charles Handy

'In the long run, failure was the only thing that worked predictably. All else was accidental.'
Joseph Heller (b. 1923), novelist

'The world breaks everyone, and afterward many are stronger at the broken places.'
Ernest Hemingway (1899–1961), novelist

'There is no loneliness greater than the loneliness of a failure. The failure is a stranger in his own house.'
Eric Hoffer (1902–83), philosopher

'Many people dream of success. To me success can only be achieved through repeated failure and introspection. In fact, success represents one percent of your work which results from the 99 percent that is called failure.'
Soichiro Honda (1906–91), Japanese industrialist

'The line between failure and success is so fine that we scarcely know when we pass it: so fine that we are often on the line and do not know it.'
Elbert Hubbard (1856–1915), American writer and business-man

'Adversity makes men, and prosperity makes monsters.'
Victor Hugo (1802–85), French writer

'We worked furiously. Because we didn't have fear, we could do something drastic.'
Masaru Ibuka (b. 1908), founder of Sony

'Man needs difficulties; they are necessary for health.'
Carl Jung (1875–1961), psychoanalyst

'Only those who dare to fail greatly can ever achieve greatly.'
Robert F. Kennedy (1925–68), politician

'Teach a highly educated person that it is not a disgrace to fail and that he must analyze every failure to find its cause. He must learn how to fail intelligently, for failing is one of the greatest arts in the world.'
Charles F. Kettering (1876–1958), engineer and inventor

'The freedom to fail is vital if you're going to succeed. Most successful people fail time and time again, and it is a measure of their strength that failure merely propels them into some new attempt at success.'
Michael Korda, failure expert

'Once you learn to quit, it becomes a habit.'
Vince Lombardi (1913–70), American football coach

'Our deepest fear is not that we are inadequate. Our deepest fear is that we are powerful beyond measure. It is our light, not our darkness, that most frightens us.'
Nelson Mandela (b. 1918), South African President

'If anything can go wrong, it will.'
Murphy's law

'There's little that is more important to tomorrow's managers than failure.'
Tom Peters (b. 1942), author and consultant

'The man who makes no mistakes does not usually make anything.'
EJ Phelps (1822–1900)

'You may have a fresh start any moment you choose, for this thing we call failure is not the falling down, but the staying down.'
Mary Pickford (1893–1979), actress

'If we do not succeed, we run the risk of failure.'
Dan Quayle (b. 1947), American politician

'Far better to dare mighty things, to win glorious triumphs, even though checkered by failure, than to take rank with those poor spirits who neither enjoy much nor suffer much, because they live in the gray twilight that knows not victory, nor defeat.'
Theodore Roosevelt (1858–1919), American President

'Never let the fear of striking out get in your way.'
Babe Ruth (1895–1948), baseball player

'Sweet are the uses of adversity which, like the toad, ugly and venomous, Wears yet a precious jewel in his head.'
William Shakespeare (1564–1616), bard

'Success covers a multitude of blunders.'
George Bernard Shaw (1856–1950), playwright

'Successful management is dead easy. Failure is complicated.'
Lord Sheppard (b. 1932), British businessman

'Keep your fears to yourself, but share your inspiration with others.'
Robert Louis Stevenson (1850–94), novelist

'If you can't stand the heat, get out of the kitchen.'
Harry S Truman (1884–1972), 33rd American President

'All men are mortal, and therefore all men are losers; our profoundest loyalty goes out to the failed.'
   John Updike (b. 1932), prolific novelist

'Sometimes adversity is what you need to face in order to become successful.'
   Zig Ziglar, American seminar presenter

THE FUTURE

The future is unwritten. Indeed, the future is anything we imagine or would like it to be. This idea is highly attractive and explains why senior managers would like to keep the future to themselves with their scenario plans and strategic visions. But, as they contemplate future vistas, the present can calmly slip by. The only thing we can be sure of is that what we did in the past to make us successful won't do so in the future.

'The future comes one day at a time.'
Dean Acheson (1893–1971), American lawyer

'Our notion of an optimist is a man who, knowing that each year was worse than the preceding, thinks next year will be better. And a pessimist is a man who knows the next year can't be any worse than the last one.'
Franklin P. Adams (1881–1960), American journalist and humorist

'There are many methods for predicting the future. For example, you can read horoscopes, tea leaves, tarot cards or crystal balls. Collectively, these methods are known as *nutty methods*. Or you can put well-researched facts into sophisticated computer models, more commonly referred to as a *complete waste of time.'*
Scott Adams (b. 1957), creator of *Dilbert*

'The future you shall know when it has come; before then, forget it.'
Aeschylus (525–456 BC) Greek soldier and playwright

'Let him who would enjoy a good future waste none of his present.'
Anon

'I've seen the future and it works.'
Anon

'If a man had half as much foresight as he had hindsight, he'd be a lot better off.'
Anon

'The longer run belongs to Oscar Wilde, who is dead.'
   BBA Group mission statement

'Future. That period of time in which our affairs prosper, our friends are true and our happiness is assured.'
   Ambrose Bierce (1842–1914), journalist and writer

'You can never plan the future by the past.'
   Edmund Burke (1729–97), statesman and writer

'Real generosity toward the future lies in giving all to the present.'
   Albert Camus (1913–60), French novelist goalkeeper

'The best way to predict the future is to create it.'
   Peter Drucker (b. 1909), accurate sage of the business futures

'I never think of the future. It comes soon enough.'
   Albert Einstein (1879–1955), physicist

'The distinction between past, present and future is only a stubbornly persistent illusion.'
   Albert Einstein

'Predicting the future is hard, especially for those who create it.'
   Anatole France (1844–1924), French writer

'Never make forecasts, especially about the future.'
   Samuel Goldwyn (1882–1974), farsighted filmmaker

'The only way to predict the future is to have power to shape the future.'
   Eric Hoffer (1902–83), popular philosopher

'Yesterday is not ours to recover, but tomorrow is ours to win or to lose.'
   Lyndon B. Johnson (1908–73), 36th American President

'You've no future unless you add value, create projects.'
   Rosabeth Moss Kanter (b. 1943), Harvard-based academic and author

'My interest is in the future because I am going to spend the rest of my life there.'
Charles F. Kettering (1876–1958), engineer and inventor

'In the long run we are all dead.'
John Maynard Keynes (1883–1946), economist

'We look at the present through a rearview mirror. We march backwards into the future.'
Marshall McLuhan (1911–80), Canadian critic and commentator

'Tomorrow is our permanent address.'
Marshall McLuhan

'The most reliable way to anticipate the future is by understanding the present.'
John Naisbitt, futurologist

'They spend their time mostly looking forward to the past.'
John Osborne (1929–94), playwright

'Everywhere I look I see the potential for growth, for discovery far greater than anything we have seen in the 20th century.'
David Packard (1912–96), computer executive

'Don't look back. Something might be gaining on you.'
Satchel Paige (1906–82), baseball pitcher

'We don't want to go back to tomorrow, we want to go forward.'
Dan Quayle (b. 1947), forever American Vice-President

'The future will be better tomorrow.'
Dan Quayle

'The future belongs to big corporations and common-interest organizations; it is the price we must pay for an assured future.'
Ernest Solvay (1838–1922), Belgian industrialist

'The trouble with our times is that the future is not what it used to be.'
   Paul Valery (1871–1945), French poet

'Hindsight is always 20–20.'
   Billy Wilder (b. 1906), actor and comedian

'The future belongs to those who prepare for it today.'
   Malcolm X (1925–65), American Muslim leader

GOING GLOBAL

It was only in the 1990s that pundits and academics began to take notice of the global reach of a growing number of businesses. They coined the phrase globalization and set about examining it. They then coined a host of even more objectionable phrases – ranging from global to transnational. As Dr. Johnson slowly revolved in a distant casket, businesspeople carried on doing what they have always done: making money through trading products and services. Globalization, as they well know, is nothing new. Business has been an international affair since the Phoenicians, and the Roman Empire Inc. was a global organization even without the miracles of instant communication.

'Men may be linked in friendship. Nations are linked only be interests.'
   Anon

'If a man be gracious and courteous to strangers, it shows he is a citizen of the world.'
   Francis Bacon (1561–1626), Elizabethan writer, wit and sage

'We are not a global business. We are a collection of local businesses with intense global coordination.'
   Percy Barnevik (b. 1941), Swedish-born global executive

'There will be two kinds of CEOs who will exist in the next five years: those who think globally and those who are unemployed.'
   Peter Drucker (b. 1909), management theorist and writer

'No nation was ever ruined by trade.'
   Benjamin Franklin (1706–90), early American all-rounder

'International life will be seen increasingly as a competition not between rival ideologies – since most economically successful states will be organized along similar lines – but between different cultures.'
Francis Fukuyama, novelist

'Merchants have no country.'
Thomas Jefferson (1743–1826), third American President

'The world is becoming a common marketplace in which people – no matter where they live – desire the same products and lifestyles. Global companies must forget the idiosyncratic differences between countries and cultures and instead concentrate on satisfying universal drives.'
Theodore Levitt (b. 1925), Harvard-based marketing guru

'We are going to win and the industrial West is going to lose out; there's not much you can do about it because the reasons for your failure are within yourselves.'
Konosuke Matsushita (1894–1989), Japanese businessman

'UK managers are very proud to be managers; the Swedish are apologetic; and Germans see themselves as specialists.'
Henry Mintzberg (b. 1939), Canadian management theorist

'Japanese people tend to be much better adjusted to the notion of work, any kind of work, as honorable.'
Akio Morita (b. 1921), co-founder of Sony

'Think globally, act locally, think tribally, act universally.'
John Naisbitt, futurologist

'No macho Western managers wants to believe it, but the Japanese win by commitment and consensus. Their enterprise is management by committee, the country is a committee, and their management moves on the lines of a sumo wrestler. Ideas develop slowly, ponderously; action strikes like lightning.'
Sir Peter Parker (b. 1924), former British Rail chief

'Tough domestic rivalry breeds international success.'
Michael Porter (b. 1947), Harvard global competitiveness guru

'A man's feet must be planted in his country, but his eyes should survey the world.'

George Santayana (1863–1952), philosopher and writer

'Every country and every organization faces dilemmas in relationships with people; dilemmas in relationship to time; and dilemmas in relations between people and the natural environment. Culture is the way in which people resolve dilemmas emerging from universal problems.'

Fons Trompenaars (b. 1952), Dutch management consultant and author

'Interest does not tie nations together; it sometimes separates them. But sympathy and understanding does unite them.'

Woodrow Wilson (1856–1924), 28th American President

GREED

'Greed is good,' proclaimed Gordon Gekko in Oliver Stone's *Wall Street*. Throughout the world, cinemagoers shook their heads at the depravity of it all. And yet, in the euphorically shortsighted eighties, beneath the surface many sympathized. Gekko was an awful human being, but he was also an awfully rich human being. Greed may not be good, but it is always tempting.

'Kill no more pigeons than you can eat.'
    Benjamin Franklin (1706–90), American inventor, writer and statesman

'Never buy what you do not want, because it is cheap; it will be dear to you.'
    Thomas Jefferson (1743–1826), third American President

'People who are greedy have extraordinary capacities for waste – they must, they take in too much.'
    Norman Mailer (b. 1923), prolific American writer notoriously short of temper and long-winded

'Man is the only creature that consumes without producing.'
    George Orwell (1903–50), British novelist

'He who wishes to be rich in a day will be hanged in a year.'
    Leonardo da Vinci (1452–1519), the Renaissance man

'You can't have everything. Where would you put it?'
    Steven Wright, American surrealist comedian

GURUS AND GODS

Gurus were once hirsute Bagwans who inhabited remote corners of the Indian subcontinent within easy reach of a plentiful supply of mind enhancing stimulants and a Rolls-Royce dealership. Today's gurus are rather less colorful. Indeed, they are usually management consultants or business school academics. The route to guru status is to come up with a catchphrase (English purists need not apply); write a book (or employ a ghostwriter); market it until it reaches the best-seller lists (this may involve buying a lot of copies) and then travelling the world giving seminars which repeat the contents of the book. Along the way you have to strenuously deny you are a guru – it demeans the quality of your research and intellectual purity. If you are lucky you can mine the lucrative world of management guru-dom for two years before your ideas are displaced.

'Ours is the age of substitutes; instead of language, we have jargon; instead of principles, slogans; and, instead of genuine ideas, bright ideas.'
Eric Bentley (b. 1916), British-born critic and commentator

'Don't follow trends, start trends.'
Frank Capra (1897–1991), Italian-born film director

'They changed all the buzzwords, but they didn't tell me.'
Leo Cullum cartoon

'Most of the change we think we see in life is due to truths being in and out of favor.'
Robert Frost (1874–1963), American poet

'If you see a bandwagon, it's too late.'
Sir James Goldsmith (1933–97), financier and politician

'It is time to stop paving the cow paths. Instead of imbedding outdated processes in silicon and software, we should obliterate them and start over.'
Michael Hammer (b. 1948), consultant and author

'When people ask me what I do for a living, I tell them that what I really do is I'm reversing the Industrial Revolution.'
Michael Hammer

'Tradition counts for nothing. Reengineering is a new beginning.'
Michael Hammer and James Champy

'I reject the term guru because it is associated with pandering to the masses, providing inspiration without substance. There is a little bit of the shaman in a guru.'
Rosabeth Moss Kanter (b. 1943), Harvard-based author, consultant and educator

'When a thing is current, it creates a currency.'
Marshall McLuhan (1911–80), Canadian sociologist and commentator

'Why don't we just stop reengineering and delayering and restructuring and decentralizing and instead start thinking?'
Henry Mintzberg (b. 1939), Canadian management thinker and educator

'There is a lot of obnoxious hype about being a guru to the extent that the medium can destroy the message.'
Henry Mintzberg

'No guru, no teacher, no method.'
Van Morrison (b. 1945), soul singer

'Guru? You find a gem here or there. But most of it's fairly obvious, you know. You go to Doubleday's business section and you see all these wonderful titles and you spend $300 and then you throw them all away.'
Rupert Murdoch (b. 1931), Australian media mogul

'Trends are bottom-up, fads top-down.'
John Naisbitt, futurologist

'Organizations churn through one technique after another and at best get incremental improvement on top of business as usual. At worst, these efforts waste resources and evoke cynicism and resignation.'
Richard Pascale (b. 1938), consultant, author and educator

'What we need now is not a savior or a guru, but an active movement so that, no matter what their culture, people work together to understand local difficulties. I'm not saying this is the final answer. There is no final answer for anything.'
Reg Revans (b. 1907), athlete and persuasive champion of action learning

'Man is a creature who lives not upon bread alone, but principally by catchwords; and the little rift between the sexes is astonishingly widened by simply teaching one set of catchwords to the girls and another to the boys.'
Robert Louis Stevenson (1850–94), novelist

'They fall for the latest isms gullibly as pups for rubber bones.'
Dylan Thomas (1914–53), Welsh poet

'The experts have looked for the magic answers – most recently in re-engineering – in globalizing – in quality – in leadership and the like. As our own strategy reflects, we, too, believe that each one of those elements is important. But none -by itself – is the answer.'
Randall Tobias, chief executive of pharmaceutical giant Eli Lilly

'If something is seen as an easy solution, it has a detrimental effect. If it develops dependency, it is bad for business. But it is a poor manager who sees it in that way. If a manager reads books or attends a seminar and as a result better understands the complexity of his or her business that is good. Indeed, anything that prompts managers to do the right thing for the right reason must be good. Often, gurus are offering sanitized, popularized versions of what has been round for a while. Hopefully, it encourages managers to stop and think. They must then decide if what the guru is suggesting is appropriate.'
Ray Wild (b. 1940), educator and author

Hard labor

Someone, somewhere, always has to do the real work. In the factories, along the production lines, outside in the fields. It can be boring. It can be dirty. But, the supervisor bellows, if a job's worth doing ...

'There are no menial jobs, only menial attitudes.'
Anon

'There's man all over for you, blaming on his boots the faults of his feet.'
Samuel Beckett (1906–89), Irish Nobel Prize–winning writer

'The factory of the future will have only two employees, a man and a dog. The man will be there to feed the dog. The dog will be there to keep the man from touching the equipment.'
Warren Bennis (b. 1925), leadership guru

'Genius is one percent inspiration and ninety-nine percent perspiration.'
Thomas Alva Edison (1847–1931), inventor and industrialist

'No one has a greater asset for his business than a man's pride in his work.'
Mary Parker Follett (1868–1933), early management thinker

'The first step forward in assembly came when we began taking the work to the men instead of the men to the work. We have now two general principles in operation – that a man shall never have to take more than one step, if possibly it can be avoided, and that no man need ever stoop over.'
Henry Ford (1863–1947), American auto manufacturer

'The workingmen have been exploited all the way up and down the line by employers, landlords, everybody.'
Henry Ford

'Satisfaction in a job may compensate for low wages. On the other hand, higher wages may compensate for a disagreeable job.'
Milton Friedman and Rose Friedman, economists

'Clearly the most unfortunate people are those who must do the same thing over and over again, every minute, or perhaps twenty to the minute. They deserve the shortest hours and the highest pay.'
JK Galbraith (b. 1908), economist

'I tell you, sir, the only safeguard of order and discipline in the modern world is a standardized worker with interchangeable parts. That would solve the entire problem of management.'
Jean Giraudoux (1882–1944), French writer

'Labor disgraces no man, but occasionally men disgrace labor.'
Ulysses S. Grant (1822–85), 18th American President

'Industrial man – a sentient reciprocating engine having a fluctuating output, coupled to an iron wheel revolving with uniform velocity. And then we wonder why this should be the golden age of revolution and mental derangement.'
Aldous Huxley (1894–1963), author

'You cannot mandate productivity, you must provide the tools to let people become their best.'
Steven Jobs (b. 1955), computer executive

'The world is moved along, not only by the mighty shoves of its heroes, but also by the aggregate of the tiny pushes of each honest worker.'
Helen Keller (1880–1968), American writer

'In a contrary and perhaps cruel way the twentieth century has relieved us of labor without at the same time relieving us of the conviction that only labor is meaningful.'
Walter C.A. Kerr (b. 1913), critic

'You'll never succeed in idealizing hard work. Before you can dig mother earth you've got to take off your ideal jacket. The harder a man works, at brute labour, the thinner becomes his idealism, the darker his mind.'
DH Lawrence (1885–1930), novelist

'Labor is prior to and independent, capital. Capital is the only the fruit of labor, and could never have existed if labor had not first existed. Labor is the superior of capital, and deserves much the higher consideration.'
Abraham Lincoln (1809–65), American President

'If a man does his best, what else is there?'
General George Patton (1885–1945), soldier

'The technology of mass production is inherently violent, ecologically damaging, self-defeating in terms of nonrenewable resources, and stultifying for the human person.'
EF Schumacher (1911–77), German economist and author of *Small is Beautiful*

'Don't go around saying the world owes you a living. The world owes you nothing. It was here first.'
Mark Twain (1835–1910), hard-working novelist

'Routine is the god of every social system; it is the seventh heaven of business, the essential component in the success of every factory, the ideal of every statesman. The social machine should run like clockwork.'
Alfred North Whitehead (1861–1947), British scientist

'If the human being is condemned and restricted to perform the same functions over and over again, he will not even be a good ant, not to mention a good human being.'
Norbert Wiener (1894–1964), cybernetician

*H*ELPFUL HINTS

Business life is never easy. Problems and complications lie around every corner. Luckily executives can take solace in immortal wisdom. It may not solve their problems, but it looks good pinned on the office wall.

'There are three ingredients in the good life: learning, earning and yearning.'

Anon

'Never take a job in a place where you can't throw cigarette butts on the floor.'

Anon

'Grit and gumption are preferable to inertia and intellect.'

BBA Group mission statement

'When working on a project, if you put away a tool that you're certain you're finished with, you will need it instantly.'

Arthur Bloch (b. 1938), American writer and educator

'Be wiser than other people if you can, but do not tell them so.'

Lord Chesterfield (1694–1773), statesman

'Never drink black coffee at lunch; it will keep you awake in the afternoon.'

Jilly Cooper (b. 1937), laureate of the shires

'We're not running an Oxford college here, we're running a business.'

Peter Ellwood (b. 1943), British businessman

'Don't ever take a fence down until you know why it was put up.'
Robert Frost (1874–1963), American poet

'Stick close to your desks and never go to sea and you all may be rulers of the Queen's navee!'
WS Gilbert (1836–1911), dramatist and writer

'Let chaos reign, then rein in chaos.'
Andrew S. Grove (b. 1936), Intel chief

'In the end, all business operations can be reduced to three words: people, product, and profits.'
Lee Iacocca (b. 1924), executive

'Never break another man's rice bowl.'
Akio Morita (b. 1921), man behind Sony

'The drowning man is not troubled by rain.'
Persian proverb

'It is wise to remember that you are one of the those who can be fooled some of the time.'
Laurence J. Peter (1919–90), Canadian author, educator and management psychologist

'In these matters the only certainty is that nothing is certainty.'
Pliny the Elder (23–79 AD), Latin writer and scientist

'The certainty of misery is better than the misery of uncertainty.'
Pogo comic strip

'If you don't find it in the index, look very carefully through the entire catalogue.'
Sears, Roebuck & Co. consumer's guide

'Add value or get out.'
Lord Sheppard (b. 1932), British executive

'There are fifty ways to leave your lover, but only six exits from this airplane.'
Southwest Airlines safety announcement

'A dinner lubricates business.'
Lord Stowell (1745–1836), hard-eating gentleman

'Distrust any enterprise that requires new clothes.'
Henry David Thoreau (1817–62), American naturalist and author

'Where the broom does not reach, the dust will not vanish of itself.'
Mao Tse-Tung (1893–1976), Chinese Communist leader

'Work hard, be brave and allow yourself no excuses.'
Marco-Pierre White, chef

*H*IERARCHIES

British Steel once had such an extensive and elaborate corporate hierarchy that its organization chart filled the entire wall of a substantial office. If commentators are to be believed, you would now be hard-pressed to find a company which can't fit its hierarchy onto the back of an envelope. But, even though the modern hierarchy is not diligently recorded, it still exists. By way of an experiment, it is worthwhile parking your battered ten-year-old car in the space where the CEO usually parks the latest in Germanic engineering.

'The number of levels of authority should be kept to a minimum.'
> **Chester Barnard (1886–1961), American executive and early management theorist**

'Hierarchies just get in the way of business, cutting off managers from their customers, insulating them from the market and creating slow bureaucracies.'
> **Percy Barnevik (b. 1941), Swedish former chief of Asea Brown Boveri**

'The effectiveness of an organization is in inverse proportion to the number of hierarchical layers.'
> **BBA Group mission statement**

'In all successful professional groups, regard for the individual is based not on title but on competence, stature and leadership.'
> **Marvin Bower (b. 1903), legendary head of consultants McKinsey & Co**

'There has to be some degree of hierarchy, because decisions actually have to be taken.'
> **George Bull (b. 1936), chief executive**

'Detestation of the high is the involuntary homage of the low.'
Charles Dickens (1812–70), Victorian novelist

'If you look at GM today versus yesterday, they've slimmed a little bit. They had 29 layers. Which means that nobody could really be considered for a top management job before age 211. This is part of the problem at GM.'
Peter Drucker (b. 1909), management thinker

'Each management job must be a rewarding job in itself rather than just a step on the promotion ladder.'
Peter Drucker

'When everyone is somebody,
Then no one's anybody.'
WS Gilbert (1836–1911), dramatist and writer

'The pyramid in an organization is typically a hierarchy of experience. What you need is a hierarchy of imagination.'
Gary Hamel (b. 1954), American consultant and best-selling author

'The integrity of the organization depends on striking a balance between the need for an equality of input and a hierarchy for judging the merits of the input.'
Charles Hampden-Turner & Fons Trompenaars, management consultants, educators and authors

'Hierarchy is the system of accountability and authority with which an organization manages the production of its products and services.'
Elliott Jaques (b. 1917), management researcher

'Subordination tends greatly to human happiness. Were we all upon an equality, we should have no other enjoyment than mere animal pleasure.'
Dr. Samuel Johnson (1709–84), the man of letters

'The good Lord sees your heart, not the braid on your jacket, before Him we are all in our birthday suits, generals and common men alike.'
Thomas Mann (1875–1955), novelist

'In a hierarchy, every employee tends to rise to his own level of incompetence.'
Laurence J. Peter (1919–90), creator of the Peter Principle

'Middle managers, as we have known them, are cooked geese.'
Tom Peters (b. 1942), consultant and author

'Every middle manager should spring out of the gate each morning as a dedicated, proactive boundary basher.'
Tom Peters

'The old hierarchical model is no longer appropriate. The new model is global in scale, an interdependent network.'
John Sculley (b. 1939), American Pepsi and Apple executive

'Titles distinguish the mediocre, embarrass the superior, and are disgraced by the inferior.'
George Bernard Shaw (1856–1950), playwright

'In the average company the boys in the mailroom, the president, the vice-presidents, and the girls in the steno pool have three things in common: they are docile, they are bored, and they are dull. Trapped in the pigeon-holes of organization charts, they've been made slaves to the rules of private and public hierarchies that run mindlessly on and on because nobody can change them.'
Robert Townsend (b. 1920), author of the unceremoniously humorous *Up the Organization*

'The organization of offices follows the principle of hierarchy; that is, each lower office is under the control and supervision of a higher one.'
Max Weber (1864–1920), sociologist and more

'Boundaryless behavior is a way of life here. People really do take ideas from A to B. And if you take an idea and share it, you are rewarded. In the old culture, if you had an idea, you'd keep it. Sharing it with someone else would have been stupid, because the bureaucracy would have made him the hero, not you.'
Jack Welch (b. 1935), American executive

'As for middle managers, they can be the stronghold of the organization, but their jobs have to be redefined. They have to see their roles as a combination of teacher, cheerleader, and liberator, not controller.'
Jack Welch

Hiring and Firing

There are few more stressful sides to corporate life than the ritual of hiring and firing. In the era of mass downsizing (and even rightsizing), hiring and firing has become a dramatic and newsworthy event. However, the humanity is being buried beneath the jargon and the corporate strategizing about becoming globally competitive.

'We want people who can hold two things in their heads at the same time, who can think in terms of their individual organizations but also in terms of the company as a whole.'
Paul Allaire (b. 1938), head of Xerox

'The days of the cattle call are over. We used to put out the word on Fridays that we needed X number of workers Monday morning. If you could walk and breathe you were in. That's not how it is anymore.'
Chrystler executive

'Some men owe most of their greatness to the ability of detecting in those they destine for their tools the exact quality of strength that matters for their work.'
Joseph Conrad (1857–1924), Polish-born novelist

'Selecting the right person for the right job is the largest part of coaching.'
Philip Crosby, quality guru

'The question "Who ought to be boss?" is like asking, "Who ought to be the tenor in the quartet?" Obviously, the man who can sing tenor.'
Henry Ford (1863–1947), American auto manufacturer

'It is all one to me if a man comes from Sing Sing or Harvard. We hire a man, not his history.'
Henry Ford

'It's a pity to shoot the piano player when it's the piano that is out of tune.'
French saying

'Few great men could pass Personnel.'
Paul Goodman (1911–72), writer and educator

'The trouble with unemployment is that the minute you wake up in the morning, you're on the job.'
Lena Horne (b. 1917), singer

'I'd really love to meet the guy I'm supposed to be, I'd hire him in a second.'
Lee Iacocca (b. 1924), American executive

'What goes on in the boardroom is a travesty. The chairman doesn't want someone under him who is a threat, so he picks someone a little less capable. It's like an anti-Darwinian theory – the survival of the unfittest – and it's getting worse.'
Carl Icahn (b. 1936), corporate raider labeled the Darth Vader of Wall Street

'We hire great attitudes, and teach them any functionality they need.'
Herb Kelleher, innovative airline executive

'If each of us hires people who are smaller than we are, we shall become a company of dwarfs. But if each of us hires people who are bigger than we are, we shall become a company of giants.'
David Ogilvy (b. 1911), founder of Ogilvy & Mather agency

'Hire people cleverer than you are and delegate more than you think is good for you.'
Sir Peter Parker (b. 1924), former head of British Rail

'Do not ask Frank Sinatra his view on the atomic bomb – ask him to croon.'
Sir Peter Parker

'Tap the energy of the anarchist.'
Anita Roddick (b. 1943), founder of The Body Shop

'I can't bear to be around people who are bland and bored and uninterested (or to employ them).'

Anita Roddick

'If you become familiar with downsizing, you may avoid the task of becoming familiar with outsourcing.'

Dr. George Schussel, President of Digital Consulting

*H*OPE AND CHARITY

The affluent business classes have little time for charity. They look down on begging letters; they sneer at the very existence of noble causes; they laugh in the face of moral dilemmas. But, if there is a camera crew and a reporter, they profess to being deeply touched by all the letters they receive; admit to investing a great deal of their precious time in causes close to their hearts; and talk of the moral difficulties of responsibility.

'We'd all like a reputation for generosity, and we'd all like to buy it cheap.'
Anon

'Hope is a good breakfast, but is a bad supper.'
Francis Bacon (1561–1626), Elizabethan man of letters

'Of every thousand dollars spent in so-called charity today, it is probable that nine hundred and fifty dollars is unwisely spent.'
Andrew Carnegie (1835–1919), industrialist and philanthropist

'It's not the despair – I can stand the despair, it's the hope.'
John Cleese (b. 1939), optimism was not part of the script in *Clockwise*

'An idealist is a man who helps other people to be prosperous.'
Henry Ford (1863–1947), auto manufacturer who idealized a car for every pocket

'The meek shall inherit the earth, but not the mineral rights.'
J. Paul Getty (1892–1976), oil tycoon

'It isn't easy making money, but giving it away is a bitch.'
Lee Iacocca (b. 1924), American executive

'Henry Ford made my kids suffer, and for that I'll never forgive him.'
Lee Iacocca

'In the factory, we make cosmetics; in the store, we sell hope.'
Charles Revlon, cosmetic king

'We are rich only through what we give, and poor only through what we refuse.'
Anne Swetchine (1782–1857)

'No one would remember the good Samaritan if he'd only had good intentions. He had money as well.'
Margaret Thatcher (b. 1925), British Prime Minister

*I*DEAS AND INNOVATION

'Men who accomplish great things in the industrial world are the ones who have faith in the money-producing power of ideas,' said Charles Fillmore. Ideas change things and can change the world. In business the perpetual hunt is for something unique, a development, a leap ahead of the competition. Innovate or die!

'Don't worry about people stealing your ideas. If your ideas are any good, you'll have to ram them down people's throats.'
Howard Aitken (1900–72), engineer

'Lack of money is no obstacle. Lack of an idea is an obstacle.'
Anon

'A good idea will keep you awake during the morning, but a great idea will keep you awake during the night.'
Anon

'One of the greatest pains to human nature is the pain of a new idea.'
Walter Bagehot (1826–77), British writer

'A good idea plus capable men cannot fail; it is better than money in the bank.'
John Berry (b. 1915), American poet and writer

'A new idea is delicate. It can be killed by a sneer or a yawn; it can be stabbed to death by a joke or worried to death by a frown on the right person's brow.'
Charles Browder, advertising executive

'To innovate is not to reform.'
Edmund Burke (1729–97), statesman and writer

'We ought not to be overanxious to encourage innovation in cases of doubtful improvement, for an old system must ever have two advantages over a new one; it is established, and it is understood.'
Charles Caleb Colton (1780–1832), writer

'Hang ideas! They are tramps, vagabonds, knocking at the backdoor of your mind, each taking a little of your substance, each carrying away some crumb of that belief in a few simple notions you must cling to if you want to live decently and would like to die easy!'
Joseph Conrad (1857–1924), Polish-born novelist

'Ideas are the root of creation.'
Ernest Dimnet (1866–1954), French writer

'Neither man or nation can exist without a sublime idea.'
Feodor Dostoyevsky (1821–81), Russian novelist

'There is no idea, no fact, which could not be vulgarized and presented in a ludicrous light.'
Feodor Dostoyevsky

'Inventors and men of genius have almost always been regarded as fools at the beginning (and very often at the end) of their careers.'
Feodor Dostoyevsky

'If at first the idea is not absurd, then there is no hope for it.'
Albert Einstein (1879–1955), physicist

'We are prisoners of ideas.'
Ralph Waldo Emerson (1803–82), poet

'There is no prosperity, trade, art, city, or great material wealth of any kind, but if you trace it home, you will find it rooted in a thought of some individual man.'
Ralph Waldo Emerson

'Ideas must work through the brains and arms of men, or they are no better than dreams.'
   Ralph Waldo Emerson

'The test of a first-rate intelligence is the ability to hold two opposed ideas in the mind at the same time, and still retain the ability to function.'
   F. Scott Fitzgerald (1896–1940), novelist

'An idea is a feat of association.'
   Robert Frost (1874–1963), American poet

'The enemy of the conventional wisdom is not ideas but the march of events.'
   JK Galbraith (b. 1908), economist

'One doesn't discover new lands without consenting to lose sight of the shore for a very long time.'
   André Gide (1869–1951), French Nobel prize winning novelist

'We are more ready to try the untried when what we do is inconsequential. Hence the remarkable fact that many inventions had their birth as toys.'
   Eric Hoffer (1902–1983), philosopher

'All human knowledge thus begins with intuitions, proceeds thence to concepts and ends with ideas.'
   Immanuel Kant (1724–1804), German philosopher

'To stay ahead, you must have your next idea waiting in the wings.'
   Rosabeth Moss Kanter (b. 1943), former editor of the *Harvard Business Review*

'Before you implement an idea that has been generated in the office, you should always take it to the field and ask for their criticisms. Pretty soon the idea will look like Swiss cheese – full of holes. They know what they're doing and we don't.'
   Herb Kelleher, airline executive

'It is ideas, not vested interests, which are dangerous for good or evil.'
   John Maynard Keynes (1883–1946), economist

'A single idea, if it is right, saves us the labor of an infinity of experiences.'
Jacques Maritain (1882–1973), philosopher and author

'Only puny secrets need protection. Big discoveries are protected by public incredulity.'
Marshall McLuhan (1911–80), commentator and critic

'Invention is the mother of necessities.'
Marshall McLuhan

'Incrementalism is innovation's worst enemy.'
Nicholas Negroponte, MIT media guru

'New ideas come from differences. They come from having different perspectives and juxtaposing different theories.'
Nicholas Negroponte

'The best way to have a good idea is to have a lot of ideas.'
Dr. Linus Pauling (1901–94), American chemist, pacifist and champion of Vitamin C

'All good ideas are eventually oversold.'
Tom Peters (b. 1942), consultant and author

'An idea is a point of departure and no more. As soon as you elaborate it, it becomes transformed by thought.'
Pablo Picasso (1881–1973), Spanish artistic genius

'Unless your ideas are ridiculed by experts they are worth nothing.'
Reg Revans (b. 1907), management academic and author

'New ideas are one of the most overrated concepts of our time. Most of the important ideas that we live with aren't new at all.'
Andrew A. Rooney (b. 1919), American journalist

'Ideas are like rabbits. You get a couple and learn how to handle them, and pretty soon you have a dozen.'
John Steinbeck (1902–68), American novelist

'Ideas that enter the mind under fire remain there securely and forever.'
   Leon Trotsky (1879–1940), revolutionary

'The man with a new idea is a crank until the idea succeeds.'
   Mark Twain (1835–1910), successful crank

'If you never had another idea, you might as well quit your job.'
   Jack Welch (b. 1935), head of General Electric

'Every time you meet somebody, you're looking for a better and newer and bigger idea. You are open to ideas from anywhere.'
   Jack Welch

'Necessity is the mother of invention is a silly proverb. "Necessity is the mother of futile dodges" is much nearer the truth.'
   Alfred North Whitehead (1861–1947), British scientist

'The value of an idea has nothing whatsoever to do with the sincerity of the man who expresses it. Indeed, the probabilities are that the more insincere the man is, the more purely intellectual will the idea be, as in that case it will not be colored by either his wants, his desires, or his prejudices.'
   Oscar Wilde (1854–1900), ideas man

'All great ideas are dangerous.'
   Oscar Wilde

'An idea is salvation by imagination.'
   Frank Lloyd Wright (1869–1959), architect

*I*DLERS AND IDLENESS

In a world of workaholics and stressed-out workers, it is refreshing to think that there are those who have time on their hands. They can contemplate life in a state of calm confidence. The only trouble is that, as one sage put it, 'The way to be nothing is to do nothing.'

'Efficiency is intelligent laziness.'
Anon

'Whenever I've got nothing to do, I open a restaurant.'
Michael Caine (b. 1933), actor

'Absence of occupation is not rest,
A mind quite vacant is a mind distressed.'
William Cowper (1731–1800), poet

'What is this life if, full of care,
We have no time to stand and stare?'
WH Davies (1870–1940), poet

'That man is idle who can do something better.'
Ralph Waldo Emerson (1803–82), poet

'Sometimes I think that idlers seem to be a special class for whom nothing can be planned, plead as one will with them – their only contribution to the human family is to warm a seat at the common table.'
F. Scott Fitzgerald (1896–1940), novelist

'Laziness may appear attractive, but work gives satisfaction.'
Anne Frank (1929–45), diarist

'Sloth makes all things difficult, but industry, all things easy. He that rises late must trot all day, and shall scarce overtake his business at night, while laziness travels so slowly that poverty soon overtakes him.'
Benjamin Franklin (1706–90), industrious American

'Sloth, like rust, consumes faster than labor wears, while the used key is always bright.'
Benjamin Franklin

'Purity of mind and idleness are incompatible.'
Mahatma Gandhi (1869–1948), Indian statesman

'It is impossible to enjoy idling thoroughly unless one has plenty of work to do.'
Jerome K. Jerome (1859–1927), Thamesside idler

'Well we can't stand here doing nothing, people will think we're workmen.'
Spike Milligan (b. 1918), comedian

'Only entropy comes easy.'
Lewis Mumford (1895–1990), philosopher and writer

'Let him that would move the world, first move himself.'
Socrates (469–399 BC), teacher of Plato executed for corrupting the young

'It takes a lot of time to be a genius, you have to sit around so much doing nothing, really doing nothing.'
Gertrude Stein (1874–1946), American writer

'A faculty for idleness implies a catholic appetite and a strong sense of personal identity.'
Robert Louis Stevenson (1850–94), novelist

'It is better to have loafed and lost than never to have loafed at all.'
James Thurber (1894–1961), American humorist and satirist

'I'm lazy. But it's the lazy people who invented the wheel and the bicycle because they didn't like walking or carrying things.'
Lech Walesa (b. 1943), shipyard worker turned political leader

'Let me say to you now that to do nothing at all is the most difficult thing in the world, the most difficult and the most intellectual.'
   Oscar Wilde (1854–1900), wit

'Idleness was a sin not against the self or against God but against Mammon and Pierce & Pierce.'
   Tom Wolfe (b. 1931), author of *The Bonfire of the Vanities*

*I*NDECISION

In a classic scene from *Bilko,* the smooth-tongued hero sorts out another poor fool: 'You said *but.* I've put my finger on the whole trouble, you're a *but* man.' Don't say *but.* That little word *but* is the difference between success and failure. Henry Ford said, 'I'm going to invent the automobile,' and Arthur T. Flanken said, 'But.' In business he who hesitates is often damned – or so, at least, we are led to believe by those who plunge bravely on no matter what the situation.

'Time is the greatest innovator.'
Francis Bacon (1561–1626), Elizabethan writer, wit and thinker

'Between saying and doing many a pair of shoes is worn out.'
Italian proverb

'There is no more miserable human being than one in whom nothing is habitual but indecision.'
William James (1842–1910), philosopher and psychologist

'Delay is preferable to error.'
Thomas Jefferson (1743–1826), American President

'Procrastination is opportunity's natural assassin.'
Victor Kiam (b. 1926), businessman

'Indecision is like the stepchild: if he doesn't wash his hands, he is called dirty; if he does, he is wasting the water.'
Madagascan Proverb

'Procrastination is the art of keeping up with yesterday.'
Donald Marquis (1878–1937), journalist and humorist

'It is human nature to stand in the middle of a thing.'
Marianne Moore (1887–1972), poet

'No problem is so big and complicated that it can't be run away from.'
Charles Schulz (b. 1922), cartoonist

'A man with a watch knows what time it is. A man with two watches is never sure.'
Segal's law

'While we are postponing, life speeds by.'
Seneca, Lucius (55 BC–39 AD), Roman master of rhetoric

'When you have avoided a tough decision on people, it usually costs you, the company and most importantly the people involved, more in the end.'
Liam Strong (b. 1945), British executive

'He who hesitates is sometimes saved.'
James Thurber (1894–1961), satirist and humorist

'He who hesitates is last.'
Mae West (1892–1980), actress

'Procrastination is the thief of time.'
Edward Young (1683–1765), poet

INFORMATION

After the British victory at Waterloo, pigeons were released conveying the good news to those at home. The pigeon which returned first belonged to banker Nathan Rothschild. He then immediately bought devalued war bonds. When news of Waterloo reached London, Rothschild had cornered the market on the now desirable bonds. Information is king.

'We are drowning in information and starved of knowledge.'
Anon

'War is 90 percent information.'
Napoleon Bonaparte (1769–1821), French General

'Where is the knowledge we have lost in information?'
TS Eliot (1888–1965), poet

'Information networks straddle the world. Nothing remains concealed. But the sheer volume of information dissolves the information. We are unable to take it all in'
Günter Grass (b. 1927), novelist

'We are standing on the verge, and for some it will be the precipice, of a revolution as profound as that which gave birth to modern industry. It will be the environmental revolution, the genetic revolution, the materials revolution, the digital revolution, and, most of all, the information revolution.'
Gary Hamel & CK Prahalad, authors and consultants

'Taking in information is only distantly related to real learning. It would be nonsensical to say, *"I just read a great book about bicycle riding – I've now learned that."* Through learning we become able to do something we were never able to do ... we reperceive the world and our relationship to it.'
Peter Senge (b. 1947), learning guru

'Life happens too fast for you ever to think about it. If you could just per-suade people of this, but they insist on amassing information.'
Kurt Vonnegut, Jr. (b. 1922), writer

'To live effectively is to live with adequate information.'
__Norbert Wiener (1894–1964), cybernetician__

'Private information is practically the source of every large modern fortune.'
Oscar Wilde (1854–1900), playwright

'Information about money has become more valuable than money itself.'
Walter Wriston, banker

'Information is not knowledge, knowledge is not wisdom, wisdom is not truth, truth is not beauty, beauty is not love, love is not music. Music is the best.'
Frank Zappa (1940–93), musician

INTUITION, GUTS AND LOGIC

> 'I am a rational man but the biggest decisions you make take no instinct,' said the soccer manager Osvaldo Ardiles. What lies behind a decision? While Ardiles relied on his instinct others are sticklers for analysis and logic – this is easier to explain at board meetings apart from anything else. Though, as Doctor Who said: 'Logic merely enables one to be wrong with authority.'

'Logic is the art of going wrong with confidence.'
   Anon

'Instinct is the nose of the mind.'
   Anon

'Logic is like the sword – those who appeal to it shall perish by it.'
   Samuel Butler (1612–80), poet and satirist

'Logic, like whisky, loses its beneficial effect when taken in too large quantities.'
   Lord Dunsany (1878–1957), novelist, poet and playwright

> *'I never discovered anything with my rational mind.'*
>   ***Albert Einstein (1879–1955), physicist***

'Intuition attracts those who wish to be spiritual without any bother, because it promises a heaven where the intuitions of others can be ignored.'
   EM Forster (1879–1970), novelist

'Call intuition cosmic fishing. You feel a nibble, then you've got to hook the fish.'
   R. Buckminster Fuller (1895–1983), architect, engineer and inventor

'There are no recipes. There are no certainties that what I'm doing is going to work. You've got to go on instinct.'
Lou Gerstner (b. 1942), American consultant and executive, CEO of IBM *et al.*

'We may take Fancy for a companion, but must follow Reason as our guide.'
Dr. Samuel Johnson (1709–84), man of letters

'Logic is neither a science or an art, but a dodge.'
Benjamin Jowett (1817–93), skeptic

'Logic doesn't apply to the real world.'
Marvin Lee Minsky (b. 1927), realist

'We have become prisoners of cerebral management. I'm sympathetic to the management process which is intuitive, based on immediate responses.'
Henry Mintzberg (b. 1939), business professor

'You can be totally rational with a machine. But if you work with people, sometimes logic often has to take a backseat to understanding.'
Akio Morita (b. 1921), co-founder of Sony

'Well-bred instinct meets reason halfway.'
George Santayana (1863–1952), philosopher and writer

'You think because you understand one you must understand two, because one and one makes two. But you must also understand *and*.'
Sufi saying

'There can never be surprises in logic.'
Ludwig Wittgenstein (1889–1951), philosopher

Investors and Investment

'I've got a rule of thumb: Anything that's worth $4 billion and costs $1 billion – buy it,' said the Saudi Prince Al-Waleed Bin Talal Bin Abdulaziz Al-Saud. The logic is good, but the figures are probably a little high for the average investor. While the newspapers bulge with information about top tips and sure things, the real investor is losing it all on the dog races

'He's called a broker because after dealing with him you are.'
Anon

'Never invest in anything that eats or needs repairing.'
Anon

'The investment of money on average return of less than three points above market should be restricted to Ascot.'
BBA Group mission statement

'Wall Street is the only place that people ride to in a Rolls Royce to get advice from those who take the subway.'
Warren Buffet (b. 1930), the investment guru

'They told me to buy this stock for my old age. It worked wonderfully. Within a week I was an old man!'
Eddie Cantor (1892–1964), comedian and singer

'Buy an annuity cheap, and make your life interesting to yourself and everybody else that watches the speculation.'
Charles Dickens (1812–70), great novelist; poor investor

'Tis sweet to know that stocks will stand
When we with daisies lie,
That commerce will continue,
And trades as briskly fly.'
Emily Dickinson (1830–86), American poet

'Time has a way of changing our assets into liabilities.'
Peter Drucker (b. 1909), author and consultant

'Human life is proverbially uncertain; few things are more certain than the solvency of a life-insurance company.'
Sir Arthur Eddington (1882–1944), astronomer

'Tis money that begets money.'
Thomas Fuller (1608–1661), doctor and writer

'The safest way to double your money is to fold over once and put it in your pocket.'
Elbert Hubbard (1856–1915), writer and businessman

'Speculation is the romance of trade, and casts contempt upon all its sober realities. It renders the stock-jobber a magician, and the exchange a region of enchantment.'
Washington Irving (1783–1859), sleepy investor in for the long haul

'Don't gamble; take all your savings and buy some good stock and hold it till it goes up, then sell it. If it don't go up, don't buy it.'
Will Rogers (1879–1935), American humorist and showman

'Buy land, they ain't makin' any more of it.'
Will Rogers

'Let Wall Street have a nightmare and the whole country has to help get them back in bed again.'
Will Rogers

'The average male likes to sit at breakfast and tell his wife and children what Adolf Hitler is going to do month after next. This is a harmless vanity. But from this it is an easy step for him to go downtown and start telling people what United States Steel is going to do month after next. That is liable to lose someone's life savings for him.'
Fred Schwed, author of *Where Are the Customers' Yachts?*

'Investment and speculation are said to be two different things, and the prudent man is advised to engage in the one and avoid the other. This is something like explaining to the troubled adolescent that Love and Passion are two different things. He perceives that they are different, but they don't seem quite different enough to clear up his problems.'

Fred Schwed

'October. This is one of the peculiarly dangerous months to speculate in stocks. The others are July, January, September, April, November, May, March, June, December, August and February.'

Mark Twain (1835–1910), creator of Huck Finn and the quotable Pudd'nhead Wilson

'On Wall Street, he and a few others – how many? three hundred, four hundred, five hundred? – had become precisely that ... Masters of the Universe. There was ... no limit whatsoever!'

Tom Wolfe (b. 1931), writer

KNOWLEDGE, KNOW-HOW AND LEARNING

'Learning is the new form of labor,' proclaims a Harvard expert. Research in the US found that a 10 percent increase in the workforce's education level led to an 8.6 percent gain in productivity. A 10 percent rise in plant and equipment values increased productivity by 3.4 percent. The conclusion? 'Knowledge and information – not just scientific knowledge, but news, advice, entertainment, communication, service – have become the economy's raw materials and its most important products. Knowledge is what we buy and sell,' says *Fortune*'s Thomas A Stewart. The downside? 'Trying to identify and manage knowledge assets is like trying to fish bare-handed.'

'Success in the marketplace increasingly depends on learning, yet most people don't know how to learn. What's more, those members of the organization that many assume to be the best at learning are, in fact, not very good at it.'
Chris Argyris (b. 1923), Harvard-based learning champion

'Real knowledge, like everything else of value, is not to be obtained easily. It must be worked for, studied for, thought for and, more than all, must be prayed for.'
Thomas Arnold (1795–1842), poet

'For knowledge itself is power.'
Francis Bacon (1561–1626), Elizabethan writer and thinker

'We can no longer compete on the cost of labor with countries like China. What we have to leverage is our know-how.'
Carlo de Benedetti, Olivetti chief

'Knowledge is the small part of ignorance that we arrange and classify.'
Ambrose Bierce (1842–1914), journalist and author

'Knowledge is like money: the more he gets, the more he craves.'
   Josh Billings (1818–85), writer

'The trouble with people is not that they don't know but that they know so much that ain't so.'
   Josh Billings (1818–85), pen name of Henry Wheeler Shaw, humorist

'The only irreplaceable capital an organisation possesses is the knowledge and ability of its people. The productivity of that capital depends on how effectively people share their competence with those who can use it.'
   Andrew Carnegie (1835–1919), industrialist

'The empires of the future are the empires of the mind.'
   Sir Winston Churchill (1874–1965), statesman

'Grace is given of God, but knowledge is born in the market.'
   Arthur Hugh Clough (1819–1861), poet

'The essence of knowledge is, having it, to apply it; not having it, to confess your ignorance.'
   Confucius (551–479 BC), Chinese philosopher

'When you say something, say what you know. When you don't know something, say that you don't know. That is knowledge.'
   Confucius

'What I hear, I forget; what I see, I remember; what I do, I understand.'
   Confucius

'Making a wrong decision is understandable. Refusing to search continually for learning is not.'
   Philip Crosby, quality guru

'Knowledge is a polite word for dead but not buried imagination.'
   ee cummings (1894–1962), lower case poet

'If you are not in a lifelong learning situation then you are the person who has five years in business and one year's experience 35 times.'
   Sir Graham Day (b. 1933), itinerant Canadian executive

'Learning is not compulsory ... neither is survival.'
W. Edwards Deming (1900–93), quality guru

'Only the organization can provide the basic continuity that knowledge workers need in order to be effective. Only the organization can convert the specialized knowledge of the knowledge worker into performance.'
Peter Drucker (b. 1909), predicted the rise of knowledge work thirty years ago

'From now on the key is knowledge. The world is becoming not labor intensive, not materials intensive, not energy intensive, but knowledge intensive.'
Peter Drucker

'The knowledge worker is both the true capitalist in the knowledge society and dependent on his job. Collectively the knowledge workers, the employed educated middle-class of today's society, own the means of production through pension funds, investment trusts, and so on.'
Peter Drucker

'We don't know a millionth of one percent about anything.'
Thomas Alva Edison (1847–1931), inventor and industrialist

'Curiosity is more important than knowledge.'
Albert Einstein (1879–1955), relativity genius

'Only two things are infinite, the universe and human stupidity, and I'm not sure about the former.'
Albert Einstein

'Of a truth, Knowledge is power, but it is a power reined by scruple, having a conscience of what must be and what may be; whereas Ignorance is a blind giant who, let him but wax unbound, would make it a sport to seize the pillars that hold up the long-wrought fabric of human good, and turn all the places of joy as dark as a buried Babylon.'
George Eliot (1819–80), novelist

'Knowledge is knowing that we cannot know.'
Ralph Waldo Emerson (1803–82), poet

'A little knowledge that acts is worth infinitely more than much knowledge that is idle.'
Kahlil Gibran (1883–1931), Syrian-born artist and writer

'Perplexity is the beginning of knowledge.'
Kahlil Gibran

'In a time of drastic change it is the learners who inherit the future. The learned usually find themselves equipped to live in a world that no longer exists.'
Eric Hoffer (1902–1983), philosopher

'A country's competitiveness starts not on the factory floor or in the engineering lab. It starts in the classroom.'
Lee Iacocca (b. 1924), executive

'Whereas at one time the decisive factor of production was the land, and later capital...today the decisive factor is increasingly man himself, that is, his knowledge.'
Pope John Paul II (b. 1920), Polish-born Pope

'Man is not weak; knowledge is more than equivalent to force.'
Dr. Samuel Johnson (1709–84), strong man

'Integrity without knowledge is weak and useless, and knowledge without integrity is dangerous and dreadful.'
Dr. Samuel Johnson

'Knowledge is of two kinds: we know a subject ourselves, or we know where we can find information upon it.'
Dr. Samuel Johnson

'A man must have a certain amount of intelligence to get anywhere.'
Charles F. Kettering (1876–1958), engineer and inventor

'Knowledge is like money: to be of value it must circulate, and in circulating it can increase in quantity and, hopefully, in value.'
Louis L'Amour (1908–88), writer

'To attain knowledge, add things every day. To attain wisdom, remove things every day.'
Lao-tzu (604–531 BC), Chinese philosopher

'What we know is not much. What we do not know is immense.'
Pierre-Simon de Laplace (1749–1827)

'That is what learning is. You suddenly understand something you've understood all your life, but in a new way.'
Doris Lessing (b. 1919), novelist

'Business, we know, is now so complex and difficult, the survival of firms so hazardous in an environment increasingly unpredictable, competitive and fraught with danger, that their continued existence depends on the day-to-day mobilization of every ounce of intelligence.'
Konosuke Matsushita (1894–1989), Japanese businessman

'The ignorance of how to use knowledge stockpiles exponentially.'
Marshall McLuhan (1911–80), Canadian sociologist and commentator

'Where there is much desire to learn, there of necessity will be much arguing, much writing, many opinions; for opinion in good men is but knowledge in the making.'
John Milton (1608–74), poet

'It's not what you don't know that will hurt you. It's what you think you know that just ain't so.'
Satchel Paige (1906–82), American baseball player

'Learning is what most adults will do for a living in the 21st century.'
SJ Perelman (1904–79), writer and humorist

'What men really want is not knowledge but certainty.'
Bertrand Russell (1872–1970), mathematician and philosopher

'Ignorance of the present, ignorance of the future – these are pardonable. But ignorance of how ignorant we are is unpardonable.'
Arthur Schlesinger, Jr. (b. 1917), historian

'Through learning we reperceive the world and our relationship to it ... This then, is the basic meaning of a "learning organization" – an organization that is continuously expanding its capacity to create its future. "Survival learning" or what is more often called "adaptive learning" is important – indeed it is necessary. But for a learning organization, "adaptive learning" must be joined by 'generative learning', learning that enhances our capacity to create.'
Peter Senge (b. 1947), educator and author

'The desire of knowledge, like the thirst of riches, increases ever with the acquisition of it.'
Laurence Sterne (1713–68), novelist

'Knowledge is the most democratic source of power.'
__Alvin Toffler (b. 1928), futurist__

'The illiterate of the 21st century will not be those who cannot read and write, but those who cannot learn, unlearn and relearn.'
Alvin Toffler

'All genuine knowledge originates in direct experience.'
Mao Tse-Tung (1893–1976), Chinese leader

'When I was a kid in the bank, the key economic indicator we looked at was freight-car loadings. Who the hell cares about them now? What we need is a way to measure the knowledge we bring to the work we do.'
Walter Wriston, banker

LAWS AND ORDERS

'Nothing is illegal if one hundred businessmen decide to do it,' said the American politician and civil rights campaigner, Andrew Young. He was probably right. Despite protestations that no one is bigger than the law, big corporations *en masse* are a difficult voice for lawmakers and enforcers to ignore. After all, it is only major companies which can now afford to hire lawyers without risking immediate bankruptcy.

'Riches without law are more dangerous than is poverty without law.'
Henry Ward Beecher (1813–87), clergyman abolitionist

'There are principals that govern human effectiveness – natural laws in the human dimension that are just as real, just as unchanging and unarguably there as laws such as gravity are in the physical dimension.'
Stephen Covey (b. 1932), self-help guru and bestselling author

'A rule to live by: I won't use anything I can't explain in five minutes.'
Philip Crosby, former executive turned quality evangelist

'If there were no bad people there would be no good lawyers.'
Charles Dickens (1812–70), novelist

'Hell, there are no rules here – we're trying to accomplish something.'
Thomas Alva Edison (1847–1931), inventor and businessman

'Life is too short to live with a bad deal.'
David Geffen (b. 1943), music executive

'In the old days, if a neighbor's apples fell into your yard, you worked it out over the back fence or picked them up and made pies. Today, you sue.'
Lee Iacocca (b. 1924), American executive

'Greenmail, in case you're wondering, is when a company pays a raider a premium for his holdings – if he'll go away. What I think it really is is blackmail in a pin-striped suit.'
Lee Iacocca

'A verbal contract isn't worth the paper it's printed on.'
Samuel Goldwyn (1882–1974), movie man

'If you obey all the rules, you miss all the fun.'
Katharine Hepburn (b. 1907), American actress

'I wish to be cremated. One tenth of my ashes shall be given to my agent, as written in our contract.'
Groucho Marx (1890–1977), comic genius

'Nordstrom Rules: Rule #1: Use your good judgement in all situations. There will be no additional rules.'
Nordstom's employee handbook

'Twenty percent of the customers account for 80 percent of the turnover; 20 percent of the components account for 80 percent of the cost and so forth.'
Pareto's Law – Vilfredo Pareto (1848–1923), Italian scientist and sociologist

'Any fool can make a rule, and any fool will mind it
Henry David Thoreau (1817–62), naturalist and writer

'Nothing is impossible for the man who doesn't have to do it himself.'
Weiler's Law

LEADERS AND LEADERSHIP

Leadership is one of the most talked about and least understood phenomena on earth. Ask anyone who they would rate as a great leader and they are as likely to say Richard Branson as Wellington, Mother Teresa as the Blessed Margaret. Confusion reigns – not surprising as there are literally hundreds of definitions of what leadership is. What can be said is that the nature of leadership appears to be undergoing fundamental changes. Leadership by dictatorship is slowly being consigned to history; to be replaced by leadership by interaction and guidance. Alfred P. Sloan has become Richard Branson.

'Now that I'm CEO, what am I supposed to actually do?'
'You're supposed to make superficial statements about how good the company is, then hope something lucky happens and profits go up.
It's called leadership, sir.'
Scott Adams (b. 1957), *Dilbert* creator

'The leadership instinct you are born with is the backbone. You develop the funny bone and the wishbone that go with it.'
Anon

He who has never learned to obey cannot be a good commander.'
Aristotle (384–322 BC), Greek philosopher

'More leaders have been made by accident, circumstance, sheer grit or will than have been made by all the leadership courses put together.'
Warren Bennis (b. 1925), leadership guru

'The capacity to create a compelling vision and translate it into action and sustain it.'
Warren Bennis

'Managers do things right. Leaders do the right thing.'
   Warren Bennis

'The new leader is one who commits people to action, who converts followers into leaders, and who may convert leaders into agents of change.'
   Warren Bennis

'If the blind lead the blind, both shall fall into the ditch.'
   Bible

'The first quality for a commander-in-chief is a cool head to receive a correct impression of things. He should not allow himself to be confused either by good or bad news.'
   Napoléon Bonaparte (1769–1821), French leader

'A leader is a dealer in hope.'
   Napoléon Bonaparte

'The leader's job is to help everyone see that the platform is burning, whether the flames are apparent or not. The process of change begins when people decide to take the flames seriously and manage by fact, and that means a brutal understanding of reality. You need to find out what the reality is so that you know what needs changing.'
   Larry Bossidy (b. 1935), CEO of Allied Signal

'Leadership over human beings is exercised when persons with certain motives and purposes mobilize, in competition or conflict with others, institutional, political, psychological and other resources so as to arouse, engage and satisfy the motives of followers.'
   James McGregor Burns (b. 19XX), political historian

'I define leadership as leaders inducing followers to act for certain goals that represent the values and motivations – the wants and needs, the aspirations and expectations – of both leaders and followers.'
   James McGregor Burns

'And when we think we lead, we are most led.'
   Lord Byron (1788–1824), Romantic poet

'No man will make a great leader who wants to do it all himself, or to get all the credit for doing it.'
   Andrew Carnegie (1835–1919), industrialist

'I am always ready to learn, although I do not always like being taught.'
Sir Winston Churchill (1874–1965), statesman

'The moment you step from independence to interdependence, you step into a leadership role.'
   Stephen Covey (b. 1932), American self-improvement guru

'You have to lead people gently toward what they already know is right.'
   Philip Crosby, quality evangelist

'Companies have to be led, not managed. It's not that difficult to manage companies. What they've got to be is led. And that leadership quality you want to get in all levels of the organization.'
   Greg Dyke (b. 1947), television executive

'You do not lead by hitting people over the head – that's assault, not leadership.'
   Dwight D. Eisenhower (1890–1969), American President

'To be a leader of men one must turn one's back on men.'
   Havelock Ellis (1859–1939), sexologist

'People try so hard to believe in leaders now, pitifully hard. But we no sooner get a popular reformer or politician or soldier or writer or philosopher – a Roosevelt, a Tolstoy, a Wood, a Shaw, a Nietzsche, than the crosscurrents of criticism wash him away. My word, no man can stand prominence these days. It's the surest path to obscurity. People get sick of hearing the same name over and over.'
   F. Scott Fitzgerald (1896–1940), prose leader

'The most successful leader of all is one who sees another picture not yet actualized.'
   Mary Parker Follett (1868–1933), neglected American management thinker

'All of the great leaders have had one characteristic in common: it was the willingness to confront unequivocally the major anxiety of their people in their time. This, and not much else, is the essence of leadership.'
   JK Galbraith (b. 1908), Canadian economist

'I believe the leader's ultimate job is to spread hope.'
   Bob Galvin, American executive

'Executives are given subordinates...they have to earn followers.'
   John W. Gardner (b. 1912), American writer and government official

'Men are of no importance. What counts is who commands.'
   Charles De Gaulle (1890–1970), French leader

'Leadership is practiced not so much in words as in attitude and in actions.'
   Harold Geneen (b. 1910), ITT chief executive during the 1960s and 1970s

'Uncertainty will always be part of the taking charge process.'
   Harold Geneen

'A leader shapes and shares a vision, which gives point to the work of others.'
   Charles Handy (b. 1932), management thinker and author

'Leadership in today's world requires far more than a large stock of gunboats and a hard fist at the conference table.'
   Hubert H. Humphrey (1911–78), American Democratic politician

'The right man comes at the right time.'
   Italian proverb

'I need to be able to look at myself in the mirror and know that tough decisions are made with a balance of commercial considerations and those arising from a deep inner faith. If you can't say this out loud, I believe that you are missing an important element of leadership.'
   Ann Iverson (b. 1944), American-born, British-based executive

'Leadership has a harder job to do than just choose sides. It must bring sides together.'
Jesse Jackson (b. 1941), American politician

'The only real training for leadership is leadership.'
Sir Antony Jay (b. 1930), British writer

'The task of the leader is to get his people from where they are to where they have not been.'
Henry Kissinger (b. 1923), American politician

'Leadership produces change. That is its primary function.'
John Kotter (b. 1947), Harvard management guru

'The quality of a leader is reflected in the standards they set for themselves.'
Ray Kroc (1902–84), man behind McDonald's

'When the effective leader is finished with his work, the people say it happened naturally.'
Lao-tzu (604–531 BC), Chinese philosopher

'A leader should be humble. A leader should be able to communicate with his people. A leader is someone who walks out in front of his people, but he doesn't get too far out in front, to where he can't hear their footsteps.'
Tommy Lasorda (b. 1927), former manager of the L.A. Dodgers

'Leaders are made, they are not born. They are made by hard effort, which is the price which all of us must pay to achieve any goal that is worthwhile.'
Vince Lombardi (1913–70), American football coach

'A man can be as great as he wants to be. If you believe in yourself and have the courage, the determination, the dedication, the competitive drive and if you are willing to sacrifice the little things in life and pay the price for the things that are worthwhile, it can be done.'
Vince Lombardi

'The leader can never close the gap between himself and the group. If he does, he is no longer what he must be. He must walk a tightrope between the consent he must win and the control he must exert.'
   Vince Lombardi

'The first method for estimating the intelligence of a ruler is to look at the men he has around him.'
   Nicolò Machiavelli (1469–1527), Florentine diplomat and author

'Leadership is the other side of the coin of loneliness, and he who is a leader must always act alone. And acting alone, accept everything alone.'
   Ferdinand E. Marcos (1917–89), dictator

'That perfect bliss and sole felicity,
The sweet fruition of an earthly crown.'
   Christopher Marlowe (1564–93), murdered poet and dramatist

'Leadership and management are in many respects the application of common sense, though this needs to be combined with humility and a willingness to recognize your own fallibility and that of others. Good leaders acknowledge their mistakes.'
   Sir Colin Marshall (b. 1933), British executive

'The tail trails the head. If the head moves fast, the tail will keep up the same pace. If the head is sluggish, the tail will droop.'
   Konosuke Matsushita (1894–1989), Japanese executive

'The real leader has no need to lead – he is content to point the way.'
   Henry Miller (1891–1980), novelist

'No one is great enough or wise enough to surrender our destiny to. The only way in which anyone can lead us is to restore to us the belief in our own thinking.'
   Henry Miller

'The leader must have infectious optimism, and the determination to persevere in the face of difficulties; he must also radiate confidence, even when he himself is not too certain of the outcome. The final test of a leader is the feeling you have when you leave his presence after a conference. Have you got a feeling of uplift and confidence?'
    Field Marshall Montgomery (1887–1976), British soldier

'I start with the premise that the function of leadership is to produce more leaders, not more followers.'
    Ralph Nader (b. 1934), American lawyer and campaigner

'To do great things is difficult; but to command great things is more difficult.'
    Friedrich Nietzsche (1844–1900), philosopher

'The high sentiments always win in the end, the leaders who offer blood, toil, tears and sweat always get more out of their followers than those who offer safety and a good time. When it comes to the pinch, human beings are heroic.'
    George Orwell (1903–50), novelist

'People prefer being led to being managed.'
    Sir Peter Parker (b. 1924), British executive

'The art of leadership is to act as a representative of a much larger constituency than those who voted for you.'
    Sir Peter Parker

'Leadership means vision, cheerleading, enthusiasm, love, trust, verve, passion, obsession, consistency, the use of symbols, paying attention as illustrated by the content of one's calendar, out-and-out drama (and the management thereof), creating heroes at all levels, coaching, effectively wandering around, and numerous other things. Leadership must be present at all levels of the organization.'
    Tom Peters (b. 1942) and Nancy Austin, consultants and authors

'A leader is someone who steps back from the entire system and tries to build a more collaborative, more innovative system that will work over the long term.'
   Robert Reich (b. 1946), economist and politician

'There is a necessary loneliness to leadership.'
   Gerry Robinson (b. 1948), Granada chief

'Most leaders in some deep sense are striving to prove something which is unprovable.'
   Gerry Robinson

'People ask the difference between a leader and a boss...the leader works in the open, and the boss is covert. The leader leads, the boss drives.'
   Theodore Roosevelt (1858–1919), American President

'Leadership is a potent combination of strategy and character. But if you must be without one, be without the strategy.'
   General H. Norman Schwarzkopf (b. 1934), soldier

'Our traditional views of leaders – as special people who set the direction, make the key decisions, and energize the troops – are deeply rooted in an individualistic and non-systemic worldview. Especially in the West, leaders are heroes – great men (and occasionally women) who *rise to the fore* in times of crises. Our prevailing leadership myths are still captured by the image of the captain of the cavalry leading the charge to rescue the settlers from the attacking Indians. So long as such myths prevail, they reinforce a focus on short-term events and charismatic heroes rather than on systemic forces and collective learning. At its heart, the traditional view of leadership is based on assumptions of people's powerlessness, their lack of personal vision and inability to master the forces of change, deficits which can be remedied only by a few great leaders.'
   Peter Senge (b. 1947), MIT-based author, researcher and educator

'To be omnipotent but friendless is to reign.'
   Percy Bysshe Shelley (1792–1822), poet

'Any one can hold the helm when the sea is calm.'
Publilius Syrus (c. 42 BC), Latin writer

'Consensus is the negation of leadership.'
Margaret Thatcher (b. 1925), Prime Minister and democrat

'A leader is someone who knows what they want to achieve and can communicate that.'
Margaret Thatcher

'Marvellous is the power which can be exercised, almost unconsciously, over a company, or an individual, or even upon a crowd by one person gifted with good temper, good digestion, good intellects and good looks.'
Anthony Trollope (1815–82), novelist

'Leadership is the ability to get men to do what they don't like to do and like it.'
Harry S Truman (1884–1972), 33rd U.S. President

'Lead, follow, or get the hell out of the way.'
Ted Turner (b. 1938), media mogul

'A leader needs to be relaxed, loose, open, stubborn, angry and unpredictable.'
Bill Walsh (b. 1931), American football coach

'The beliefs that mold great organizations frequently grow out of the character, the experience and the convictions of a single person.'
Thomas Watson, Jr. (1914–93), IBM chief and diplomat

LOVE AND EMOTION

'Every man has business and desire,' claimed Shakespeare. In the corporate-man era this was difficult to believe. After all, while the rest of the world was smoking its way through the summer of love, managers discovered strategic management. Instead of Jimi Hendrix they had Igor Ansoff. Things have changed. Offices aren't exactly palaces of brotherly love, but they are open plan.

'It is the heart always that sees, before the head can see.'
Thomas Carlyle (1795–1881), essayist

'I love Mickey Mouse more than any woman I have ever known.'
Walt Disney (1901–66), frank admission from the man behind the ears

'You don't need a Harvard MBA to know that the bedroom and the boardroom are just two sides of the same ballgame.'
Stephen Fry (b. 1957), British writer and comedian

'Management must have a purpose, a dedication and that dedication must have an emotional commitment. It must be built in as a vital part of the personality of anyone who truly is a manager.'
Harold Geneen (b. 1910), not renowned for his emotional life

'There are two worlds: the world we measure with line and rule, and the world we feel with our hearts and imaginations.'
James Henry Leigh Hunt (1784–1859), poet and essayist

'If you're going to play together as a team, you've got to care for one another. You've got to love each other...The difference between mediocrity and greatness ... is the feeling these guys have for each other. Most people call it team spirit.'
Lee Iacocca (b. 1924), team player

'We are not afraid to talk to our people with emotion. We're not afraid to tell them, *We love you,* because we do.'
Herb Kelleher, airline chief based at Love Field

'It is better to be feared than loved, if you cannot be both.'
Nicolò Machiavelli (1469–1527), Florentine diplomat and writer

'People, including managers, do not live by pie charts alone – or by bar graphs or three-inch statistical appendices to 300 page reports. People live, reason, and are moved by symbols and stories.'
Tom Peters (b. 1942), managerial Billy Graham

'The word love is never mentioned in big business.'
Anita Roddick (b. 1943), founder The Body Shop

'Never marry for money. Ye'll borrow it cheaper.'
Scottish proverb

'Don't just put your heart into the business. Put the business into your heart.'
Thomas Watson, Jr. (1914–93), IBM chief and diplomat

'To love is to be engaged is to work is to be interested is to create.'
Lina Wertmuller (b. 1929), filmmaker

LUCK AND TIMING

Is being in the right place at the right time a finely honed skill? Some people seem to do it repeatedly. Is it mere luck on their part or the result of sharpened commercial antennae?

'The only thing sure about luck is that it will change.'
Anon

'Fortunes ... come tumbling into some men's laps.'
Francis Bacon (1561–1626), Elizabethan writer

'Good luck needs no explanation.'
Shirley Temple Black (b. 1928), child star turned diplomat

'Luck is not chance, it's toil. Fortune's expensive smile is earned.'
Emily Dickinson (1830–86), poet

'Shallow men believe in luck ... Strong men believe in cause and effect.'
Ralph Waldo Emerson (1803–82), poet

'Chance fights ever on the side of the prudent.'
Euripedes (484–406 BC), tragedian

'Failure or success seem to have been allotted to men by their stars. But they retain the power of wriggling, of fighting with their star or against it, and in the whole universe the only really interesting movement is this wriggle.'
EM Forster (1879–1970), novelist

'He that waits upon fortune is never sure of a dinner.'
Benjamin Franklin (1706–90), realist

'Only learn to seize good fortune, for good fortune is always here.'
Johann Wolfgang von Goethe (1749–1832), German writer

'You can resist an invading army; you cannot resist an idea whose time has come.'
Victor Hugo (1802–85), French writer

'I'm still not sure what is meant by good fortune and success. I know fame and power are for the birds. But then life suddenly comes into focus for me. And, ah, there stand my kids.'
Lee Iacocca (b. 1924), sentimentalist

'I find that the harder I work, the more luck I seem to have.'
Thomas Jefferson (1743–1826), American President (also attributed to virtually anyone who has been successful)

'Those who solely by good fortune become princes from being private citizens have little trouble in rising, but much in keeping atop; they have not any difficulties on the way up, because they fly, but they have many when they reach the summit.'
Nicolò Machiavelli (1469–1527), diplomat and writer

'Fortune knocks but once, but misfortune has much more patience.'
Dr. Laurence J. Peter (1919–90), creator of the Peter Principle

'Nine tenths of wisdom consists in being wise in time.'
Theodore Roosevelt (1858–1919), American President

'Luck is what happens when preparation meets opportunity.'
Lucius Seneca (55 BC–39 AD), Roman master of rhetoric

'Fortune knocks at every man's door once in a life, but in a good many cases the man is in a neighboring saloon and does not hear her.'
Mark Twain (1835–1910), novelist

'The two prime movers in the Universe are Time and Luck.'
Kurt Vonnegut, Jr. (b. 1922), novelist

'Luck is not something you can mention in the presence of self-made men.'
EB White (b. 1899), humorist and writer

'Luck is a matter of preparation meeting opportunity.'
Oprah Winfrey (b. 1954), broadcaster

MANAGEMENT

The meaning of management is a matter of continuing debate. Alternatively, there is the equally perennial – and redundant – debate about what it is that managers actually do. There appears to be universal surprise that the answers to these questions aren't instantly available. This overlooks the fact that management, more than any other professional discipline, is in a state of perpetual flux. Its meaning and what it involves change constantly: Hard and fast definitions are inevitably short-lived and unhelpful.

'Management is an activity or art where those who have not yet succeeded and those who have proved unsuccessful are led by those who have not yet failed.'
Anon

'The manager is a hero in the Western world, but an impostor. The concept of management has proved a huge distraction. The management side of running a company is trivial compared to the importance of being commercial or entrepreneurial, or having a particular specialist skill. Any organization needs to have people with the skills relevant to its business rather than concentrating on turning the marketing director into a rounded general manager.'
Andrew Campbell (b. 1950), British author and academic

'Management is more art than science. No one can say with certainty which decisions will bring the most profit, any more than they can create instructions over how to sculpt a masterpiece. You just have to feel it as it goes.'
Richard D'Aveni, academic-based at Amos Tuck School of Business

'A manager's job should be based on a task to be performed in order to attain the company's objectives...the manager should be directed and controlled by the objectives of performance rather than by his boss.'
Peter Drucker (b. 1909), creator of modern management theory

'Management means, in the last analysis, the substitution of thought for brawn and muscle, of knowledge for folklore and superstition, and of co-operation for force.'
Peter Drucker

'I would be a very poor manager. Hopeless. And a company job would bore me to death.'
Peter Drucker

'Management is the organ of institutions, the organ that converts a mob into an organization, and human efforts into performance.'
Peter Drucker

'Before World War II most managers did not know they were managing.'
Peter Drucker

'Management will remain a basic and dominant institution perhaps as long as Western civilization itself survives.'
Peter Drucker

'Management is tasks. Management is discipline. But management is also people. Every achievement of management is the achievement of a manager. Every failure is the failure of a manager. People manage, rather than forces or facts. The vision, dedication and integrity of managers determine whether there is management or mismanagement.'
Peter Drucker

'The function which distinguishes the manager above all others is his educational one. The one contribution he is uniquely expected to make is to give others vision and ability to perform. It is vision and more responsibility that, in the last analysis, define the manager.'
Peter Drucker

'The more efficient business you have, the easier it is to run that business, and win.'
Tom Farmer (b. 1940), Kwik-Fit chief

'To manage is to forecast and plan, to organize, to command, to coordinate and to control.'
   Henri Fayol (1841–1925), French industrialist and management thinker

'The art of management is to promote people without making them managers.'
   Bill Gates (b. 1955), billionaire boffin

'Management must manage.'
   Harold Geneen (b. 1910), former ITT chief

'Running a conglomerate requires working harder than most people want to work and taking more risks than most people want to take.'
   Harold Geneen

'The traditional concept of management is reaching the end of the road.'
   Michael Hammer (b. 1948), reengineering guru

'There are three simple things to remember about running a business. One, encourage youth ... Two, give them responsibility as soon as you can and they will seldom let you down. Three, you must show an interest in what they are doing and have them report to you frequently on a fairly informal basis.'
   Lord Hanson (b. 1922), industrialist

'Most ideas on management have been around for a very long time, and the skill of the manager consists in knowing them all and, rather as he might choose the appropriate gold club for a specific situation, choosing the particular ideas which are most appropriate for the position and time in which he finds himself.'
   Sir John Harvey-Jones (b. 1924), former ICI chief

'I believe that management is an art – and possibly one of the most difficult ones. Just as the artist constantly and consciously works to perfect his technique and to gain mastery of his relevant skills, so must the manager. Mere technical command of the skills does not, however, produce a virtuoso or a superb manager. It is that extra something which each of us brings from within ourselves that makes the difference – vision, judgement, awareness of the world around us, and responsiveness to that world, which leads to success. Managing is a matter of the mind and the character.'

Sir John Harvey-Jones

'You can compare our roles in the front office to the military: we're the supply corps, not the heroes. We supply the heroes, period. The heroes are out there.'

Herb Kelleher, airline executive

'A good manager is best when people barely know that he exists. Not so good when people obey and acclaim him. Worse when they despise him.'

Lao-tzu (604–531 BC), Chinese philosopher

'Managing is like holding a dove in your hand. Squeeze too tight, you kill it. Open your hand too much, you let it go.

Tommy Lasorda (b. 1927), former manager of the L.A. Dodgers

'It takes no more actual sagacity to carry on the everyday hawking and haggling of the world, or to ladle out its normal doses of bad medicine and worse law, than it takes to operate a taxicab or fry a pan of fish.'

HL Mencken (1880–1956), journalist and writer

'If you ask managers what they do, they will most likely tell you that they plan, organize, coordinate and control. Then watch what they do. Don't be surprised if you can't relate what you see to those four words.'

Henry Mintzberg (b. 1939), Canadian academic and author

'My perception of what constitutes effective management is not so different as it was. But now there is a lot more ineffective management.'

Henry Mintzberg

'Managing at any time, but more than ever today, is a symbolic activity. It involves energizing people, often large numbers of people, to do new things they previously had not thought important. Building a compelling case – to really deliver a quality product, to double investment in research and development, to step out and take risks each day (e.g. make suggestions about cost-cutting when you are already afraid of losing your job) – is an emotional process at least as much as it is a rational one.'

Tom Peters (b. 1942), consultant and best-selling author

'Management is like taking a bath. First you wash yourself. Then second, you think. The problem with managers today is that too many are taking showers.'

Antoine Riboud, head of French company, BSN

'The achievement of stability, which is the manager's objective, is a never-to-be-attained ideal. He is like a symphony orchestra conductor, endeavoring to maintain a melodious performance in which the contributions of the various instruments are coordinated and sequenced, patterned and paced, while the orchestra members are having various personal difficulties, stage hands are moving music stands, alternating excessive heat and cold are creating audience and instrumental problems, and the sponsor of the concert is insisting on irrational changes in the program.'

Leonard Sayles, academic

'Behaving like a manager means having command of the whole range of management skills and applying them as they become appropriate.'

Herbert Simon (b. 1916), cognitive scientist and economist

MARKETING

'While great devices are invented in the laboratory, great products are invented in the Marketing Department,' says author William Davidow. This might help in clearing up the mystery as to what marketing actually involves. The confusion is inevitable when you are told (by Alfred Taubman): 'There is more similarity in the marketing challenge of selling a precious painting by Degas and a frosted mug of root beer than you ever thought possible.' I have never thought it but, in the hands of persuasive marketers, anything is possible.

'Marketing's job is to convert societal needs into profitable opportunities.'
Anon

'Marketing consists of all activities by which a company adapts itself to its environment – creatively and profitably.'
Anon

'Marketing is so basic that it cannot be considered a separate function. It is the whole business seen from the point of view of its final result, that is, from the customer's point of view...Business success is not determined by the producer but by the customer.'
Peter Drucker (b. 1909), management writer

'Marketing is the distinguishing, the unique function of the business. A business is set apart from all other human organizations by the fact that it markets a product or a service.'
Peter Drucker

'Not everything that goes by the name of *marketing* deserves it. It has become too fashionable. A grave-digger remains a grave-digger even when called a mortician. Only the cost of burial goes up.'
Peter Drucker

'Marketing is not a function, it is the whole business seen from the customer's point of view.'
Peter Drucker

'There is only one valid definition of business purpose: to create a customer. Markets are not created by God, nature or economic forces, but by businessmen. The want they satisfy may have been felt by the customer before he was offered the means of satisfying it. It may indeed, like the want of food in a famine, have dominated the customer's life and filled all his waking moments. But it was a theoretical want before; only when the action of businessmen makes it an effective demand is there a customer, a market.'
Peter Drucker

'Production only fills a void that it has itself created.'
JK Galbraith (b. 1908), economist

'We defined personality as a market niche.'
Herb Kelleher, personable airline chief

'Although it only takes a semester to learn marketing, it takes a lifetime to master it.'
Philip Kotler, author of seminal marketing texts

'Good companies will meet needs; great companies will create markets. Market leadership is gained by envisioning new products, services, lifestyles, and ways to raise living standards. There is a vast difference between companies that offer me-too products and those that create new product and service values not even imagined by the marketplace. Ultimately, marketing at its best is about value creation and raising the world's living standards.'
Philip Kotler

'Companies pay too much attention to the cost of doing something. They should worry more about the cost of not doing it.'
Philip Kotler

'Every company should work hard to obsolete its own product line...before its competitors do.'
Philip Kotler

'Your company does not belong in any market where it can't be the best.'
Philip Kotler

'Marketing takes a day to learn. Unfortunately it takes a life time to master.'
Philip Kotler

'Management must think of itself not as producing products but as providing customer-creating value satisfactions.'
Theodore Levitt (b. 1925), Harvard Business School marketing expert

'The railroads collapsed because they thought they were in the railroad business, when really they were in the transportation business. They let others take customers away from them because they assumed themselves to be in the railroad business rather than in the transportation business. The reason they defined their industry wrong was because they were railroad-oriented instead of transportation-oriented; they were product-oriented instead of customer-oriented.'
Theodore Levitt

'Marketing is too important to be left to the marketing department.'
David Packard (1912–96), computer company founder

'Thanks to our free-enterprise system and phenomenal advances in marketing, we now stand on the threshold of an era when the American palate, stimulated by delicacies formerly reserved only for a Maecenas, will one day hold aloft a gustatory torch for the entire world.'
SJ Perelman (1904–79), humorist

'Strategy and timing are the Himalayas of marketing. Everything else is the Catskills.'
Al Ries & Jack Trout, mountaineers of marketing

'Marketing strategy is a series of integrated actions leading to a sustainable competitive advantage.'
John Sculley (b. 1939), Pepsi marketer undone at Apple

Measurement

'What gets measured gets done; what gets rewarded gets done repeatedly,' observed the engagingly named Barcy C. Fix of St Louis University. Measurement has dominated much of the business thinking of the century. This can largely be attributed to Frederick Taylor and his development of scientific management – which involved timing every single part of a job. The men with stop watches are still with us though their techniques are now more subtle.

'Time is the measure of business.'
Francis Bacon (1561–1626), writer and thinker

'Measure not the work
Until the day's out and the labor done,
Then bring your gauges.'
Elizabeth Barrett Browning (1806–61), poet

'Not everything that can be counted counts, and not everything that counts can be counted.'
Albert Einstein (1879–1955), relativity genius

'Measure what is measurable and make measurable what is not so.'
Galileo Galilei (1564–1642), astronomer

'Whenever you can, count.'
Sir Francis Galton (1822–1911), scientist and explorer

'Companies should measure their success not by the fact they are still around and making money, but how many opportunities they have missed.'
Gary Hamel (b. 1954), author and London Business School academic

'The first step is to measure whatever can be easily measured. That is okay as far as it goes. The second step is to disregard that which can't be easily measured or to give it an arbitrary quantitative value. This is artificial and misleading. The third step is to presume that what can't be measured easily really isn't important. This is blindness. The fourth step is to say that what can't be easily measured really doesn't exist. This is suicide.'

Robert McNamara (b. 1916), businessman and politician

MEDIA PACKS

Love them or hate them, the media are now an indispensable part of modern business. No major corporate action is complete without a press release and a series of interviews. Some executives seem to spend more time with profile writers than in their offices. They know that our reputations are what history remembers.

'Everything you do or say is public relations.'
Anon

'There is no such thing as a free lunch.'
Anon

'There is no such thing as bad publicity except your own obituary.'
Brendan Behan (1923–64)

'Journalists say a thing that they know isn't true, in the hope that if they keep on saying it long enough it will be true.'
Arnold Bennett (1867–1931), writer

'Have regard for your name, since it will remain for you longer than a great store of gold.'
Bible

'Four hostile newspapers are more to be feared than a thousand bayonets.'
Napoleon Bonaparte (1769–1821), French General

'A great reputation is a great noise, the more there is of it, the further does it swell. Land, monuments, nations, all fall, but the noise remains, and will reach to other generations.'
Napoléon Bonaparte

'Public behavior is merely private character writ large.'
Stephen Covey (b. 1932), self-improvement guru

'The easiest way to get a reputation is to go outside the fold, shout around for a few years as a violent atheist or a dangerous radical, and then crawl back to the shelter.'
   F. Scott Fitzgerald (1896–1940), novelist

'You can't build a reputation on what you are going to do.'
   Henry Ford (1863–1947), automobile manufacturer

'You must stir it and stump it,
And blow your own trumpet,
Or trust me, you haven't a chance.'
   WS Gilbert (1836–1911), dramatist and writer

'The blaze of reputation cannot be blown out, but it often dies in the socket; a very few names may be considered as perpetual lamps that shine unconsumed.'
   Dr. Samuel Johnson (1709–84), media man

'The function of the press in society is to inform, but its role is to make money.'
   AJ Liebling (1904–63), journalist

'My reputation is a media creation.'
   John Lydon (b. 1956), aka Johnny Rotten

'Until you've lost your reputation, you never realize what a burden it was or what freedom really is.'
   Margaret Mitchell (1900–49), author

'Reputation, reputation, reputation! O, I ha' lost my reputation, I ha' lost the immortal part of myself, and what remains is bestial!'
   William Shakespeare (1564–1616), bard

'Newspapers are unable, seemingly, to discriminate between a bicycle accident and the collapse of civilization.'
   George Bernard Shaw (1856–1950), playwright

'The way to gain a good reputation is to endeavor to be what you desire to appear.'
   Socrates (469–399 BC), teacher of Plato

'Better a quiet death than a public misfortune.'
Spanish proverb

'A good reputation is more valuable than money.'
Publilius Syrus (c. 42 BC), Latin writer

Missions, mottos and mantras

'Never have a mission, my dear child,' says Mr. Jellyby in *Bleak House*. It's too late. Every business in the country now proclaims that it has a mission. From Indian restaurants to the Foreign Office, grandiose statements of intent are fashionable. Their usefulness has long been forgotten as slogans, jargon and catchphrases are condensed into weighty paragraphs which every executive is expected to memorize and – even more unlikely – put into practice.

'Think differently.'
    Apple slogan

'A sense of mission is essentially an emotional feeling by the people in the organization. An organization with a sense of mission has captured the emotional support of its people.'
    Andrew Campbell (b. 1950), British expert on corporate missions

'Grow industry, grow! grow! grow!
Harmony and sincerity,
Matsushita Electric.'
    Company song

'Mission and philosophy is the key starting point in business. A business is not defined by its name, statutes, or articles of incorporation. It is defined by the business mission. Only a clear definition of the mission and purpose of the organization makes possible clear and realistic business objectives.'
    Peter Drucker (b. 1909), thinker and writer

'The management that does not ask *What is our mission?* when the company is successful is, in effect, smug, lazy and arrogant. It will not be long before success will turn into failure.'
    Peter Drucker

'Any color – so long as it's black.'
Henry Ford (1863–1947), champion of choice

'Think.'
IBM slogan

'Never knowingly undersold.'
John Lewis Partnership

'Being great at everything is not an actionable message.'
Floris Maljers (b. 1933), former Unilever chief executive

'The worst newspaper in the world.'
***The Marshall Islands Journal* slogan**

'We are in the business of preserving and improving human life. All of our actions must be measured by our success in achieving this goal.'
Merck Internal management guide

'All the news that's fit to print.'
Adolph Ochs (1858–1935), *New York Times* mission

'Say it with flowers.'
Patrick O'Keefe (1872–1934) slogan for Society of American Florists

'To do all in our power to pack the customer's dollar full of value, quality and satisfaction.'
JC Penney (1875–1971), American businessman

'Our mission is to be the best-managed company in the world in the [fill in the blank] industry through our commitment to total customer satisfaction delivered by our totally empowered employees who work in the new team paradigm to continuously improve our position of unequalled quality and lowest costs, and in so doing, produce superior returns for our shareholders.'
Eileen Shapiro, management consultant

'Make a little, sell a little.'
3M motto

'Take small steps.'
3M motto

'We Sell for Less.'
Wal-Mart slogan

Mistakes

To err is human, but try telling your boss that. How we react to and learn from our mistakes is emerging as an important area of research for academics and theorists. You could try telling your boss that the catastrophic error you have just committed is more profitably regarded as a learning experience. However, you may value your job.

'Learn all you can from the mistakes of others. You won't have time to make them all yourself.'
   Anon

'Who has enough credit in this world to pay for his mistakes?'
   Anon

'Truth comes out of error more readily than out of confusion.'
   Francis Bacon (1561–1626), Elizabethan writer

'The errors of young men are the ruin of business, but the errors of aged men amount to this, that more might have been done, or sooner.'
   Francis Bacon

'An expert is a man who has made all the mistakes which can be made in a very narrow field.'
   Niels Bohrs (1885–1962), physicist

'To swear off making mistakes is very easy. All you have to do is swear off having ideas.'
   Leo Burnett, founder of advertising agency

'Truth is a good dog; but beware of barking too close to the heels of an error, lest you get your brains kicked out.'
   Samuel Taylor Coleridge (1772–1834), poet

'Even a mistake may turn out to be the one thing necessary to a worthwhile achievement.'
Henry Ford (1863–1947), auto manufacturer

'From error to error, one discovers the entire truth.'
Sigmund Freud (1856–1939), psychoanalyst

'We're all human and we all goof. Do things that may be wrong, but do something.'
Newt Gingrich (b. 1943), American politician

'One of the measures of a good leader is that when he makes a mistake, and the company suffers for it, people still follow him.'
Richard Giordano (b. 1934), American-born, British-based executive

'Man must strive, and striving he must err.'
Johann Wolfgang von Goethe (1749–1832), German writer

'If a man has money, it is usually a sign, too, that he knows how to take care of it; don't imagine his money is easy to get simply because he has plenty of it.'
Edgar Watson Howe (1853–1937), American writer

'The greatest mistake you can make in life is to be continually fearing you will make one.'
Elbert Hubbard (1856–1915), writer and businessman

'Mistakes are a part of life; you can't avoid them. All you can hope is that they won't be too expensive and that you don't make the same mistake twice.'
Lee Iacocca (b. 1924), former chairman of Chrysler

'If you own up to your mistakes, you don't suffer as much. But that's a tough lesson to learn.'
Lee Iacocca

'Mistakes are the portals of discovery.'
James Joyce (1882–1941), Irish novelist

'To err is human; to admit it, superhuman.'
  Doug Larson, cartoonist

'Clever people learn from others' mistakes. Fools learn from their own.'
  Alexander Lebed, Russian politician

'All men are liable to error; and most men are, in many points, by passion or interest, under temptation to it.'
  John Locke (1632–1704), British philosopher

'I have learned the novice can often see things that the expert overlooks. All that is necessary is not to be afraid of making mistakes or of appearing naive.'
  Abraham Maslow (1908–70), motivational theorist

'Give me the fruitful error any time, full of seeds, bursting with its own corrections. You can keep your sterile truth for yourself.'
  Vilfredo Pareto (1848–1923), Italian scientist and sociologist

'The man who makes no mistakes does not usually make anything.'
  EJ Phelps (1822–1900), writer

'He who never made a mistake never made a discovery.'
  Samuel Smiles (1812–1904), social reformer

'Once we realize that imperfect understanding is the human condition, there is no shame in being wrong, only in failing to correct our mistakes.'
  George Soros (b. 1930), investor

'I have learned throughout my life as a composer chiefly through my mistakes and pursuits of false assumptions, not by my exposure to founts of wisdom and knowledge.'
  Igor Stravinsky (1882–1971), Russian-born composer

'A man should never be ashamed to own he has been in the wrong, which is but saying, in other words, that he is wiser today than he was yesterday.'
  Jonathan Swift (1667–1745), author of *Gulliver's Travels*

'The progress of rivers to the ocean is not so rapid as that of man to error.'
  Voltaire (1694–1778), French philosopher and writer

'Here at the head office, we don't go very deep into much of anything, but we have a smell of everything. Our job is capital allocation – intellectual and financial. Smell, feel, touch, listen, then allocate. Make bets, with people and dollars. And make mistakes – but we're big enough to make mistakes.'

Jack Welch (b. 1935), American executive

'There is no mistake; there has been no mistake; and there shall be no mistake.'

Arthur Wellesley, Duke of Wellington (1769–1852)

'Why do you necessarily have to be wrong just because a few million people think you are?'

Frank Zappa (1940–93), iconoclastic musician

MONEY GO ROUND

Money makes the world go round. It is the meaning of life, which leaves an unpleasant smell in your hands and fills a space in your trousers. It is the very blood of capitalism, which communist societies have failed to do without. Bartering is the only alternative – but it is less fun (none of that maniacal revolution of money from one to another) and who wants a chicken anyway?

'Most of the people living on [earth] were unhappy for pretty much of the time. Many solutions were suggested for this problem, but most of these were largely concerned with the movements of small green pieces of paper, which is odd because on the whole it wasn't the small green pieces of paper that were unhappy.'
> **Douglas Adams (b. 1952), author of *The Hitchhiker's Guide to the Galaxy***

'Money is the root of all evil, and yet it is such a useful root that we cannot get on without it any more than we can without potatoes.'
> **Louisa May Alcott (1832–88), American author**

'Money is better than poverty, if only for financial reasons.'
> *** Woody Allen (b. 1935), filmmaker***

'Money doesn't mind if we say it's evil, it goes from strength to strength. It's a fiction, an addiction and a tacit conspiracy.'
> **Martin Amis (b. 1949), British novelist and author of *Money***

'When money talks, nobody notices what grammar it uses.'
> **Anon**

'Money can't buy happiness; it can, however, rent it.'
> **Anon**

'Business, you know, may bring money, but friendship hardly ever does.'
> **Jane Austen (1775–1817), English novelist**

'Money is like mulch, not good except it be spread.'
Francis Bacon (1561–1626), Elizabethan writer

'Money is a good servant but a bad master.'
Francis Bacon

'Money, it turned out, was exactly like sex. You thought of nothing else if you didn't have it and thought of other things if you did.'
James Baldwin (1924–87), American novelist

'Money is a terrible master but an excellent servant.'
Phineas T. Barnum (1810–91), promoter

'It is the heart that makes a man rich. He is rich according to what he is not according to what he has.'
Henry Ward Beecher (1813–87), American abolitionist, clergy-man and brother of best-selling author Harriet Beecher Stowe

'A feast is made for laughter and wine maketh merry: but money answereth all things.'
Bible

'The love of money is the root of all evil.'
Bible

'Money, *n*. A blessing that is of no advantage to us excepting when we part with it.'
Ambrose Bierce (1842–1914), journalist and writer

'One must choose, in life, between making money and spending it. There's no time to do both.'
Edouard Bourdet (b. 1887), French playwright

'Life is short and so is money.'
Bertolt Brecht (1898–1956), German dramatist

'We all need money, but there are degrees of desperation.'
Anthony Burgess (1917–93), prolific novelist

'Money has a power above
The stars and fate, to manage love:
Whose arrows, learned poets hold,
That never miss, are tipped with gold.'
  Samuel Butler (1612–80), poet and satirist

'What makes all doctrines plain and clear?
About two hundred pounds a year.
And that which was proved true before,
Prove false again? Two hundred more.'
  Samuel Butler

'The want of money is the root of all evil.'
  Samuel Butler

'I have imbibed such a love for money that I keep some sequins in a drawer to count and cry over them once a week.'
  Lord Byron (1788–1824), Romantic poet

'Yes! Ready money is Aladdin's lamp.'
  Lord Byron

'Cash payment never was, or could except for a few years be, the union bond of man to man. Cash never yet paid one man fully his desserts to another; nor could it, nor can it, now or henceforth to the end of the world.'
  Thomas Carlyle (1795–1881), essayist

'The only thing money gives is the freedom of not worrying about money.'
  Johnny Carson (b. 1925), American TV host

'No honest hardworking official likes to see good money disappearing into the hands of the Treasury at the end of the financial year.'
  Joyce Cary (1888–1957), novelist

'However toplofty and idealistic a man may be, he can always rationalize his right to earn money.'
  Raymond Chandler (1888–1959), novelist

'Dollars! All their cares, hopes, joys, affections, virtues and associations seemed to be melted down into dollars.'
Charles Dickens (1812–70), novelist

'In any country where talent and virtue produce no advancement, money will be the national god.'
Denis Diderot (1713–84), French thinker and writer

'Money doesn't talk, it swears.'
Bob Dylan (b. 1941), singer, songwriter

'Money often costs too much.'
Ralph Waldo Emerson (1803–82), poet

'Money, which represents the prose of life, and which is hardly spoken of in parlours without an apology, is in its effects and laws as beautiful as roses.'
Ralph Waldo Emerson

'Money is the sinews of love, as of war.'
George Farquhar (1678–1707), playwright

'If you make money your god, it will plague you like the devil.'
Henry Fielding (1707–54), creator of *Tom Jones*

'Sir, money, money, the most charming of all things; money, which will say more in one moment than the most elegant lover can in years. Perhaps you will say a man is not young; I answer he is rich. He is not genteel, handsome, witty, brave, good-humored, but he is rich, rich, rich, rich, rich – that one word contradicts everything you can say against him.'
Henry Fielding

'The quality of life is in the mind, not in material.'
Malcolm S. Forbes (1919–90), publisher

'A business that makes nothing but money is a poor kind of business.'
Henry Ford (1863–1947), maker of cars as well as cash

'People do not care for money as money, as they once did. Certainly they do not stand in awe of it, nor of him who possesses it.'
   Henry Ford

'If money is your hope for independence you will never have it. The only real security that a man will have in this world is a reserve of knowledge, experience and ability.'
   Henry Ford

'The use of money is all the advantage there is in having it.'
   Benjamin Franklin (1706–90), inventor and much more

'He that is of the opinion money will do everything may well be suspected of doing everything for money.'
   Benjamin Franklin

'Money is a singular thing. It ranks with love as man's greatest source of joy. And with death as his greatest source of anxiety. Over all history it has oppressed nearly all people in one of two ways: either it has been abundant and very unreliable or reliable and very scarce.'
   JK Galbraith (b. 1908), economist

'We're in the business of making money, not cars.'
   General Motors executive

'Politics, war, marriage, crime, adultery. Everything that exists in the world has something to do with money.'
   Graham Greene (1904–91), novelist

'They had been corrupted by money, and he had been corrupted by sentiment. Sentiment was the more dangerous, because you couldn't name its price. A man open to bribes was to be relied upon below a certain figure, but sentiment might uncoil in the heart at a name, a photograph, even a smell remembered.'
   Graham Greene

'Money is seldom the measure of much, once you have enough.'
   Charles Handy (b. 1932), best-selling business thinker

'Put not your trust in money, but put your money in trust.'
   Oliver Wendell Holmes, Jr. (1841–1935), long-lived American jurist

'When a man says money can do anything, that settles it; he hasn't any.'
   Edgar Watson Howe (1853–1937), writer

'If little kids don't aspire to make money like I did, what the hell good is this country?'
   Lee Iacocca (b. 1924), executive

'The almighty dollar, that great object of universal devotion.'
   Washington Irving (1783–1859), writer

'Money's a horrid thing to follow, but a charming thing to meet.'
Henry James (1843–1916), American novelist

'There are few ways in which a man can be more innocently employed than in getting money.'
   Dr. Samuel Johnson (1709–84), man of letters

'Go into the street, and give one man a lecture on morality, and another a shilling, and see which will respect you most.'
   Dr. Samuel Johnson

'That for which all virtue now is sold, and almost every vice – almighty gold.'
   Ben Jonson (1572–1637), Elizabethan dramatist

'It is better that a man should tyrannize over his bank balance than over his fellow citizens and whilst the former is sometimes denounced as being but a means to the latter, sometimes at least it is an alternative.'
   John Maynard Keynes (1883–1946), economist

'The materialistic idealism that governs American life, that on the one hand makes a chariot of every grocery wagon, and on the other a mere hitching post of every star, lets every man lead a very enticing double life.'
   Louis Kronenberger (b. 1904), writer

'I don't like money, actually, but it quiets my nerves.'
Joe Louis (1914–81), undefeated heavyweight champion

'Money is the alienated essence of man's work and existence; the essence dominates him and he worships it.'
Karl Marx (1818–83), economist and revolutionary

'Money is like a sixth sense without which you cannot make a complete use of the other five.'
W. Somerset Maugham (1874–1965), novelist

'Money is the poor man's credit card.'
Marshall McLuhan (1911–80), commentator and critic

'The nature of people demands that most of them be engaged in the most frivolous possible activities – like making money.'
Marshall McLuhan

'The chief value of money lies in the fact that one lives in a world in which it is overestimated.'
HL Mencken (1880–1956), writer and journalist

'Money couldn't buy friends, but you got a better class of enemy.'
Spike Milligan (b. 1918), comedian and Goon

'Money writes books, money sells them. Give me not righteousness, O Lord, give me money, only money.'
George Orwell (1903–50), journalist and novelist

'Having money is rather like being a blonde. It is more fun but not vital.'
Mary Quant (b. 1934), former model

'Without money, honour is a malady.'
Jean Baptiste Racine (1639–99), French playwright

'The great dynamic success of capitalism had given us a power weapon in our battle against Communism – money.'
Ronald Reagan (b. 1911), film actor and President

'I know of nothing more despicable and pathetic than a man who devotes all the hours of the waking day to the making of money for money's sake.'
John D. Rockefeller (1839–1937), oil tycoon

'If companies are in business solely to make money, you can't fully trust whatever else they do or say.'
Anita Roddick (b. 1943), founder of The Body Shop

'I do not care about money. I really mean it. I care about being able to do things right and winning. Cash is a happy consequence of doing those things.'
Gordon Roddick, founder of The Body Shop

'Money is power, freedom, a cushion, the root of all evil, the sum of blessings.'
Carl Sandburg (1878–1967), poet

'Lack of money is the root of all evil.'
George Bernard Shaw (1856–1950), playwright

'Money is indeed the most important thing in the world; and all sound and successful personal and national morality should have this fact for its basis.'
George Bernard Shaw

'The universal regard for money is the one hopeful fact in our civilization. Money is the most important thing in the world. It represents health, strength, honour, generosity and beauty...not the least of its virtues is that it destroys base people as certainly as it fortifies and dignifies noble people.'
George Bernard Shaw

'Money alone sets all the world in motion.'
Publilius Syrus (c. 42 BC), Latin writer

'The dollar is innocent.'
Henry David Thoreau (1817–62), naturalist and writer

'We Americans worship the almighty dollar! Well, it is a worthier god than Heredity Privilege.'
Mark Twain (1835–1910), novelist

'I concluded that my mind was so ordinary, which is to say empty, that I could never buy anything but a reasonably good camera. So I would content myself with a more common and general sort of achievement than serious art, which was money.'
Kurt Vonnegut, Jr. (b. 1922), author of *Slaughterhouse Five*

'Algebra and money are essentially levellers; the first intellectually, the second effectively.'
Simone Weil (1909–43), philosopher

'There is only one class in the community that thinks more about money than the rich, and that is the poor. The poor can think of nothing else.'
Oscar Wilde (1854–1900), wit

'It is better to have a permanent income than to be fascinating.'
Oscar Wilde

'You can be young without money but you can't be old without it.'
Tennessee Williams (1911–83), American dramatist

'Money, big money (which is actually a relative concept) is always, under any circumstances, a seduction, a test of morals, a temptation to sin.'
Boris Yeltsin (b. 1931), Russian politician

*M*OTIVATION

There has to be a reason why we wake at six o'clock, rush for a train and then spend the day wading through a morass of problems. Take away the monthly salary check, and great minds have to labor long and hard to find what this reason might be.

'The man who would lift others must be uplifted himself, and he who would command others must learn to obey.'
   Anon

'The worst mistake a boss can make is not to say "well done." '
   John Ashcroft (b. 1948), British executive

'Any fool can criticize, condemn and complain – and most fools do.'
   Dale Carnegie (1888–1955), author of *How to Make Friends and Influence People*

'The single-minded ones, the monomaniacs, are the only true achievers. The rest, the ones like me, may have more fun; but they fritter themselves away. The monomaniacs carry out a "mission"; the rest of us have "interests." Whenever anything is being accomplished, it is being done...by a monomaniac with a mission.'
   Peter Drucker (b. 1909), author

'The reward of a thing well done is to have done it.'
   Ralph Waldo Emerson (1803–82), poet

'I have never found anybody yet who went to work happily on a Monday that had not been paid on a Friday.'
   Tom Farmer (b. 1940), Kwik-Fit founder

'My best friend is the one who brings out the best in me.'
   Henry Ford (1863–1947), auto manufacturer

'I have come to the conclusion that my subjective account of my motivation is largely mythical on almost all occasions. I don't know why I do things.'
   JBS Haldane (1860–1936), scientist

'Too many organizations seem to believe that the only motivation to work is an economic one. Treating knowledge assets like Skinnerian rats is hardly the way to get the best out of people.'
   Gary Hamel (b. 1954), consultant and author

'People will always work harder if they're getting well paid and if they're afraid of losing a job which they know will be hard to equal. As is well known, if you pay peanuts, you get monkeys.'
   Armand Hammer (1898–1990), businessman with legendary contacts

'Good work must, in the long run, receive good rewards or it will cease to be good work.'
   Charles Handy (b. 1932), Irish-born business thinker and best-selling author

'People are self-motivated. They do their best work when they have come to believe, through their own processes, that what they are going to do is worthwhile. The free man is always better than the slave.'
   Sir John Harvey-Jones (b. 1924), former ICI chief

'If you do anything just for the money you don't succeed.'
   Barry Hearn (b. 1948), snooker manager, boxing promoter and football club owner

'Man has two sets of needs, his need as an animal to avoid pain and his need as a human to grow psychologically.'
   Frederick Herzberg (b. 1923), motivational theorist

'If you have someone on a job, use him. if you can't use him on the job, get rid of him, either via automation or by selecting someone with lesser ability. If you can't use him and you can't get rid of him, you will have a motivation problem.'
   Frederick Herzberg

'Ability is what you're capable of doing. Motivation determines what you do. Attitude determines how well you do it.'
   Lou Holtz (b. 1937), American football coach

'Motivation is everything. You can do the work of two people, but you can't be two people. Instead, you have to inspire the next guy down the line and get him to inspire his people.'
   Lee Iacocca (b. 1924), best-selling author

'March on with IBM/Work hand in hand/Stouthearted men go forth/In every land.'
   IBM anthem

'The deepest principle in human nature is the craving to be appreciated.'
   William James (1842–1910), philosopher and psychologist

'Treat a person as he is and he will remain as he is. Treat him as he could be, and he will become what he should be.'
   Jimmy Johnson (b. 1943), American football coach

'He who praises everybody praises nobody.'
   Dr. Samuel Johnson (1709–84), man of letters

'Motivating people for a short period is not very difficult. A crisis will often do just that, or a carefully planned special event. Motivating people over a longer period of time, however, is far more difficult. It is also far more important in today's business environment.'
   John Kotter (b. 1947), Harvard-based management thinker

'Where there is no desire, there will be no industry.'
   John Locke (1632–1704), British philosopher

'Human life will never be understood unless its highest aspirations are taken into account. Growth, self-actualization, the striving toward health, the quest for identity and autonomy, the yearning for excellence (and other ways of phrasing the striving "upward") must by now be accepted beyond question as a widespread and perhaps universal human tendency.'
   Abraham Maslow (1908–70), motivational theorist and businessman

'The philosophy of management by direction and control – regardless of whether it is hard or soft – is inadequate to motivate because the human needs on which this approach relies are relatively unimportant motivators of behavior in our society today. Direction and control are of limited value in motivating people whose important needs are social and egotistic.'

Douglas McGregor (1906–64), author of *The Human Side of Enterprise*

'*Keep up the good work, whatever it is, whoever you are.*'
New Yorker *cartoon*

'Caring about what you are doing is considered either unimportant or taken for granted.'

Robert M. Pirsig (b. 1928), author and philosopher

'People become motivated when you guide them to the source of their own power and when you make heroes out of employees who personify what you want to see in the organization.'

Anita Roddick (b. 1943), founder of The Body Shop

OFFICE LIFE

Office life is sustained through regular doses of caffeine and gossip. One of the reasons that teleworking and the like have never taken off is that they reduce the opportunities to gossip about the man on the third floor who may or may not have marital problems and an unhealthy liking for extra strong European beer.

'A desk is a wastebasket with drawers.'
Anon

'A rumor is one thing that gets thicker instead of thinner as it is spread.'
Anon

'1. Face forward. 2. Fold hands in front. 3. Do not make eye contact. 4. Watch the numbers. 5. Don't talk to anyone you don't know. 6. Stop talking with anyone you do know when anyone you don't know enters the elevator. 7. Avoid brushing bodies.'
Longfellow's Rules of the Elevator

'Organizational politics is the bane of most organizations. People who spend their entire time trying to understand people's motives in order to manipulate them are a double liability. Usually they haven't got enough to do.'
Martin Taylor (b. 1952), journalist and businessman

'The image of the office of the future is too neat, too smooth, too disembodied to be real. Reality is always messy. But it is clear that we are rapidly on our way, and even a partial shift towards the electronic office will be enough to trigger an eruption of social, psychological, and economic consequences. The coming word-quake means more than just new machines. It promises to restructure all the human relationships and roles in the office as well.'
Alvin Toffler (b. 1928), futurologist

'It is perfectly monstrous the way people go about nowadays saying things against one behind one's back, that are absolutely and entirely true.'
Oscar Wilde (1854–1900), wit

*O*PPORTUNITY KNOCKS

'Small opportunities are often the beginning of great enterprises,' said Demosthenes, and he had never even heard of Microsoft. Opportunism is all. 'It is better to be prepared for an opportunity and not to have one than to have an opportunity and not be prepared,' noted one observer. In business you are perpetually waiting for the golden chance to double market share; the miracle ingredient which will revolutionize the product; the earth-shattering discovery. You sometimes have to wait a long time and often it proves far from worthwhile, but there is a joy in anticipation.

'The person who is waiting for something to turn up might start with their shirtsleeves.'
   Anon

'All that we do is done with an eye to something else.'
   Aristotle (384–322 BC), Greek philosopher

'A wise man will make more opportunities than he finds.'
   Francis Bacon (1561–1626), Elizabethan writer

'Opportunity makes a thief.'
   Francis Bacon

'When one door closes another door opens; but we so often look so long and so regretfully upon the closed door, that we do not see the ones which open for us.'
   Alexander Graham Bell (1847–1922), inventor

'If opportunity doesn't knock, build a door.'
   Milton Berle (b. 1908), American comedian and actor

'Intentions often melt in the face of unexpected opportunity.'
   Shirley Temple Black (b. 1928), actress and diplomat

'Ability is of little account without opportunity.'
Napoléon Bonaparte (1769–1821), French General

'Everyone is surrounded by opportunities. But they only exist once they have been seen. And they will only be seen if they are looked for.'
Edward de Bono (b. 1933), creative-thinking champion

'The lure of the distant and the difficult is deceptive. The great opportunity is where you are.'
John Burroughs (1837–1921), American naturalist and writer

'When fate hands us a lemon, let's try to make a lemonade.'
Dale Carnegie (1888–1955), motivational expert and author of *How to Make Friends and Influence People*

'Make the iron hot by striking it.'
Oliver Cromwell (1599–1658), statesman

'There are so many good opportunities out there, but we have only so many laser bombs we can use. We have to concentrate on optimizing this opportunity.'
Michael Dell (b. 1964), youthful computer pioneer

'Opportunity is missed by most people because it is dressed in overalls and looks like work.'
Thomas Alva Edison (1847–1931), industrialist and inventor

'Everything comes to him who hustles while he waits.'
Thomas Alva Edison

'In the middle of difficulty lies opportunity.'
Albert Einstein (1879–1955), author of *The General Theory of Relativity and physicist*

'It's them as take advantage that get advantage i' this world.'
George Eliot (1819–80), novelist

'There are always opportunities through which businessmen can profit handsomely if they will only recognize and seize them.'
J. Paul Getty (1892–1976), oil tycoon

'Art is long, life short; judgment difficult, opportunity transient.'
Johann Wolfgang von Goethe (1749–1832), German writer (adapting the words of Hippocrates)

'I skate to where I think the puck will be.'
Wayne Gretzky (b. 1961), ice hockey's Great One

'An age of unreason is an age of opportunity even if it looks at first sight like the end of all ages.'
Charles Handy (b. 1932), author of *The Age of Unreason* and *The Empty Raincoat*

'He who refuses to embrace a unique opportunity loses the prize as surely as if he had failed.'
William James (1842–1910), philosopher and psychologist

'Unmet needs always exist.'
Philip Kotler, American marketing guru

'There is no security on this earth; there is only opportunity.'
General Douglas MacArthur (1880–1964), American soldier

'The difference is whether you are capable of taking your chances. We are all presented with them.'
Sophie Mirman (b. 1956), entrepreneur

'If a window of opportunity appears, don't pull down the shade.'
Tom Peters (b. 1942), the original modern management guru

'I always tried to turn every disaster into an opportunity.'
John D. Rockefeller (1839–1937), oil tycoon

'The best place to succeed is where you are with what you have.'
Charles Schwab (1862–1939), American executive

'I invent things when I perceive people's need – it is then a matter of convincing people they need it.'
Sir Clive Sinclair (b. 1940), British inventor

'Men who are resolved to find a way for themselves will always find opportunities enough; and if they do not find them, they will make them.'
Samuel Smiles (1812–1904), champion of self-help

'Opportunities multiply as they are seized.'
***Sun-Tzu (500 BC), author of* The Art of War**

ORIGINALITY

'Don't follow everybody else. Get off the beaten track. Be a little mad,' advises Jean Paulucci. This is not something which goes down well with a room full of middle managers who know that the beaten track usually leads straight out the door. Originality need not be madness and it usually provides a much cherished competitive advantage. But, with the corporate world getting ever better at copying and responding, the shelf life of originality is rapidly shortening.

'Originality is unexplored territory. You get there by carrying a canoe – you can't take a taxi.'
Alan Alda (b. 1936), American actor

'Novelties *please* less than they *impress*.'
Lord Byron (1788–1824), Romantic poet

'Pioneering don't pay.'
Andrew Carnegie (1835–1919), American industrialist and philanthropist

'People go through four stages before any revolutionary development:
1. It's nonsense, don't waste my time.
2. It's interesting, but not important.
3. I always said it was a good idea.
4. I thought of it first.'
Arthur C. Clarke (b. 1917), science fiction writer

'Only God and some few rare geniuses can keep forging ahead into novelty.'
Denis Diderot (1713–84), French thinker and writer

'There is no subject so old that something new cannot be said about it.'
Fyodor Dostoyevsky (1821–81), Russian novelist

'No one can possibly achieve any real and lasting success or get rich in business by being a conformist.'
J. Paul Getty (1892–1976), oil tycoon

'The thing I am most aware of is my limits. And this is natural; for I never, or almost never, occupy the middle of my cage; my whole being surges toward the bars.'
André Gide (1869–1951), Nobel Prize winning French novelist

'Everything has been said before, but since nobody listens we have to keep going back and beginning all over again.'
André Gide

'If you can't be different, you might as well be damned.'
Roberto Goizueta (b. 1931), Cuban-born former head of Coca-Cola

'The key to success for Sony, and to everything in business, science and technology is never to follow the others.'
Masaru Ibuka (b. 1908), Sony co-founder

'The principal mark of genius is not perfection but originality, the opening of new frontiers.'
Arthur Koestler (1905–83), Hungarian-born writer

'The more original a discovery, the more obvious it seems afterward.'
Arthur Koestler

'All good things which exist are the fruits of originality.'
John Stuart Mill (1806–73), British philosopher and economist

'We should do something when people say it is crazy. If people say something is *good*, it means that someone else is already doing it.'
Hajime Mitari, president of Canon

'Copy from one, it's plagiarism; copy from two, it's research.'
Wilson Mizner (1876–1933), researcher

'Everybody wants the same, everybody is the same: whoever feels different goes voluntarily into a madhouse.'
Friedrich Nietzsche (1844–1900), philosopher

'Let no one say that I have said nothing new; the arrangement of the subject is new.'
Blaise Pascal (1623–62), French writer and philosopher

'*What's new?* is an interesting and broadening eternal question, but one which, if pursued exclusively, results only in an endless parade of trivia and fashion, the silt of tomorrow.'
Robert M. Pirsig (b. 1928), author of *Zen and the Art of Motorcycle Maintenance*

'One thing about pioneers that you don't hear mentioned is that they are invariably, by their nature, mess-makers. They go forging ahead, seeing only their noble, distant goal, and never notice any of the crud and debris they leave behind them.'
Robert M. Pirsig

'A mere copier of nature can never produce anything great.'
Sir Joshua Reynolds (1723–92), British artist

'If you want to be successful in business, find someone who has achieved the results you want and copy what they do, and you'll achieve the same results.'
Anthony Robbins, American self-motivation guru

'Everything of importance has been said before by somebody who did not discover it.'
Alfred North Whitehead (1861–1947), British scientist

'It requires a very unusual mind to undertake the analysis of the obvious.'
Alfred North Whitehead

'The man who is swimming against the stream knows the strength of it.'
Woodrow Wilson (1856–1924), 28th American President

PEOPLE

People matter. The trouble is that it is only in the last decade that this blindingly obvious fact of business life has been widely trumpeted. The reasons for the silence are easy. People are troublesome. They refuse to get out of beds whistling songs from the corporate song sheet. They complain about the new computers and always want to take time off to attend their daughter's sports day. 'The soft stuff is always harder than the hard stuff,' reflects PepsiCo's Roger Enrico. You're right, Roger, but executives are paid to master both.

'If you don't have the best people, you hurt everyone.'
Larry Bossidy (b. 1935), American executive

'You bet on people, not on strategies.'
Larry Bossidy

'In my experience, people can face almost any problem except the problems of people. They can work long hours, face declining business, face loss of jobs, but not the problems of people.'
W. Edwards Deming (1900–93), American quality guru

'Of all the things I've done, the most vital is coordinating the talents of those who work for us and pointing them toward a certain goal.'
Walt Disney (1901–66), creator of Mickey Mouse

'No institution can possibly survive if it needs geniuses or supermen to manage it. It must be organized in such a way as to be able to get along under a leadership composed of average human beings.'
Peter Drucker (b. 1909), father of management theory

'Developing men still requires a basic quality in the manager which cannot be created by supplying skills or by emphasizing the importance of the task. It requires integrity of character.'
Peter Drucker

'You can learn good manners to deal with people, but you can't learn to trust people. And you must trust to be comfortable with them.'
Peter Drucker

'We can never wholly separate the human from the mechanical side.'
Mary Parker Follett (1868–1933), multitalented and much neglected business thinker

'The study of human relations in business and the study of the technology of operating are bound up together.'
Mary Parker Follett

'I do not think that we have psychological and ethical and economic problems. We have human problems, with psychological, ethical and economical aspects, and as many others as you like.'
Mary Parker Follett

'How come when I want a pair of hands I get a human being as well.'
Henry Ford (1863–1947), the first mass-market automaker

'The micro-division of labor has fostered a basic distrust of human beings. People weren't allowed to put the whole puzzle together. Instead they were given small parts because companies feared what people would do if they knew and saw the whole puzzle. Human assets shouldn't be misused. Brains are becoming the core of organizations – other activities can be contracted out.'
Charles Handy (b. 1932), author and broadcaster

'The best way to run a business is to put your trust in people. If they let you down, you can make changes.'
Lord Hanson (b. 1922), industrialist

'It is the responsibility of the leadership and the management to give opportunities and put demands on people which enable them to grow as human beings in their work environment.'
Sir John Harvey-Jones (b. 1924), former ICI chief

'Amazing things happen when you make people feel they are valued as individuals, when you dignify their suggestions and their ideas, when you show your respect for them by allowing them to exercise their own wisdom and judgment and discretion.'
Herb Kelleher, airline executive

'If then the case as to the state of your inanimate machines can produce such beneficial results, what may not be expected if you devote equal attention to your vital machines, which are far more wonderfully constructed.'
Robert Owen (1771–1858), British industrialist

'Your most precious possession is not your financial assets. Your most precious possession is the people you have working there, and what they carry around in their heads, and their ability to work together.'
Robert Reich (b. 1946), American economist and politician

'If you treat people right they will treat you right – 90 percent of the time.'
Franklin D. Roosevelt (1882–1945), architect of the New Deal

'By the time people become CEOs they are preoccupied with survival and money. They respond to capital markets, stockholders, etc. Even if they try or want to be people-oriented, a financial crisis will always get their attention.'
Edgar H. Schein (b. 1928), MIT-based educator and champion of corporate culture

'Ultimately, whatever the form of economic activity, it is people that count most.'
Lord Sieff (1889–1972), practiced what he preached with Marks & Spencer

'The only way to make a man trustworthy is to trust him.'
Henry Stimson (1867–1950), American Secretary of War

'A personnel man with his arm around an employee is like a treasurer with his hand in the till.'
   Robert Townsend (b. 1920), author of *Up the Organization*

'If only it weren't for the people, the goddamned people always getting tangled up in the machinery. If it weren't for them, earth would be an engineer's paradise.'
   Kurt Vonnegut, Jr. (b. 1922), in *Player Piano,* drawn from his experiences working for General Electric

'The person who figures out how to harness the collective genius of the people in his or her organization is going to blow the competition away.'
   Walter Wriston, banker

Persistence ... or not

American football coach, Mike Dikta, sums up the general view in his observation that 'You never really lose until you quit trying.' Ever since Robert the Bruce watched his spider, persistence has been regarded as a good thing. It may be character building, but that does not always make good business sense. It can be bad for your health as well as your bank balance. When Jake DiMotta mouths to Sugar Ray, 'You never got me down Ray' at the end of the epic *Raging Bull,* your sympathies lie with the loser who persisted rather than the winner. Jake got it wrong. It is sometimes better to call it quits than to blindly press on.

'Obstinacy alone is not a virtue.'
Albert Camus (1913–60), French writer and part-time goal-keeper

'Most of the important things in the world have been accomplished by people who have kept on trying when there seemed to be no hope at all.'
Dale Carnegie (1888–1955), the first self-help guru

'Never, never, never, never give up.'
Sir Winston Churchill (1874–1965), and he didn't

'Never give in – in nothing, great or small, large or petty – except to convictions of honor and good sense.'
Sir Winston Churchill

'Nothing in this world can take the place of persistence. Talent will not; nothing is more common than unsuccessful people with talent. Genius will not; unrewarded genius is almost a proverb. Education will not; the world is full of educated derelicts. Persistence and determination alone are omnipotent. The slogan *press on* has solved and always will solve the problems of the human race.'
  Calvin Coolidge (1872–1933), 30th American President

'If at first you don't succeed, failure may be your style.'
  Quentin Crisp (b. 1908), writer

'Never confuse a single defeat with a final defeat.'
  F. Scott Fitzgerald (1896–1940), author of *The Great Gatsby* and more

'It is not always by plugging away at a difficulty and sticking at it that one overcomes it; but, rather, often by working on the one next to it. Certain people and certain things require to be approached on an angle.'
  André Gide (1869–1951), Nobel Prize–winning French writer

'Perseverance is the hard work you do after you get tired of doing the hard work you already did.'
  Newt Gingrich (b. 1943), American right-wing politician

'Life is often compared to a marathon, but I think it is more like being a sprinter; long stretches of hard work punctuated by brief moments in which we are given the opportunity to perform at our best.'
  Michael Johnson (b. 1967), Olympic athlete

'Few things are impossible to diligence and skill ... Great works are performed not by strength, but perseverance.'
  Dr. Samuel Johnson (1709–84), man of letters

'We can do anything we want to do if we stick to it long enough.'
  Helen Keller (1880–1968), American writer

'Those who have the desire – win or lose – to say: again!'
  Phil Knight, Nike founder

'Always bear in mind that your own resolution to succeed is more important than any other one thing.'
Abraham Lincoln (1809–65), American President

'It's not how many times you get thrown, it's how many times you get back on.'
Marlboro advertisement

'Character consists of what you do on the third and fourth tries.'
James Michener (1907–97), American novelist

'Most people give up just when they're about to achieve success. They quit on the one yard line. They give up at the last minute of the game one foot from a wining touch.'
H. Ross Perot (b. 1930), executive and politician

'Never accept failure, no matter how often it visits you. Keep on going. Never give up. Never.'
Dr. Michael Smurfit, executive

'Stubbornness and stupidity are twins.'
Sophocles (496–406 BC), Athenian tragedian

'You have to kiss a lot of frogs to find a prince.'
3M slogan

'Obstacles cannot crush me
Every obstacle yields to stern resolve
He who is fixed to a star does not change his mind.'
Leonardo Da Vinci (1452–1519), inventor, artist and genius

PLANES, TRAINS AND AUTOMOBILES

The homes of executives throughout the world enjoy a constant stock of shampoos which can't be opened; unused shower caps and thick white bathrobes with the word Hilton or Sheraton on their fronts. International travel is a perk of the job. Some executives now spend more time in the air than at their desks and are more able to open a mini-bar than their garage doors. Even in business class, travelling can be stressful and demanding unless certain rules are obeyed. The first and most simple of these is that if you look like your passport photo, you are too ill to travel.

'It can hardly be a coincidence that no language on earth has ever produced the expression "as pretty as an airport."'
Douglas Adams (b. 1952), British author of *The Hitchhiker's Guide to the Galaxy*

'An American is a man with two arms and four wheels.'
Anon

'What affects men sharply about a foreign nation is not so much finding or not finding familiar things; it is rather not finding them in the familiar place.'
GK Chesterton (1874–1936), British writer

'Why do the wrong people travel, travel, travel,
When the right people stay back home?'
Noël Coward (1899–1973), writer, actor and composer

'In traveling: a man must carry knowledge with him, if he would bring home knowledge.'
Dr. Samuel Johnson (1709–84), traveler to Scotland, among other places

'To George F. Babbitt, as to most prosperous citizens of Zenith, his motor car was poetry and tragedy, love and heroism. The office was his pirate ship but the car his perilous excursion ashore.'
Sinclair Lewis (1885–1951), American novelist

'Travelers are always discoverers, especially those who travel by air. There are no signposts in the sky to show that a man has passed that way before.'
Anne Morrow Lindbergh (b. 1906), American writer

'Take a little of home with you, and leave a little of yourself at home.'
Mark McCormack (b. 1930), sports agent and author

'The car has become an article of dress without which we feel uncertain, unclad, and incomplete.'
Marshall McLuhan (1911–80), commentator, critic and traveler

'Business class is not just something in an airline.'
Henry Mintzberg (b. 1939), Canadian management thinker

'There is not much to say about most airplane journeys. Anything remarkable must be disastrous, so you define a good flight by negatives: you didn't get hijacked, you didn't crash, you didn't throw up, you weren't late, you weren't nauseated by the food.'
Paul Theroux (b. 1941), well-traveled writer

'Commuter – one who spends his life
In riding to and from his wife;
A man who shaves and takes a train,
And then rides back to shave again.'
EB White (1899–1985), American writer and humorist

PLANS AND PLANNING

'Planning, of course, is not a separate, recognizable act. ... Every managerial act, mental or physical is inexorably intertwined with planning. It is as much a part of every managerial act as breathing is to the living human,' concludes the weighty *History of Management Thought*. Planning is like preparing a room to be decorated: a tedious but essential task which always takes far longer than you expected. The real joy is applying the paint, and so it is with plans where the real joy is in implementing them. Turning planning into action is interesting. But the constant frustration for managers is that plans often lead to nothing more than additional plans. 'A good deal of corporate planning ... is like a ritual rain dance. It has no effect on the weather that follows, but those who engage in it think it does,' says American academic Brian Quinn. With customary accuracy, Ambrose Bierce defined a plan as 'to bother about the best method of accomplishing an accidental result.'

'Planning is the design of a desired future and of effective ways of bringing it about.'
  Russell L. Ackoff (b. 1919), management researcher and writer

'I was in a warm bed, and suddenly I'm part of a plan.'
  Woody Allen (b. 1935), filmmaker

'Baldrick, you wouldn't recognize a cunning plan if it painted itself purple and danced naked on top of a harpsichord singing "Cunning plans are here again." '
  Edmund Blackadder (c. 1600), in *Blackadder*

'The best-laid plans o' mice an' men gang aft a-gley.'
  Robert Burns (1759–96), Scottish poet

'There are so many plans, so many schemes, and so many reasons why there should be neither plans nor schemes.'
Benjamin Disraeli (1804–81), British statesman

'Unless commitment is made, there are only promises and hopes ... but no plans.'
Peter Drucker (b. 1909), management thinker and author

'Long-range planning does not deal with future decisions. It deals with the futurity of present decisions.'
Peter Drucker

'Just because something doesn't do what you planned it to do doesn't mean it's useless.'
Thomas Alva Edison (1847–1931), inventor and industrialist

'Plans are nothing; planning is everything.'
Dwight D. Eisenhower (1890–1969), 34th American President

'It is true that if foresight is not the whole of management at least it is an essential part of it.'
Henri Fayol (1841–1925), French businessman and one of the first management thinkers

'The making of plans is mostly an uppish, presumptuous mental exercise insofar as the planner claims some creative genius when he demands of others what he cannot himself deliver, or blames others for what he could not do himself.'
Immanuel Kant (1724–1804), philosopher

'Life is what happens while you are making other plans.'
John Lennon (1940–80), Beatle

'People don't plan to fail. They fail to plan.'
Mark McCormack (b. 1930), spectacularly itinerant sports agent

'Planning by its very nature defines and preserves categories. Creativity, by its very nature, creates categories or rearranges established ones. This is why strategic planning can neither provide creativity, nor deal with it when it emerges by other means.'
Henry Mintzberg (b. 1939), Canadian management thinker and author

'The classic view of the manager as planner is not in accord with reality. If the manager does indeed plan, it is not by locking his door, puffing on his pipe, and thinking great thoughts.'
Henry Mintzberg

'The very madness of the scheme protects it.'
Iris Murdoch (b. 1919), British novelist

'Plans get you into things but you got to work your way out.'
Will Rogers (1879–1935), American humorist and showman

'What I'm really thinking about is the 300–year plan.'
Masayoshi Son, Japanese banker

'Anyone who talks five-year plans talks crap.'
Alan Sugar (b. 1942), forward-thinking computer businessman

'Amid a multitude of projects, no plan is devised.'
Publilius Syrus (c. 42 BC), Latin writer

'It is a bad plan that admits of no modification.'
Publilius Syrus

'Plans seem to exist in a context of justification more than in a context of anticipation. They refer more to what has been accomplished than to what is yet to be accomplished.'
Karl Weick, American academic

PLEASURES

Your average executive is a human being. Some are not and those that are may successfully hide their humanity behind managerial bluster, but they always have a lighter side. Something, somewhere gives them a kick. You or I may consider that an obsession with collecting used bottle tops is an unlikely source of orgasmic excitement but we *might* be wrong, and, if it gives them pleasure, who are we to criticize? Businesspeople take pleasure in some pretty peculiar things, profit and loss accounts being one of the more inoffensive.

'If you break 100, watch your golf. If you break 80, watch your business.'
   Anon

'The man who attends strictly to his business usually has plenty of business to attend to.'
   Anon

'To make pleasures pleasant, shorten them.'
   Anon

'All business is show business.'
   Jan Carlzon, Swedish businessman

'It's kind of fun to do the impossible.'
   Walt Disney (1901–66), creator of the entertainment empire

'Business was his pleasure; pleasure was his business.'
   Maria Edgeworth (1767–1849), British writer

'I never did a day's work in my life; it was all fun.'
   Thomas Alva Edison (1847–1931), industrialist and inventor

'My work is a game, a very serious game.'
   MC Escher, artist

'Putting deals together beats spending every day playing golf.'
Harold Geneen (b. 1910), famed ITT leader and author

'I love to build companies more than anything else.'
Lou Gerstner (b. 1942), IBM chief and former consultant

'I have no private life; I have a wife who understands. When the phone doesn't ring at home I get depressed. So my wife says, *Why not go out and sell something, Lew?* And that always cheers me up.'
Lord Grade (b. 1906), television and film mogul

'It's important for young people to remember that when you get up in the morning and go to work it must be enjoyable. You must have in your sights enjoyment in what you're going to do. If you have that, you don't take it too seriously, have a joke and a bit of fun out of life.'
Lord Hanson (b. 1922), industrialist

'Our purpose is to make products with pleasure, that we can sell with pleasure and that our customers can use with pleasure.'
Honda advertisement

'It is neither wealth nor splendor, but tranquillity and occupation, which give happiness.'
Thomas Jefferson (1743–1826), third American President

'It really gets my adrenalin flowing to hear the ping of the cash registers.'
Stanley Kalms (b. 1931), Dixons supremo

'Too much work and too much energy kill a man just as effectively as too much assorted vice or too much drink.'
Rudyard Kipling (1865–1936), British writer

'Damn the great executives, the men of measured merriment, damn the men with careful smiles, damn the men that run the shops, oh, damn their measured merriment.'
Sinclair Lewis (1885–1951), American novelist, author of *Babbit*

'Our minds need relaxation, and give way
Unless we mix with work a little play.'
Molière (1622–73), French dramatist

'By putting business before every other manifestation of life, our mechanical and financial civilization has forgotten the chief business of life, namely, growth, reproduction, development. It pays infinite attention to the incubator – and it forgets the egg!'
Lewis Mumford (1895–1990), writer, teacher and philosopher

'True leisure is not freedom from work but freedom in work, and, along with that, the time to converse, to ruminate, to contemplate the meaning of life.'
Lewis Mumford

'In our play we reveal what kind of people we are.'
Ovid (43 BC–17 AD), Roman poet

'Men, some to business, some to pleasure take.'
Alexander Pope (1688–1744), British poet

'Perpetual devotion to what a man calls his business is only to be sustained by perpetual neglect of many other things.'
Robert Louis Stevenson (1850–94), British author

'At Amstrad the staff start early and finish late. Nobody takes lunches – they may get a sandwich slung on their desk – there's no small talk. It's all action and the atmosphere is amazing, and the esprit de corps is terrific. Working hard is fun.'
Alan Sugar (b. 1942), pugnacious British businessman

'All fits of pleasure are balanced by an equal degree of pain or languor; 'tis like spending this year's part of the next year's revenue.'
Jonathan Swift (1667–1745), author of *Gulliver's Travels*

'The supreme accomplishment is to blur the line between work and play.'
Arnold Toynbee (1889–1975), British historian

'As a rule, from what I've observed, the American captain of industry doesn't do anything out of business hours. When he has put the cat out and locked up the office for the night, he just relapses into a state of coma from which he emerges only to start being a captain of industry again.'
PG Wodehouse (1881–1975), comic creator of Jeeves and Wooster

POWER

'Power is the ultimate aphrodisiac,' noted the sexually alluring and once extremely powerful Henry Kissinger. But there is more to power than sex. Power is the ability to have things your own way; to change and shape things; to create and to improve. It is also the ability to drive people into the ground, to engage in Machiavellian schemes and to engage in corporate megalomania. It is not pretty to watch.

'Power tends to corrupt, and absolute power corrupts absolutely. Great men are almost always bad men.'
   Lord Acton (1834–1902), British statesman

'There are kings and prophets, I was always told. The kings have the power and the prophets have the principles.'
   Tony Benn (b. 1925), British politician

'Those who have been once intoxicated with power, and have derived any kind of emolument from it, even but for one year, can never willingly abandon it.'
   Edmund Burke (1729–97), statesman and writer

'All power is trust.'
   Benjamin Disraeli (1804–81), statesman and writer

'Adversarial power relationships work only if you never have to see or work with the bastards again.'
   Peter Drucker (b. 1909), still prolific management thinker and author

'Power is not something that can be assumed or discarded at will like underwear.'
   JK Galbraith (b. 1908), economist

'In the main it will be found that a power over a man's support [compensation] is a power over his will.'
Alexander Hamilton (1755–1804), American man of letters and statesman

'Managers have been brought up on a diet of power, divide and rule. They have been preoccupied with authority rather than making things happen.'
Charles Handy (b. 1932), Irish-born oil executive turned educator and author

'Positions of power are, by definition, ephemeral, while one's personal characteristics remain with one until death.'
Sir John Harvey-Jones (b. 1924), former ICI chief

'As power grows, so does the chorus of flattery. Some is obvious and sickening, but much is invidious. In common with many people I am vain, and I would like to like myself.'
Sir John Harvey-Jones

'Unused power slips imperceptibly into the hands of another.'
Konrad Heiden (1901–75), German author

'The problem of power is how to achieve its responsible use rather than its irresponsible and indulgent use – of how to get men of power to live *for* the public rather than *off* the public.'
Robert F. Kennedy (1925–68), politician

'Knowing others is intelligence; knowing yourself is true wisdom. Mastering others is strength; mastering yourself is true power.'
Lao-tzu (604–531 BC), Chinese philosopher who founded Taoism

'Power corrupts. Absolute power is kind of neat.'
John Lehman (b. 1942), Secretary of the U.S. Navy

'Nearly all men can stand adversity, but if you want to test a man's character, give him power.'
Abraham Lincoln (1809–65), assassinated American President

'Whoever is the cause of another becoming powerful, is ruined himself; for that power is produced by him either through craft or force; and both of these are suspected by the one who has been raised to power.'
Nicolò Machiavelli (1469–1527), Florentine diplomat and author

'Lost in the solitude of his immense power, he began to lose direction.'
Gabriel Garcìa Márquez (b. 1928), author of *One Hundred Years of Solitude*

'So long as commerce specializes in business methods which take no account of human nature and social motives, so long may we expect strikes and sabotage to be the ordinary accompaniment of industry.'
Elton Mayo (1880–1949), Australian-born management researcher and thinker

'Powerlessness is a state of mind. If you think you're powerless, you are.'
Tom Peters (b. 1942), contemporary guru of gurus

'We were not born to use, but to command.'
William Shakespeare (1564–1616), the bard

'What you cannot enforce, do not command.'
Socrates (469–399 BC), teacher of Plato

'Power does not corrupt. Fear corrupts ... perhaps the fear of a loss of power.'
John Steinbeck (1902–68), American novelist

'Being powerful is like being a lady. If you have to tell people you are, you aren't.'
Margaret Thatcher (b. 1925), British Prime Minister

'All power is trust.'
Margaret Thatcher

'Power games kill an organization.'
Jan Timmer, Dutch executive

'They say that power corrupts and perhaps it does. What I know, in myself, is quite a different thing. That power corrupts the people it is exercised over.'
Raymond Williams (b. 1921), British academic

'When I resist ... the concentration of power, I am resisting the processes of death, because the concentration of power is what always preceded the destruction of human initiative, and therefore of human energy.'
Woodrow Wilson (1856–1924), American President

'Power never takes a back step – only in the face of more power.'
Malcolm X (1925–65), confrontational black leader

PREDICTIONS AND PROPHECIES

Don't bother with crystal balls or complex economic models. The future, as has been proved time and time again, is unknowable. The more you get it wrong the more likely it is that your words will come back to haunt you. 'The problem with television is that people must sit and keep their eyes glued to the screen. The average American family doesn't have time for it,' said *The New York Times* in 1939. This was 40 years after Charles Duell's brilliantly arrogant claim that 'everything that can be invented has been invented.' Fools rush in.

'Forecasting is like trying to drive a car blindfolded and following directions given by a person who is looking out of the back window.'
Anon

'When in doubt, predict that the present trend will continue.'
Anon

'Forecasting is difficult, especially about the future.'
Victor Borge (b. 1909), Danish-born entertainer

'I always avoid prophesying beforehand, because it is a much better policy to prophesy after the event has already taken place.'
Sir Winston Churchill (1874–1965), shrewd statesman

'When a distinguished but elderly scientist states that something is possible, he is almost certainly right. When he states that something is impossible, he is almost certainly wrong.'
Arthur C. Clarke (b. 1917), science fiction writer

'What we anticipate seldom occurs; what we least expected generally happens.'
Benjamin Disraeli (1804–81), statesman and author

'Prophecy is the most gratuitous form of error.'
 George Eliot (1819–80), author of *Middlemarch*

'Airplanes are interesting toys but of no military value.'
 Ferdinand Foch (1851–1929), French soldier and Professor of Strategy

'It would appear that we have reached the limits of what it is possible to achieve with computer technology, although one should be careful with such statements, as they tend to sound pretty silly in five years.'
 John von Neumann (1903–57), mathematical genius, whose 1949 comment proved ill-advised

'We may become the makers of our fate when we have ceased to pose as its prophets.'
 Sir Karl Popper (1902–89), Austrian-born philosopher

'The mission Columbus has proposed is folly. Among the many reasons that might be cited as to the folly of his enterprise is the well-known fact that the Atlantic ocean is infinite and therefore impossible to traverse.'
 Talevera Commission (1491)

'Denial ain't just a river in Egypt.'
 Mark Twain (1835–1910), waterways expert

'The art of prophecy is very difficult – especially with respect to the future.'
 Mark Twain

'Who the hell wants to hear actors talk?'
 HM Warner (1881–1958), film mogul

'I think there is a world market for maybe five computers.'
 Thomas Watson, Jr. (1914–93), IBM chief, understating his own market

'The concept is interesting and well-formed, but in order to earn better than a C, the idea must be feasible.'
 A Yale management professor to Federal Express Founder Fred Smith's paper proposing reliable overnight delivery service

PRICES

Products and services which are of poor quality are invariably cheaper than those of higher quality. There are no bargains. While the nitty-gritty of price tends to preoccupy our minds, the heart of the matter is value. Value can defy reason and price. One man's priceless collection of football programs is another's wastepaper.

'Free is good – but read the small print.'
Anon

'The cheap, no matter how charming, how immediate, does not wear so well. It has a way of telling its story the first time through.'
Anon

'That which sorts little is less valued.'
Miguel de Cervantes (1547–1616), Spanish writer

'In the market economy the price that is offered is counted upon to produce the result that is sought.'
JK Galbraith (b. 1908), economist

'I paid too much for it, but it's worth it.'
Samuel Goldwyn (1882–1974), filmmaker

'People want economy, and they will pay any price to get it.'
Lee Iacocca (b. 1924), American business executive

'Where quality is the thing sought after, the thing of supreme quality is cheap, whatever the price one has to pay for it.'
William James (1842–1910), psychologist and philosopher

'An idea without a price tag is never acceptable.'
Inguar Kamprad, founder of IKEA

'Nothing can have value without being an object of utility.'
Karl Marx (1818–83), writer and political thinker

'What we obtain too cheap we esteem too little; it is dearness only that gives everything its value.'
Thomas Paine (1737–1809), political thinker

'That which is honored is produced.'
Plato (c. 428–348 BC), philosopher

'There is nothing in the world that some man cannot make a little worse and sell a little cheaper, and he who considers price only is that man's lawful prey.'
John Ruskin (1819–1900), writer

'The real price of everything, what everything really costs to the man who wants to acquire it, is the toil and trouble of acquiring it.'
Adam Smith (1723–90), original free marketer

'They're only puttin' in a nickel, but they want a dollar song.'
Song title

'Cheat me in price, but not in the goods I purchase.'
Spanish proverb

'One pays for everything; the trick is not to pay too much of anything for anything.'
John Steinbeck (1902–68), author of *The Grapes of Wrath*

'Nowadays people know the price of everything and the value of nothing.'
Oscar Wilde (1854–1900), wit

PROBLEM SOLVING

Managers no longer have problems. Instead, they have challenges. Both pose difficulties. Indeed, so many difficulties that a full 40–hour week is usually spent on problem solving. The remaining 20 hours are then spent on identifying next week's problems. Actually solving the problems is the only way out. But how do you solve them? Helpful advice comes from the reliable source of Homer Simpson: 'The answers to life's problems aren't at the bottom of a bottle, they're on TV!'

'Each problem has hidden in it an opportunity so powerful that it literally dwarfs the problem. The greatest success stories were created by people who recognized a problem and turned it into an opportunity.'
Anon

'The real problem is what to do with the problem solvers after the problems are solved.'
Anon

'It isn't that they can't see the solution. It is that they can't see the problem.'
Grover Cleveland (1837–1908), American President

'When you have eliminated the impossible, that which remains, however improbable, must be the truth.'
Sir Arthur Conan Doyle (1859–1930), creator of Sherlock Holmes

'The significant problems we face cannot be solved at the same level of thinking we were at when we created them.'
Albert Einstein (1879–1955), genius and physicist

'A problem is a chance for you to do your best.'
Duke Ellington (1899–1974), bandleader

'Don't find a fault. Find a remedy.'
Henry Ford (1863–1947), boy racer turned automaker

'When I am working on a problem I never think about beauty, I only think about how to solve the problem. But when I have finished, if the solution is not beautiful, I know it is wrong.'
R. Buckminster Fuller (1895–1983), architect, inventor and engineer

'Problems are only opportunities in work clothes.'
Henry J. Kaiser (1882–1967), American executive

'Our problems are man-made, therefore they may be solved by man. And man can be as big as he wants. No problem of human destiny is beyond human beings.'
John F. Kennedy (1917–63), 35th American President

'If you only have a hammer, you tend to see every problem as a nail.'
Abraham Maslow (1908–70), psychologist and creator of the 'hierarchy of needs'

'The answers are always inside the problem, not outside.'
Marshall McLuhan (1911–80), commentator and critic of the modern world

'For every problem there is a solution which is simple, clean and wrong.'
Henry Louis Mencken (1880–1956), American journalist and writer

'Focus on remedies, not faults.'
Jack Nicklaus (b. 1940), golfing great

'The level of intellectual inquiry among managers and organizations is not robust enough to cope with the complexity of our problems.'
Richard Pascale (b. 1938), management thinker and author of *Managing on the Edge*

'I am grateful for all my problems. I became stronger and more able to meet those that were still to come.'
JC Penney, American businessman

'In the life of a nation, few ideas are more dangerous than good solutions to the wrong problems.'
Robert B. Reich (b. 1946), economist and politician

'I need problems. A good problem makes me come alive.'
Tiny Rowland, former head of Lonrho

'The greatest challenge to any thinker is stating the problem in a way that will allow a solution.'
Bertrand Russell (1872–1970), mathematician and philosopher

'No problem is so formidable that you can't walk away from it.'
Charles Schulz (b. 1922), creator of *Peanuts*

'True proactiveness comes from seeing how we contribute to our own problems.'
Peter Senge (b. 1947), MIT-based academic and author

*P*ROFIT

'It is not the aim of Marks and Spencer to make more money than is prudent,' said Lord Rayner when he was the retailer's chairman. It is not a sentiment shared by many in business. Profit is the founding principle of capitalism. More is unquestionably better. But when does more become too much?

'The smell of profit is clean
And sweet, whatever the source.'
Juvenal (60–140?), Roman satirist

'Those who profit are the ones at the top. They keep the doughnut for themselves and give the hole to the people.'
Alexander Lebed, Russian politician

'Medicine is for the patient; not for the profits. The profits follow.'
George Merck, founder of a pharmaceutical company

'One of our most important management tasks is maintaining the proper balance between short-term profit performance and investment for future strength and growth.'
David Packard (1912–96), computer company founder

'It is just as easy to make a profit today as it will be tomorrow. Actions taken which result in reducing short-term profit in the hope of increasing long-term profit are very seldom successful. Such actions are almost always the result of wishful thinking and almost always fail to achieve an overall optimum performance.'
David Packard

'Putting profits after people and products was magical at Ford.'
Don Petersen, Ford chief executive

'No one can long make a profit producing anything unless the customer makes a profit using it.'
Samuel Pettengill (1886–1974), American congressman

'Profit is the payment you get when you take advantage of change.'
Joseph Schumpeter (1883–1950), Czech-born economist

'The trouble with the profit system has always been that it was highly un-profitable to most people.'
EB White (1899–1985), American writer and humorist

PROGRESS

Progress is necessary for business survival. It does not occur spontaneously. 'Our company has, indeed, stumbled onto some of its new products. But never forget that you can only stumble if you're moving,' said former 3M chief executive, Richard Carlton. Progress only comes to those
with their eyes open and their feet moving.

'A thousand things advance; nine hundred and ninety-nine retreat: that is
progress.'
Henri Frédéric Amiel (1821–81), Swiss philosophical poet

'All human progress is the result of standing on the shoulders of our predecessors.'
Anon

'The whole history of civilization is strewn with creeds and institutions
which were invaluable at first and deadly afterwards.'
Water Bagehot (1826–77), British writer

'What is now proved was once only imagined.'
  William Blake (1757–1827), Romantic poet

'All progress is based upon a universal innate desire on the part of every
organism to live beyond its income.'
Samuel Butler (1612–80), poet and satirist

'If the automobile had followed the same development cycle as the computer, a Rolls-Royce would today cost $100, get a million miles per gallon,
and explode once a year, killing everybody inside.'
Robert X. Cringely, American writer

'You don't leap a chasm in two bounds.'
Chinese proverb

'Be not afraid of going slowly; be only afraid of standing still.'
Chinese proverb

'Nobody in his right mind tries to cross a broad ditch in two steps.'
Carl von Clausewitz (1780–1831), Prussian soldier and writer

'If there is no struggle, there is no progress.'
Frederick Douglass (1817–95), American campaigner and journalist

'Products are always gonna be obsolete, so you'd better enjoy doing the next version. It's like pinball – if you play a good game, the reward is that you get to play another one.'
Bill Gates (b. 1955), Microsoft founder

'If you're not making progress all the time, you're slipping backwards.'
Sir John Harvey-Jones (b. 1924), businessman, television presenter and author

'Progress with distinction.'
Honda Motor Company mission statement

'All progress is precarious, and the solution of one problem brings us face to face with another problem.'
Martin Luther King (1929–68), American civil rights champion

'Unquestionably, there is progress. The average American now pays out twice as much in taxes as he formerly got in wages.'
HL Mencken (1880–1956), journalist and writer

'You think you understand the situation, but what you don't understand is that the situation just changed.'
Putnam Investments advertisement

'It is only through labor and painful effort, by grim energy and resolute courage that we move on to better things.'
Theodore Roosevelt (1858–1919), American President

'Change is scientific, progress is ethical; change is indubitable, whereas progress is a matter of controversy.'
   Bertrand Russell (1872–1970), mathematician and philosopher

'Man's *progress* is but a gradual discovery that his questions have no meaning.'
   Antoine de Saint-Exupéry (1900–44), French writer and aviator

'Progress occurs when courageous, skillful leaders seize the opportunity to change things for the better.'
   Harry S Truman (1884–1972), American President

'Progress imposes not only new possibilities for the future but new restrictions.'
   Norbert Wiener (1894–1964), one of the founders of cybernetics

'Fundamental progress has to do with the reinterpretation of basic ideas.'
   Alfred North Whitehead (1861–1947), British mathematician, logician and metaphysician

Quality

The business world was reintroduced to the world of quality in the 1980s when an aging American, W. Edwards Deming, was featured on an American television program. Ignored in the West, he had been preaching his quality gospel successfully in Japan for decades. The program was a watershed. Before long every company in the Western world claimed to be implementing Total Quality Management. Quality circles and continuous improvement teams were everywhere. Some even achieved Japanese-like quality. Unfortunately, the Japanese had raised their standards.

'Quality is the totality of features and characteristics of a product or service that bear on its ability to satisfy stated or implied needs.'
American Society for Quality Control

'More will mean worse.'
Kingsley Amis (1922–95), British novelist

'I have never known a concern to make a decided success that did not do good, honest work, and even in these days of the fiercest competition when everything would seem to be a matter of price, there lies still at the root of great business success the very much more important factor of quality.'
Andrew Carnegie (1835–1919), American industrialist and philanthropist

'Reducing the cost of quality is in fact an opportunity to increase profits without raising sales, buying new equipment, or hiring new people.'
Philip Crosby, author of best-selling quality gospel, *Quality Is Free*

'Quality is conformance to requirements, not goodness.'
Philip Crosby

'Quality has to be caused, not controlled.'
  Philip Crosby

'People all over the world think that it is the factory worker that causes problems. He is not your problem. Ever since there has been anything such as industry, the factory worker has known that quality is what will protect his job. He knows that poor quality in the hands of the customer will lose the market and cost him his job. He knows it and lives with that fear every day. Yet he cannot do a good job. He is not allowed to do it because the management wants figures, more products, and never mind the quality.'
  W. Edwards Deming (1900–93), quality guru ignored in the West until the 1980s

'We have learned to live in a world of mistakes and defective products as if they were necessary to life. It is time to adopt a new philosophy in America.'
  W. Edwards Deming

'Quality is characteristic of a product or service that helps somebody and which has a market.'
  W. Edwards Deming

'Quality in a product or service is not what the supplier puts in. It is what the customer gets out and is willing to pay for. A product is not quality because it is hard to make and costs a lot of money, as manufacturers typically believe. This is incompetence. Customers pay only for what is of use to them and gives them value. Nothing else constitutes quality.'
  Peter Drucker (b. 1909), management author

'If there's a way to do it better ... find it.'
  Thomas Alva Edison (1847–1931), inventor and businessman

'I believe that there is hardly a single operation in the making of our car that is the same as when we made our first car of the present model. That is why we make them so cheaply.'
  Henry Ford (1863–1947), quality auto manufacturer

'The best brewer sometimes makes bad beer.'
  German proverb

'It is the quality of our work which will please God and not the quantity.'
Mahatma Gandhi (1869–1948), Indian statesman

'Quality is remembered long after the price is forgotten.'
Gucci slogan

'The only job security anybody has in this company comes from quality, productivity, and satisfied customers.'
Lee Iacocca (b. 1924), former chairman of Chrysler

'Be a yardstick of quality. Some people aren't used to an environment where excellence is expected.'
Steve Jobs (b. 1955), computer executive

'Quality is not a thing. It is an event.'
Robert M. Pirsig (b. 1938), author of *Zen and the Art of Motorcycle Maintenance*

'Quality doesn't have to be defined. You understand it without definition. Quality is a direct experience independent of and prior to intellectual abstractions.'
Robert M. Pirsig

'"What the hell is Quality? What *is* it?" "And what is good, Phaedrus, and what is not good – need we ask anyone to tell us these things?"'
Robert M. Pirsig

'Continuous improvement is desirable – but think of its implications. We are telling employees, "If you do not become more efficient, you will lose your job to your competitor." The employees can understand that. But we are also saying, "If you become very efficient, you will lose your job to productivity improvement" – and that they don't understand. How long do you expect employees to continuously improve without them recognizing the implication of such improvement is loss of jobs?'
CK Prahalad, co-author of *Competing for the Future*

'Quality is never an accident; it is always the result of intelligent effort.'
John Ruskin (1819–1900), critic and writer

'Good management techniques are enduring. Quality control, for instance was treated as a fad here, but it's been part of the Japanese business philosophy for decades. That's why they laugh at us.'
Peter Senge (b. 1947), author of _The Fifth Discipline_

> _'Continuous improvement is better than delayed perfection.'_
> **_Mark Twain (1835–1910), literary perfectionist_**

'The superfluous is very necessary.'
Voltaire (1694–1778), writer and philosopher

'Quality is our best assurance of customer allegiance, our strongest defense against foreign competition, and the only path to sustained growth and earnings.'
Jack Welch (b. 1935), General Electric chief

QUESTIONS AND ANSWERS

One of the most touching things about executives is their perennial faith in answers. In their action-centered world, if there is a problem there has to be a solution. This, of course, is naive, tinged with executive arrogance. Some problems don't have solutions or, at least, not ones we are capable of coming up with. Some things are insoluble. This is inconvenient and leads to two possible reactions: a philosophical shrug of the shoulders or a studious insistence that the solution is just around the corner. Managers usually choose the latter.

'There aren't any embarrassing questions – just embarrassing answers.'
   Anon

'A prudent question is one half of wisdom.'
   Francis Bacon (1561–1626), wise Elizabethan

'If a man will begin with certainties, he shall end in doubts; but if he will be content to begin with doubts, he shall end in certainties.'
   Francis Bacon

'Left to themselves, people will elaborate, not simplify solutions.'
   Chester Barnard (1886–1961), executive and thoughtful commentator on the nature of management

'The important thing is not to stop questioning.'
   Albert Einstein (1879–1955), genius and physicist

'The important thing is not to stop questioning. Curiosity has its own reason for existing.'
   Albert Einstein

'There is always a best way of doing everything, if it be to boil an egg.'
   Ralph Waldo Emerson (1803–82), poet

'The questions that are beyond the reach of economics – the beauty, dignity, pleasure, and durability of life – may be inconvenient but they are important.'
JK Galbraith (b. 1908), economist and more

'It is by losing himself in the objective, in inquiry, creation, and craft, that a man becomes something.'
Paul Goodman (1911–72), writer, educator and analyst

'There is no formula or perfect solution. This is the tide of events. We can't turn the tide, but we can ride it.'
Charles Handy (b. 1932), best-selling author and commentator

'Find interest in the most mundane of things.'
Sir John Harvey-Jones (b. 1924), inquisitive author and businessman

'The uncreative mind can spot wrong answers, but it takes a creative mind to spot wrong questions.'
Sir Antony Jay (b. 1930), writer

'Curiosity is one of the permanent and certain characteristics of a vigorous mind.'
Dr. Samuel Johnson (1709–84), man of letters

'It is fashionable stupidity to regard everything one cannot explain as a fraud.'
Carl Jung (1875–1961), psychoanalyst

'I keep six honest serving-men
(They taught me all I knew);
Their names are What and Why and When
And How and Where and Who.'
Rudyard Kipling (1865–1936), author

'The wise man doesn't give the right answers, he poses the right questions.'
__Claude Lévi-Strauss (b. 1908), social anthropologist__

'I go into factories, offices, stores and look out the window and just see things and ask Why? Why are they doing that? Why are things this way and not that? You ask questions and pretty soon you come up with answers. When you begin to try to answer your own questions, you become much more receptive to reading things which help you to answer questions. Seeing is one thing but perception requires cognitive effort and personal involvement. You bring something to what you see.'
Theodore Levitt (b. 1925), marketing thinker and question master

'It is not the business of the botanist to eradicate the weeds. Enough for him if he can tell us just how fast they grow.'
C. Northcote Parkinson (1909–93), academic and author

'There are no answers. Just, at best, a few guesses that might be worth a try.'
Tom Peters (b. 1942), consultant and author

'Live your questions now, and perhaps even without knowing it, you will live along some distant day into your answers.'
Rainer Maria Rilke (1875–1926), Austrian poet

'How can you ennoble the spirit when you are selling something as inconsequential as a face cream?'
Antia Roddick (b. 1943), founder of The Body Shop

'Good questions outrank easy answers.'
Paul A. Samuelson (b. 1915), economist

'It is better to know some of the questions than all of the answers.'
James Thurber (1894–1961), writer and humorist

'The outcome of any serious research can only be to make two questions grow where only one grew before.'
Thorstein Veblen (1857–1929), economist and philosopher

'The *silly question* is the first intimation of some totally new development.'
Alfred North Whitehead (1861–1947), scientist

'Even when all the possible scientific questions have been answered, the problems of life remain completely untouched.'
Ludwig Wittgenstein (1889–1951), Austrian philosopher

'The riddle does not exist. If a question can be put at all, then it can also be answered.'
Ludwig Wittgenstein

RESPONSIBILITY

After starting a typically rambunctious brawl during an ice hockey match, Barry Beck of the New York Rangers commented: 'We have only one person to blame, and that's each other.' Taking responsibility does not come easy – even for those who are paid to take responsibility. 'There will be no whitewash in the White House,' said Richard Nixon, but executives, politicians and human beings in general have an instinctive tendency to reach for the whitewash at the slightest sign of trouble.

'We can delegate authority, but not responsibility.'
   Anon

'Never mind whom you praise, but be very careful who you blame.'
   Anon

'Responsibility should always be coupled with corresponding authority.'
   Chester Barnard (1886–1961), American executive and management thinker

'The price of greatness is responsibility.'
   Sir Winston Churchill (1874–1965), British statesman, greatness assured

'What is the first duty – and continuing responsibility – of the business manager? To strive for the best possible economic results from the resources currently employed or available.'
   Peter Drucker (b. 1909), author and Japanese art expert

'Responsibility is the great developer of men.'
   Mary Parker Follett (1868–1933), management thinker

'A man who enjoys responsibility usually gets it. A man who merely likes exercising authority usually loses it.'
   Malcolm S. Forbes (1919–90), publisher

'There is one and only one social responsibility of business – to use its resources and engage in activities designed to increase its profits so long as it engages in open and free competition without deception or fraud.'
   Milton Friedman (b. 1912), American economist

'Somebody has to do something, and it's just incredibly pathetic that it has to be us.'
   Jerry Garcia (1942–95), leader of *The Grateful Dead*

'We are not here for ourselves alone.'
   Václav Havel (b. 1936), Czech President

'While you're saving your face, you're losing your ass.'
   Lyndon B. Johnson (1908–73), American President

'You cannot escape the responsibility of tomorrow by evading it today.'
   Abraham Lincoln (1809–65), American President

'I believe that every right implies a responsibility; every opportunity an obligation; every possession a duty.'
   John D. Rockefeller, Jr. (1839–1937), oil tycoon

'People need responsibility. They resist assuming it, but they cannot get along without it.'
   John Steinbeck (1902–68), novelist

'Human beings were held accountable long before there were corporate bureaucracies. If the knight didn't deliver, the king cut off his head.'
   Alvin Toffler (b. 1928), futurist author of *The Third Wave*

'The buck stops here.'
   Harry S Truman (1884–1972), 33rd American President

Retirement

One of the great attractions of the business world is that age is no bar. You can come up with a bright idea when you are sixty and make a million. You can run a major corporation when you are in your seventies. Despite the pressure and demands, the upper executive echelons are dominated by fifty-year old men in full suits. However, none can go on indefinitely. They should heed the example of Professor Scott Elledge who retired from Cornell University with the words: 'It is time I stepped aside for a less experienced and less able man.'

'Old age is always 15 years older than I am.'
Bernard Baruch (1870–1965), American financier and economic adviser

'Cessation of work is not accompanied by cessation of expenses.'
Cato the Elder (234–149 BC), Roman statesman

'The worst of work nowadays is what happens to people when they cease to work.'
GK Chesterton (1874–1936), writer

'When a man fell into his anecdotage it was a sign for him to retire for the world.'
Benjamin Disraeli (1804–81), statesman and writer

'Raking over the past and sifting its dust is an occupation for the idle or the elderly retiree.'
Armand Hammer (1898–1990), businessman

'Dismiss the old horse in good time, lest he fail in the lists and the spectators laugh.'
Horace (65–8 BC), Roman poet

'You can plan everything in life, and then the roof caves in on you because you haven't done enough thinking about who you are and what you should do with the rest of your life.'
Lee Iaccoca (b. 1924), Chrysler savior

'It is one of the enjoyments of retirement that you are able to drift through the day at your own pace, easy in the knowledge that you have put hard work and achievement behind you.'
Kazuo Ishiguro (b. 1954), novelist

'Don't think of retiring from the world until the world will be sorry that you retire. I hate a fellow whom pride or cowardice or laziness drove into a corner, and who does nothing when he is there but sit and growl. Let him come out as I do, and bark.'
Dr. Samuel Johnson (1709–84), retiring man of letters

'I don't know any executive who ever thought about stress, although a lot of other people do. No one ever dies of hard work, but a lot of people die once they retire from an active job.'
Sir Ian Macgregor (b. 1912), American executive imported to Britain

'Few men of action have been able to make a graceful exit at the appropriate time.'
Malcolm Muggeridge (1903–90), British journalist

'It is better to be a has-been than a never-was.'
Cecil Parkinson (b. 1931), British politician

Risk and risk taking

'To be alive at all involves some risk,' said the outwardly risk-averse Harold Macmillan. Risks in the business world usually revolve around money. How big a bet are you prepared to make? It takes a steely nerve and steadfast confidence to make the grade. And then, hopelessly addicted, you have an irresistible urge to do it all again.

'We pay for security with boredom, for adventure with bother.'
   Anon

'Rashness succeeds often, still more often fails.'
   Napoléon Bonaparte (1769–1821), French General

'When firmness is sufficient, rashness is unnecessary.'
   Napoléon Bonaparte

'Take a chance! All life is a chance. The man who goes the furthest is generally the one who is willing to do and dare.'
   Dale Carnegie (1888–1955), author of *How to Make Friends and Influence People*

'Those who trust to chance must abide by the results of chance.'
   Calvin Coolidge (1872–1933), American President

'When you ain't got nothing you've got nothing to lose.'
   Bob Dylan (b. 1941), songwriter

'However well organized the foundations of life may be, life must always be full of risks.'
   Havelock Ellis (1859–1939), sexologist

'One does not discover new continents without consenting to lose sight of the shore for a very long time.'
   André Gide (1869–1951), French novelist and Nobel Prize winner

'Whatever you can do,
or dream you can, begin it,
Boldness has genius,
power and magic in it.'
   Johann von Wolfgang Goethe (1749–1832), writer

'What would life be if we had no courage to attempt anything?'
   Vincent Van Gogh (1853–90), artist

'You miss 100 percent of the shots you never take.'
__Wayne Gretzky (b. 1961), ice hockey player__

'Half the failures in life arise from pulling in one's horse as he is leaping.'
   Augustus William Hare (1792–1834), clergyman author

'Nothing will ever be attempted if all possible objections must first be overcome.'
   Dr. Samuel Johnson (1709–84), man of letters

'And the trouble is, if you don't risk anything, you risk even more.'
   Erica Jong (b. 1942), writer

'The policy of being too cautious is the greatest risk of all.'
   Jawaharlal Nehru (1889–1964), India's first Prime Minister

'Take calculated risks. That is quite different from being rash.'
   General George S. Patton (1885–1945), soldier

'The country needs and, unless I mistake, the country demands, bold persistent experimentation. It is common sense to take a method and try it. If it fails, admit it frankly and try another. But above all, try something.'
   Franklin D. Roosevelt (1882–1945), American President

'So long as money can answer, it were wrong in any business to put the life in danger.'
  Sa'di (1184–1291), Persian poet

'Everything is sweetened by risk.'
  Alexander Smith (1830–67), Scottish poet and writer

'Ignorance is bold, and knowledge reserved.'
  Thucydides (460–400? BC), historian

'Don't play for safety. It's the most dangerous game in the world.'
  Sir Hugh Walpole (1884–1941), English novelist

SELL SELL SELL

Selling has changed. 'Buying shoes has become an emotional experience. Our business now is selling excitement rather than shoes,' says the excitement selling Francis C. Rooney. The hard sell has become the constant sell. There is no hiding place. Brands are built up and projected in Technicolor right in front of our eyes. And yet, take away the color and glamor, and the salesman or saleswoman is still a persuader. You take the bait or you don't, but it is becoming ever harder to ignore.

'Don't confuse selling with art.'
    Anon

'These are my new shoes. They're good shoes. They won't make you rich like me, they won't make you rebound like me, they definitely won't make you handsome like me. They'll only make you have shoes like me. That's it.'
    Charles Barkley (b. 1963), basketball player in a commercial for basketball shoes

'You can make more friends in two months by becoming more interested in other people than you can in two years by trying to get people interested in you.'
    Dale Carnegie (1888–1955), self-improvement guru

'To please people is a great step towards persuading them.'
    Lord Chesterfield (1694–1773), statesman

'Would you persuade, speak of interest, not of reason.'
    Benjamin Franklin (1706–90), inventor and writer

'When a man is try to sell you something, don't imagine he is that polite all the time.'
    Edgar Watson Howe (1853–1937), American writer

'Selling focuses on the needs of the seller; marketing on the needs of the buyer. Selling is preoccupied with the seller's need to convert his product into cash; marketing with the idea of satisfying the needs of the customer by means of the product and the whole cluster of things associated with creating, delivering and finally consuming it.'
Theodore Levitt (b. 1925), Harvard-based marketing guru

'I see
that everywhere among the race of men
it is the tongue that wins and not the deed.'
Sophocles (496–406 BC), tragedian

'Every one lives by selling something.'
Robert Louis Stevenson (1850–1894), author of Kidnapped

'In all important respects, the man who has nothing but his physical power to see has nothing to sell which it is worth anyone's money to buy.'
Norbert Wiener (1894–1964), cybernetician

SIMPLICITY

If you can make something simple, you can make a fortune. KISS – Keep It Simple Stupid – is one of the more enduring managerial acronyms and useful *aide memoire* next time you have to write a plan, deliver a presentation or even write an E-mail.

'Everything should be made as simple as possible, but not simpler.'
Albert Einstein (1879–1955), physicist

'Simple solutions seldom are.'
Forbes *magazine*

'I have no use for a motor car which has more spark plugs than a cow has teats.'
Henry Ford (1863–1947), purveyor of spark plugs to the people

'You press the button, and we'll do the rest.'
Kodak advertisement (c. 1888)

'Business is actually a rotten intellectual exercise – the essence of business is very straightforward. A lot of great things are the result of an incredibly narrow focus and great drive and a lot of bad things have come out of enormously complex and sophisticated strategizing.'
Gerry Robinson (b. 1948), Granada chief

'Less is more. God is in the details.'
Mies van der Rohe, architect

'The great fault all over the world in business is that people overcomplicate and forget that the main ingredients for success are common sense and simplicity. I use lawyers and accountants as little as possible.'
Peter de Savary (b. 1944), British businessman and property developer

'Any intelligent fool can make things bigger, more complex, and more violent. It takes a touch of genius – and a lot of courage – to move in the opposite direction.'

EF Schumacher (1911–77), German author of *Small Is Beautiful*

'Small is beautiful. Less is more.'
    EF Schumacher

'Tis the gift to be simple.'
    Shaker hymn

'Our life is frittered away by detail ... Simplify, simplify.'
    Henry David Thoreau (1817–62), naturalist and writer

'Seek simplicity and distrust it.'
    Alfred North Whitehead (1861–1947), scientist

SPECIALISTS AND GENERALISTS

Managers have yearned for decades to be recognized as professionals in an honorable and noble profession. Recognition has been slow in coming. This is largely due to the all-embracing nature of business. There is an unquenchable demand for general managers who have moved from discipline to discipline, picking up a little of each along the way. The well-rounded generalist is usually preferred to the narrowness of the marketer or financier.

'My definition of an expert in any field is a person who knows enough about what's really going to be scared.'
Anon

'The work of every person in the organization should be confined as far as possible to the performance of a single leading function.'
Chester Barnard (1886–1961), executive and author

'An expert is a person who avoids the small errors while sweeping on to the grand fallacy.'
Arthur Bloch (b. 1938), American writer

'A professional is a person who can do his best at a time when he doesn't particularly feel like it.'
Alistair Cooke (b. 1908), 'Letter from America' journalist and broadcaster

'As a rule, the man who can do all things equally well is a very mediocre individual.'
Elbert Hubbard (1856–1915), writer and businessman

'Specialized meaninglessness has come to be regarded, in certain circles, as a kind of hallmark of true science.'
Aldous Huxley (1894–1963), author of *Brave New World*

'The essence of the expert is that his field shall be very special and narrow: one of the ways in which he inspires confidence is to rigidly limit himself to the little toe; he would scarcely venture an off-the-record opinion on an infected little finger.'

Louis Kronengerger (b. 1904), critic and writer

'We are moving from the specialist who is soon obsolete to the generalist who can adapt.'

John Naisbitt, futurist

SPEECHES

There comes a moment in everyone's life when you find yourself getting to your feet with a strange feeling in your stomach and a light-headed sensation. The other symptoms may be a mouth as dry as the Sahara, a body shaking as if it were holding a pneumatic drill and the loss of all muscular control with twitches which can take you half across a room. The joys of public speaking may escape you at this point.

'The habit of common and continuous speech is a symptom of mental deficiency. It proceeds from not knowing that is going on in other people's minds.'
Walter Bagehot (1826–77), writer

'Nothing is so unbelievable that oratory cannot make it acceptable.'
Marcus Tullius Cicero (106–43 BC), Roman writer and statesman

'By inflection you can say much more than your words do.'
Malcom S. Forbes (1919–90), publisher

'Hell is a half-filled auditorium.'
Robert Frost (1874–1963), American poet

'Speak clearly, if you speak at all; carve every word before you let it fall.'
Oliver Wendell Holmes, Jr. (1841–1935), jurist

'Talking and eloquence are not the same thing; to speak and to speak well are two things. A fool may talk, but a wise man speaks.'
Ben Jonson (1572–1637), Elizabethan playwright

'Think before you speak and don't say everything you think.'
Alexander Lebed, Russian politician

'Do not say a little in many words but a great deal in a few.'
   Pythagoras (582–507? BC)

'Public speaking is very easy.'
   Dan Quayle (b. 1947), politician

'In oratory the greatest art is to hide art.'
   Jonathan Swift (1667–1745), author of *Gulliver's Travels*

'It is the man determines what is said, not the words.'
   Henry David Thoreau (1817–62), naturalist and writer

'It usually takes me more than three weeks to prepare a good impromptu speech.'
   Mark Twain (1835–1910), novelist

'Talk low, talk slow, and don't say too much.'
   John Wayne (1907–79), actor who was true to his words

SPEED FREAKS

'We intend to move as fast as we can, ripping up the road behind us,' says Intel's Craig Barrett which leads to a fact of business life: if you are quicker than your competitors (at developing, delivering or making products) you will be more successful. This startlingly obvious truism provided a lucrative income for Boston Consulting Group when it became the height of managerial fashion. Speed also means that your mistakes tend to be made quicker and are more dramatic. If you must run across a tightrope, don't be surprised when you plunge to the ground.

'If everything seems under control, you're just not going fast enough.'
Mario Andretti (b. 1940), race driver

'The backbone of surprise is fusing speed with secrecy.'
Carl von Clausewitz (1780–1831), Prussian soldier and writer

'In this business, there are two kinds of people, really, the quick and the dead.'
Michael Dell (b. 1964), computer entrepreneur

'When skating over thin ice our safety is in our speed.'
Ralph Waldo Emerson (1803–82), poet

'In this business, by the time you realize you're in trouble, it's too late to save yourself.'
Bill Gates (b. 1955), billionaire computer enthusiast

'You have no choice but to operate in a world shaped by globalization and the information revolution. There are two options: adapt or die. The new environment dictates two rules: first, everything happens faster; second, anything than can be done will be done, if not by you, then by someone else, somewhere. Let there be no misunderstanding: these changes lead to a less kind, less gently, and less predictable workplace. As managers in such a workplace, you need to develop a higher tolerance for disorder.'
   Andrew S. Grove (b. 1936), Intel chief

'There are two classes of pedestrians in these days of reckless motor traffic: the quick and the dead.'
   George Robey (1869–1954), comedian

'We're a 93–year old company, and we have our own way of doing things. We couldn't keep pace. We used to take four days from getting raw material to putting the product on the truck, and now we take 25 minutes. It's still not good enough.'
   3M statement

'The nineties will be a decade in a hurry, a nanosecond culture. There'll be only two kinds of managers: the quick and the dead.'
   David Vice, vice chairman of Nortel

Spend Spend Spend

There's no point pouring all your filthy lucre into a pension fund, savings account, off-shore trust or those obscure unit trusts. Nor do you want to leave a hefty inheritance for the children to fight over. You could be dead tomorrow, so get out there and shop!

'Riches are for spending.'
   Francis Bacon (1561–1626), Elizabethan spendthrift

'I am money's medium. It passes through me – taxes, insurance, mortgage, child support, rent, legal fees. All this dignified blundering costs plenty.'
   Saul Bellow (b. 1915), literary master

'Expense, and great expense, may be an essential part of true economy.'
   Edmund Burke (1729–97), statesman and writer

'The miser is the man who starves himself, and everybody else, in order to worship wealth in its dead form, as distinct from its living form.'
   GK Chesterton (1874–1936), writer

'I'm living so far beyond my income that we may almost be said to be living apart.'
   ee cummings (1894–1962), lower-case poet

'My problem lies in reconciling my gross habits with my net income.'
   Errol Flynn (1909–59), Tasmanian-born actor

'The urge to consume is fathered by the value system which emphasises the ability of the society to produce.'
   JK Galbraith (b. 1908), economist

'We have constructed in our civilization a false world of plastic flowers and Astro-Turf, air-conditioning and fluorescent lights, windows that don't open and background music that never stops, days when we don't know whether it has rained, nights when the sky never stops glowing, Walkman and Watchman, entertainment cocoons, frozen food for the microwave oven, sleepy hearts jump-started by caffeine, alcohol, drugs and illusions.'
Al Gore (b. 1948), American Vice President

'Acquisition means life to miserable mortals.'
Hesiod (8th century BC), Greek poet

'America is good at three things: basketball, making war and buying stuff.'
Watts Wacker, futurist

'It is better to have a permanent income than to be fascinating.'
Oscar Wilde (1854–1900), fascinatingly frivolous

'The world is too much with us; late and soon
Getting and spending, we lay waste our powers:
Little we see in Nature that is ours;
We have given our hearts away, a sordid boon!'
William Wordsworth (1770–1850), poet

STANDARDS

Only the best will do. But, given the time constraints, the lack of finance, the manpower shortage, the impossibly high quality of the competing product, the proximity of the weekend, aching feet, our track record, the money involved and low standards, it hardly seems worthwhile.

'Doing a thing well is often a waste of time.'
Anon

'I can't honestly see the reason for doing something unless you want to be the best at it. Otherwise what's the point?'
Will Carling (b. 1965), England rugby player

'I am easily satisfied with the best.'
Sir Winston Churchill (1874–1965), statesman

'We'll never be 100% satisfied until you are, too.'
Cigna advertisement

'The superior man is easy to serve and difficult to please.'
Confucius (551–479 BC), Chinese philosopher

'Either dance well or quit the ballroom.'
Greek proverb

'Perhaps the reason so many people are satisfied with our automobiles is because we aren't.'
Honda advertisement

'I emphasise the importance of details. You must perfect every fundamental of your business if you expect it to perform well.'
Ray Kroc (1902–84), McDonald's founder

'If you refuse to accept anything but the best, you very often get it.'
  W. Somerset Maugham (1874–1965), novelist

'The nicest thing about standards is that there are so many of them to choose from.'
  Ken Olsen (b. 1926), founder of DEC

'There are no excellent companies.'
  Tom Peters (b. 1942), co-author of *In Search of Excellence*

'High expectations are the key to everything.'
  Sam Walton (1918–92), founder of the Wal-Mart retail chain

STRATEGY

The sheer amount of words dedicated to strategy is unbelievable. Harvard's Alfred Chandler defines strategy as 'the determination of the long-term goals and objectives of an enterprise, and the adoption of courses of action and the allocation of resources necessary for carrying out these goals.' Many others beg to differ and some even remember that actually turning strategy into action is still the real challenge.

'One person's strategy is another's tactics.'
   Anon

'The end product of strategic decisions is deceptively simple; a combination of products and markets is selected for the firm. This combination is arrived at by addition of new product markets, divestment from some old ones, and expansion of the present position.'
   Igor Ansoff (b. 1918), strategy guru

'Strategy is the art of making use of time and space. I am less chary of the latter than the former; space we can recover, time never.'
   Napoléon Bonaparte (1769–1821), ambitious soldier

'Unhappy the general who comes on the field of battle with a system.'
   Napoléon Bonaparte

'Strategies are intellectually simple; their execution is not.'
   Larry Bossidy (b. 1935), industrialist

'Unless structure follows strategy, inefficiency results.'
   Alfred Chandler (b. 1918), historian

'A strategy is no good if people don't fundamentally believe in it.'
   Robert Haas, businessman

'We all know a strategy when we see one.'
Gary Hamel (b. 1954), consultant, academic and author

'Our view of strategy has changed from the classic Coca-Cola versus Pepsi market share fight to how do you shape the emergence of the new opportunity areas, whether it's branchless banking, satellite telephony, or genetic engineering.'
Gary Hamel

'Companies don't produce strategies, just plans.'
Gary Hamel

'Strategy doesn't come from a calendar-driven process; it isn't the product of a systematic search for ways of earning above average profits; strategy comes from viewing the world in new ways. Strategy starts with an ability to think in new and unconventional ways.'
Gary Hamel

'Strategy is, above all else, the search for above average returns.'
Gary Hamel

'Strategy is extraordinarily emotional and demanding. It is not a ritual or a once-a-year exercise, though that is what it has become. We have set the bar too low.'
Gary Hamel

'The real challenge in crafting strategy lies in detecting their subtle discontinuities that may undermine a business in the future. And for that there is no technique, no program, just a sharp mind in touch with the situation.'
Henry Mintzberg (b. 1939), Canadian strategist, author of *The Rise and Fall of Strategic Planning*

'Planning by its very nature defines and preserves categories. Creativity, by its very nature, creates categories or rearranges established ones. This is why strategic planning can neither provide creativity, nor deal with it when it emerges by other means.'
Henry Mintzberg

'Strategy is not the consequence of planning but the opposite: its starting point.'
   Henry Mintzberg

'Perception is strong and sight weak. In strategy it is important to see distant things as if they were close and to take a distanced view of close things.'
   Miyamoto Musashi (1584–1645)

'In strategic thinking, one first seeks a clear understanding of the particular character of each element of a situation and then makes the fullest possible use of human brain power to restructure the elements in the most advantageous way.'
   Kenichi Ohmae (b. 1943), flautist, nuclear physicist, consultant, author and politician

'The job of the strategist is to achieve superior performance, relative to competition, in the key factors for success of the business.'
   Kenichi Ohmae

'The strategist's method is very simply to challenge the prevailing assumptions with a single question: Why? and to put the same question relentlessly to those responsible for the current way of doing things until they are sick of it.'
   Kenichi Ohmae

'Strategies are okayed in boardrooms that even a child would say are bound to fail. The problem is, there is never a child in the boardroom.'
   Victor Palmieri, turnaround expert

'Strategic planning, at best, is about posing questions, more than attempting to answer them.'
   Richard Pascale (b. 1938), academic, consultant & author

'Those oft are strategems which errors seem,
Nor is it Homer nods, but we that dream.'
   Alexander Pope (1688–1744), poet

'Strategic thinking rarely occurs spontaneously.'
   Michael Porter (b. 1947), Harvard Business School star

'Self-generated strategic change requires the stamina, the endurance and the resilience to just keep coming back to that strategy. You get knocked partly off, but you come back again. You get knocked the other way off, but you come back. You're not going to arrive if you get diverted.'

Allen Sheppard (b. 1932), British executive

'Deploy forces to defend the strategic points; exercise vigilance in preparation, do not be indolent. Deeply investigate the true situation, secretly await their laxity. Wait until they leave their strongholds, then seize what they love.'

Sun Tzu (500 BC), author of *The Art of War*

'To subdue the enemy's forces without fighting is the summit of skill. The best approach is to attack the other side's strategy; next best is to attack his alliances; next best is to attack his soldiers; the worst is to attack cities.'

Sun Tzu

STRESS

In an age of overwork for some and underwork for others, there is stress attached to each and every job. The mistake is to think that executives have a monopoly over stress. It is just that stress is more obvious with executives because they are not doing anything else.

'Executive: an ulcer with authority.'
   Fred Allen (1894–1956), American comedian

'It is not work that kills men; it is worry. Worry is rust upon the blade.'
   Henry Ward Beecher (1813–87), clergyman campaigner

'If you can't sleep, then get up and do something instead of lying there worrying. It's the worry that gets you, not the lack of sleep.'
   Dale Carnegie (1888–1955), motivational guru

'Let our advance worrying become advance thinking and planning.'
   Sir Winston Churchill (1874–1965), statesman

'I enjoy pressure, can't do without it.'
   George Davies (b. 1941), British businessman

'Worry – a God, invisible but omnipotent. It steals the bloom from the cheek and lightness from the pulse; it takes away the appetite, and turns the hair grey.'
   Benjamin Disraeli (1804–81), statesman and writer

'As a cure for worrying, work is better than whiskey.'
   Thomas Alva Edison (1847–1931), inventor

'If you have a job without aggravations, you don't have a job.'
   Malcolm S. Forbes (1919–90), magazine publisher

'When I can't handle events, I let them handle themselves.'
Henry Ford (1863–1947), automobile manufacturer

'There is nothing that wastes the body like worry, and one who has any faith in God should be ashamed to worry about anything whatsoever.'
Mahatma Gandhi (1869–1948), Indian leader

'What you do at GE is you kill yourself, work hard, fall on your sword and hope someone notices – and then you hope that they don't raise the bar five times more. At GE, you perform or you die.'
General Electric manager

'We often hear of people breaking down from overwork, but in nine out of ten they are really suffering from worry or anxiety.'
Sir John Lubbock (1834–1913), author and financier

'It is my profound belief that a man or woman who rises up through the hierarchy of a corporation must justify his or her position every single day. They must also be in a state of perpetual anxiety, the healthy anxiety that makes one reject complacency.'
Jacques Maisonrouge, former senior vice president of IBM

'How Sunday into Monday melts!'
Ogden Nash (1902–71), light versifier

'How happy the life unembarrassed by the cares of business!'
Publilius Syrus (c. 42 BC), Latin writer

'For fast acting relief, try slowing down.'
Lily Tomlin (b. 1939), actress and comedienne

'Worry, the interest paid by those who borrow trouble.'
George Washington (1732–99), first American President

'An overburdened, stretched executive is the best executive, because he or she doesn't have time to meddle, to deal in trivia, to bother people.'
Jack Welch (b. 1935), American executive

SUCCESS

According to the Peter Principle, success is the 'final placement at the level of incompetence.' Once you are top dog, you can recline in your heavily upholstered executive swivel chair and survey the view over the city from your office. You can then contemplate the big issues – executive parking spaces, menus in the executive restaurant, company cars, personalized number plates, your choice for Desert Island Discs and the need for an executive retreat to Grand Cayman.

'80 percent of success is showing up.'
Woody Allen (b. 1935), filmmaker

'The road to success is lined with many tempting parking spaces.'
Anon

'Nothing succeeds like the appearance of success.'
Anon

'Success seems to be largely a matter of hanging on after others have let go.'
Anon

'Success is not the key to happiness. Happiness is the key to success. If you love what you are doing, you will be successful.'
Anon

'There are two rules for success:
1.   Never tell everything you know.'
Anon

'Success is that old ABC – ability, breaks and courage.'
Anon

'In civil business; what first? Boldness; what second, and third? Boldness.
And yet boldness is a child of ignorance and baseness.'
   Francis Bacon (1561–1626), Elizabethan writer and thinker

'One's religion is whatever he is most interested in, and yours is success.'
   Sir James Barrie (1860–1937), writer

'Yes, success is everything. Failure is more common. Most achieve a sort of
middling thing, but fortunately one's situation is always blurred, you never
know absolutely quite where you are.'
   Donald Barthelme (1931–89), American writer

'The toughest thing about success is that you've got to keep on being a success.'
   Irving Berlin (1888–1989), songwriter

'My formula for success is to be found in three words – work – work –
work.'
   Silvio Berlusconi (b. 1936), Italian businessman and politician

'Too much success can ruin you as surely as too much failure.'
   Marlon Brando (b. 1924), actor

'If at first you do succeed, quit trying.'
   Warren Buffet (b. 1930), investor

'The only infallible criterion of wisdom to vulgar minds – success.'
   Edmund Burke (1729–97), statesman and writer

'It takes 20 years to make an overnight success.'
   Eddie Cantor (1892–1964), comedian and singer

'Success is following the pattern of life one enjoys most.'
   Al Capp (1909–79), comedian

'The key to success is preparation. I want to be part of the best team in the
world. What you say to people on the pitch is not as important as everything you do before you get onto it. The image is made before the game.'
   Will Carling (b. 1965), rugby player

'Firmness of purpose is one of the most necessary sinews of character and one of the best instruments of success. Without it genius wastes its efforts in a maze of inconsistencies.'
Lord Chesterfield (1694–1773), statesman

'Success is going from failure to failure without a loss of enthusiasm.'
Sir Winston Churchill (1874–1965), inspirational statesman

'I can do it; I am responsible; I am self-reliant; I can choose.'
Stephen Covey (b. 1932), self-improvement guru

'Success is counted sweetest
By those who ne'er succeed.
To comprehend a nectar
Requires sorest need.'
Emily Dickinson (1830–86), poet

'The secret of success is constancy of purpose.'
Benjamin Disraeli (1804–81), statesman and writer

'There are no recipes for success, only failure.'
Peter Drucker (b. 1909), consultant and author

'A man is a success if he gets up in the morning and gets to bed at night, and in between he does what he wants to do.'
Bob Dylan (b. 1941), songwriter

'If A equals success, then the formula is A = X + Y + Z. X is work, Y is play, Z is keep your mouth shut.'
Albert Einstein (1879–1955), genius and physicist

'Success is relative: it is what we can make of the mess we have made of things.'
TS Eliot (1888–1965), American-born poet

'If to grow is success, then one must wake up anew each morning and keep awake all day.'
Henry Ford (1863–1947), industrialist and automaker

'Don't aim for success if you want it; just do what you love and believe in, and it will come naturally.'
   Sir David Frost, broadcaster

'Success is a lousy teacher – it seduces smart people into thinking they can't lose.'
   Bill Gates (b. 1955), industrialist

'My view is that you perpetuate success by continuing to run scared, not by looking back at what made you great, but looking forward at what is going to make you ungreat, so that you are constantly focusing on the challenges that keep you humble, hungry and nimble.'
   Lou Gerstner (b. 1942), consultant and businessman

'The key to survival is to learn to add more value today, and every day.'
   Andrew S. Grove (b. 1936), Hungarian-born Intel chip master and author

'The way to get on in the world is to be neither more nor less wise, neither better nor worse than your neighbors.'
   William Hazlitt (1778–1830), essayist

'He was a self-made man who owed his lack of success to nobody.'
   Joseph Heller (b. 1923), novelist

'The ability to concentrate and to use your time well is everything if you want to succeed in business – or almost anywhere else, for that matter.'
   Lee Iacocca (b. 1924), former chairman of Chrysler

'Better quality + less price = value
+ spiritual attitude of our employees = unbeatable.'
   Herb Kelleher, airline chief

'Get a sun lamp to keep you looking as if you have just come back from somewhere expensive.'
   Aristotle Onassis (1906–75), shipping magnate

'The secret of success is to know something nobody else knows.'
   Aristotle Onassis

'Nothing fails like success.'
Richard Pascale (b. 1938), author, consultant and educator

'Simply identifying attributes of success is like identifying attributes of people in excellent health during the age of the bubonic plague.'
Richard Pascale

'Great strengths are inevitably the root of weakness.'
Richard Pascale

'Success is how high you bounce when you hit bottom.'
General George S. Patton (1885–1945), soldier

'There are no secrets to success. It is the result of preparation, hard work, learning from failure.'
General Colin Powell (b. 1937), soldier

'Success is a tricky mistress. It's nice to have, but it's a tricky thing to embrace.'
Robert Redford (b. 1936), actor

'The secret of success is learning how to use pain and pleasure instead of having pain and pleasure use you. If you do that, you're in control of your life. If you don't, life controls you.'
Anthony Robbins, motivational speaker

'First, you have to have fun. Second, you have to put love where your labour is. Third, you have to go in the opposite direction to everyone else.'
Anita Roddick (b. 1943), founder of The Body Shop

'Constant improvement and continuous change are the hallmarks of our business.'
David Sainsbury (b. 1940), retailer

'The only place where success comes before work is in the dictionary.'
Vidal Sassoon (b. 1928), master hairstylist

'You will only succeed if you know that what you are doing is right and you know how to bring out the best in people.'
Margaret Thatcher (b. 1925), politician

'Live your life, do your work, then take your hat.'
Henry David Thoreau (1817–62), naturalist and writer

'All you need in this life is ignorance and confidence; then success is sure.'
Mark Twain (1835–1910), novelist

'It is not enough to succeed. Others must fail.'
Gore Vidal (b. 1929), generous hearted writer

'To succeed in the world it is not enough to be stupid, you must also be well-mannered.'
Voltaire (1694–1778), writer

'What I have become has almost nothing to do with Cornell, where, on the bad advice of my brother and my father, I was attempting and failing to become a biochemist....The advice I give myself at the age of 71 is the best advice I could have given myself in 1940, when detraining for the first time at [Cornell], "Keep your hat on. We may end up miles from here."'
Kurt Vonnegut, Jr. (b. 1922), novelist

'Success is to be measured not so much by the position that one has reached in life as by the obstacles which he has overcome while trying to succeed.'
Booker T. Washington (1856–1915), educator and writer

*T*ACTICS

Tactics are the often nasty underside of corporate life. They are the tricks and diversions which allow managers to achieve their ends. It is not that tactics are inherently underhanded, but their foundation is often greed, ambition or suspicion and cynicism. Hagar the Horrible, the font of much managerial wisdom, warned: 'As you journey through life take a minute every now and then to give a thought for the other fellow. He could be plotting something.' Plots and machinations abound.

'Not all brilliancy prizes go to dazzling attacks, sometimes sly, unpretentious subtlety wins.'
   Anon

'Tactics is what you do when there's something to do, strategy is what you do when there isn't.'
   Anon

'Choose your friends carefully. Your enemies will choose you.'
   Yasir Arafat (b. 1929), Palestinian leader

'We often get in quicker by the back door than by the front.'
   Napoléon Bonaparte (1769–1821), French General and gate crasher

'To chop a tree quickly, spend twice the time sharpening your axe.'
   Chinese proverb

'Never give a sucker an even break.'
   WC Fields (1880–1946), American comedian

'Attempt easy tasks as if they were difficult, and difficult as if they were easy: in the one case that confidence may not fall asleep, in the other that it may not be dismayed.'
   Baltasar Graci·n (1601–58), Spanish priest and writer

'Strategy is revolution; everything else is tactics.'
  Gary Hamel (b. 1954), consultant and author

'The best armor is to keep out of range.'
  Italian proverb

'A man who is always ready to believe what is told him will never do well, especially a businessman.'
  Gaius Petronius (first century AD), court writer

'In baiting a mousetrap with cheese, always leave room for the mouse.'
  Saki (1870–1916), master of the short story

'Keep your friends close, but keep your enemies closer.'
  Sicilian proverb

'Divide the fire, and you will the sooner put it out.'
  Publilius Syrus (c. 42 BC)

'It pays to know the enemy – not least because at some time you may have the opportunity to turn him into a friend.'
  Margaret Thatcher (b. 1925), former British Prime Minister

'One arrow does not bring down two birds.'
  Turkish proverb

'For to win one hundred victories in one hundred battles is not the acme of skill. To subdue the enemy's forces without fighting is the summit of skill.'
  Sun-Tzu (500 BC), master tactician

'If you are near the enemy, make him believe you are far from him. If you are far from the enemy, make him believe you are near.'
  Sun-Tzu

TARGETS

The bane of many an executive's life are the targets which can appear to determine their very existence. Budgets have targets; projects have targets; careers have targets. There is no escape, though management jargon has done its best, with objectives, goals and aims now being virtually interchangeable with the demanding t-word.

'The impossible often has a kind of integrity which the merely improbable lacks.'
Douglas Adams (b. 1952), British writer and producer

'A budget is just a method of worrying before you spend money as well as afterwards.'
Anon

'A budget is a numerical check of your worst suspicions.'
Anon

'If there are obstacles, the shortest line between two points may be the crooked line.'
Bertolt Brecht (1898–1956), German dramatist

'A man without a goal is like a ship without a rudder.'
Thomas Carlyle (1795–1881), essayist

'If you cry "forward!" you must without fail make plain in which direction to go. Don't you see that if, without doing so, you call out the word to both a monk and revolutionary, they will go in directions precisely opposite?'
Anton Chekov (1860–1904), Russian writer

'If you aspire to the highest place, it is no disgrace to stop at the second, or even the third, place.'
Marcus Tullius Cicero (104–43 BC), Roman writer of *On Oratory*

'Begin with the end in mind.'
Stephen Covey (b. 1932), Mormon guru

'It is important than an aim never be defined in terms of activity or methods. It must always relate directly to how life is better for everyone...the aim of the system must be clear to everyone in the system. The aim must include plans for the future. The aim is a value judgement.'
W. Edwards Deming (1900–93), quality champion

'We aim above the mark to hit the mark.'
Ralph Waldo Emerson (1803–82), poet

'When you aim for perfection, you discover it's a moving target.'
George Fisher, American executive and head of Kodak

'Performance is your reality. Forget everything else.'
Harold Geneen (b. 1910), former ITT chief

'Set your goals high, and don't stop till you get there.'
Bo Jackson (b. 1962), American baseball and football player

'The mind's direction is more important than its progress.'
Joseph Joubert (1754–1824), French writer

'Setting a goal is not the main thing. It is deciding how you will go about achieving it and staying with that plan.'
Tom Landry, American football coach and commentator

'Establishing goals is all right if you don't let them deprive you of interesting detours.'
Doug Larson, cartoonist

'If your train's on the wrong track every station you come to is the wrong station.'
Bernard Malamud (1914–86), writer

'The person who makes a success of living is the one who sees his goal steadily and aims for it unswervingly. That is dedication.'
Cecil B. de Mille (1881–1959), epic filmmaker

'Reality is something you rise above.'
Liza Minnelli (b. 1946), actress and singer

'Don't bunt. Aim out of the ballpark.'
David Ogilvy (b. 1911), ad man turned guru

'Give me a stock clerk with a goal and I'll give you a man who will make history. Give me a man with no goals and I'll give you a stock clerk.'
JC Penney, businessman

'If you don't know where you are going, you will probably end up somewhere else.'
Laurence J. Peter (1919–90), author and academic

'To live only for some future goal is shallow. It's the sides of the mountain that sustain life, not the top.'
Robert M. Pirsig (b. 1928), novelist philosopher

'You have to erect a fence and say *Okay, scale this.*'
Linda Ronstadt (b. 1946), American singer

'What sets us against one another is not our aims – they all come to the same thing – but our methods, which are the fruit of our varied reasoning.'
Antoine de Saint-Exupéry (1900–40), writer and flier

'Whoever wants to reach a distant goal must take many small steps.'
__Helmut Schmidt (b. 1918), German politician__

'To be in hell is to drift; to be in heaven is to steer.'
George Bernard Shaw (1856–1950), playwright

'In the long run men hit only what they aim at.'
Henry David Thoreau (1817–62), American naturalist and writer

'A goal properly set is halfway reached.'
Zig Ziglar, improbably named American motivational speaker

'What you get by achieving your goals is not as important as what you become by achieving your goals.'
Zig Ziglar

TAXES AND DEATH

There are people (usually residents of California) who put their corpses into cold storage in the belief that a few packs of ice will assure mortality. Some people also try and avoid paying taxes. Both are wasting their time. The grim reaper is as sure as the nice man with a fistful of complex forms—or as Mr. Barkis says in *David Copperfield*, 'It was as true as taxes is. And nothing's truer than them.'

'The saddest summary of a life contains three descriptions: could have, might have and should have.'
   Anon

'No matter how rich you become, how famous or powerful, when you die the size of your funeral will still pretty much depend on the weather.'
   Anon

'The state is never so efficient as when it wants money.'
   Anthony Burgess (1917–93), novelist

'Why do we want organizations to thrive forever? On average, organizations survive for less time than the working life of an individual. They become dysfunctional and, at that point, they should be killed off. What is encouraging is that, first through management buyouts and now through demergers, we are becoming more adept at bringing an end to corporate lives which have run their course and creating new organizations in their place.'
   Andrew Campbell (b. 1950), British academic

'Men pass away, but their deeds abide.'
   Augustin-Louis Cauchy (1789–1857)

'The only thing that hurts more than paying an income tax is not having to pay an income tax.'
   Thomas Robert Dewar (1864–1930)

'A billion here, a billion there, pretty soon it adds up to real money.'
Everett Dirksen (1896–1969), politician

'The hardest thing in the world to understand is the income tax.'
Albert Einstein (1879–1955), genius

'Every advantage has its tax.'
Ralph Waldo Emerson (1803–82), poet

'Only the little people pay taxes.'
Leona Helmsley (b. 1920?), hotel owner and prisoner

'The avoidance of taxes is the only intellectual pursuit that carries any reward.'
John Maynard Keynes (1883–1946), economist

'Unquestionably, there is progress. The average American now pays out twice as much in taxes as he formerly got in wages.'
HL Mencken (1880–1956), humorous writer

'Giving money and power to the government is like giving whiskey and car keys to teenage boys.'
PJ O'Rourke (b. 1947), acerbic American commentator

'The income tax has made liars out of more Americans than golf.'
Will Rogers (1879–1935), American comedian and showman

'If you make any money, the government shoves you in the creek once a year with it in your pockets, and all that don't get wet you can keep.'
Will Rogers

'Income tax returns are the most imaginative fiction being written today.'
Herman Wouk (b. 1915), novelist

TECHNOLOGY

'Technology: No Place For Wimps!' warns Dilbert, overturning the long-standing stereotype of techno-freaks and nerds. It may never be the manly thing – there are no action heroes running the computer giants – but it is imperative to embrace technology. Corporate luddites have a short shelf life at a time when the life cycle of technology becomes shorter by the day.

'Technology has replaced hot cars as the new symbol of robust manhood. Men know that unless they get a digital line to the Internet no woman is going to look at them twice.'
Scott Adams (b. 1957), cartoonist

'Automatic simply means that you can't repair it yourself.'
Anon

'Whatever the country, capitalist or socialist, man was everywhere crushed by technology, made a stranger to his own work, imprisoned, forced into stupidity.'
Simone de Beauvoir (1908–86), writer and feminist

'Any technology sufficiently advanced is indistinguishable from magic.'
Arthur C. Clarke (b. 1917), science fiction writer

'It was naive of nineteenth-century optimists to expect paradise from technology, and it is equally naive of twentieth-century pessimists to make technology the scapegoat for such old shortcomings as man's blindness, cruelty, immaturity, greed and sinful pride.'
Peter Drucker (b. 1909), management thinker and writer

'It has become appallingly obvious that our technology has exceeded our humanity.'
Albert Einstein (1879–1955), physicist and full-time genius

'Technology: the knack of so arranging the world that we don't have to experience it.'
Max Frisch (1911–91), Swiss writer

'The danger of the past was that men became slaves. The danger of the future is that men may become robots.'
Erich Fromm (1900–80), author of *The Sane Society*

'It is a commonplace of modern technology that there is a high measure of certainty that problems have solutions before there is knowledge of how they are to be solved.'
JK Galbraith (b. 1908), Canadian economist

'Customers have become very sceptical of the constant flood of new information technology. Customers are saying – give us technology we can manage, that is easy to use, that evolves at a reasonable pace and, most of all, helps us to achieve measurable competitive advantage.'
Lou Gerstner (b. 1942), IBM chief

'Business is about communications, sharing data and instantaneous decision making. If you have on your desk a device that enables you to communicate and share data with your colleagues around the world, you will have a strategic advantage.'
Andrew S. Grove (b. 1936), chip-maker and managerial thinker

'With telephone and TV it is not so much the message as the sender that is sent.'
Marshall McLuhan (1911–80), Canadian sociologist and commentator

'Technocrats are deadly when they're in charge.'
Henry Mintzberg (b. 1939), Canadian management thinker

'Technology presumes there's just one right way to do things and there never is.'
Robert M. Pirsig (b. 1928), novelist and philosopher

'Sometimes you might think the machines we worship make all the chief appointments, promoting the human beings who seem closest to them.'
JB Priestley (1894–1984), British dramatist

'We cannot get grace from gadgets. In the bakelite house of the future, the dishes may not break, but the heart can.'
JB Priestley

'Technology is dominated by two types of people: those who understand what they do not manage, and those who mange what they do not understand.'
Putt's law

'The machine does not isolate man from the great problems of nature but plunges him more deeply into them.'
Antoine de Saint-Exupéry (1900–44), French flier and writer

'The machine yes the machine
never wastes anybody's time
never watches the foreman
never talks back.'
Carl Sandburg (1878–1967), American poet

'Measuring managerial productivity is the key to knowing how to invest in information technologies. Improve management before you systemize or automate. Make management more productive, by electronic means, if you know where, when and how. Automate success, not failure.'
Paul A. Strassmann (b. 1929), American executive and educator

'Those who live by electronics die by electronics. *Sic semper tyrannis.*'
Kurt Vonnegut (b. 1922), American novelist

*T*HEORY AND THINKING

> Management is a young discipline which has spawned an unhealthily large number of theories. This is ironic. Management is action-oriented and yet knee-deep in theoretical mire. It has more theories than economics and yet remains as mysterious as psychology. Theories are neat and alluring. There are believers aplenty; but where are the practitioners?

'If human beings don't keep exercising their lips, he thought, their mouths probably seize up. After a few months' consideration and observation he abandoned this theory in favor of a new one. If they don't keep on exercising their lips, he thought, their brains start working.'

Douglas Adams (b. 1952), writer and producer

> *'All great theorems were discovered after midnight.'*
> ***Anon***

'To think is to say no.'

Anon

'Our life is what our thoughts make it.'

Marcus Aurelius Antonius (121–80), Roman Emperor and philosopher

'In theory there is no difference between theory and practice. In practice there is.'

Yogi Berra (b. 1925), baseball player and pontificator

'Brain: an apparatus with which we think we think.'

Ambrose Bierce (1842–1914), journalist and writer

'Don't think. Thinking is the enemy of creativity. It's self-conscious and anything self-conscious is lousy. You can't try to do things. You simply must do things.'

Ray Bradbury (b. 1920), writer

'Your theory is crazy, but it's not crazy enough to be true.'
   Bertolt Brecht (1898–1956), German dramatist

'A public opinion poll is no substitute for thought.'
   Warren Buffet (b. 1930), legendary investor

'A thing may look specious in theory, and yet be ruinous in practice; a thing may look evil in theory, and yet be in practice excellent.'
   Edmund Burke (1729–97), statesman and writer

'Remember happiness doesn't depend upon who you are or what you have; it depends solely on what you think.'
   Dale Carnegie (1888–1965), writer and motivator

'I think; therefore I am.'
   René Descartes (1595–1650), philosopher

'It is a capital mistake to theorize before one has data.'
   Sir Arthur Conan Doyle (1859–1930), creator of Sherlock Holmes

'All the great business builders we know of – from the Medici of Renaissance Florence and the founders of the Bank of England in the late seventeenth century down to IBM's Thomas Watson in our day – had a clear theory of the business which informed all their actions and decisions.'
   Peter Drucker (b. 1909), writer and thinker

'The only thing worse than slavishly following management theory is ignoring it completely.'
   The Economist

'It is the theory that decides what we can observe.'
   Albert Einstein (1879–1955), physicist

'Thinking is the hardest work there is, which is probably the reason so few engage in it.'
   Henry Ford (1863–1947), automobile manufacturer

'Thought is action in rehearsal.'
   Sigmund Freud (1856–1939), psychoanalyst

'The conventional view serves to protect us from the painful job of thinking.'
 JK Galbraith (b. 1908), economist

'Those that think must govern those that toil.'
 Oliver Goldsmith (1730?–74), Irish-born writer

'Thought is the wind, knowledge the sail, and mankind the vessel.'
 August Hare (1792–1834), writer

'There is no ultimate theory of the universe, just an infinite sequence of theories that describe the universe more and more accurately.'
 Stephen Hawking (b. 1942), scientist and best-selling author

'A moment's thinking is an hour in words.'
 Thomas Hood (1799–1845), poet

'A theory is no more like a fact than a photograph is like a person.'
 Edgar Watson Howe (1853–1937), American writer

'To meditate is to labor; to think is to act.'
 Victor Hugo (1802–85), French writer

'A great many people think they are thinking when they are merely rearranging their prejudices.'
 William James (1842–1910), psychologist and philosopher

'Ideas shape the course of history.'
 John Maynard Keynes (1883–1946), economist

'Practical men, who believe themselves to be quite exempt from any intellectual influences, are usually the slaves of some defunct economist. Madmen in authority, who hear voices in the air, are distilling their frenzy from some academic scribbler of a few years back.'
 John Maynard Keynes

'Nothing is so practical as a good theory.'
 Kurt Lewin (1890–1947), psychologist

'The majority of businessmen are incapable of original thought because they are unable to escape from the tyranny of reason.'
  David Ogilvy (b. 1911), ad man

'There is no expedient to which man will not resort to avoid the real labor of thinking.'
  Sir Joshua Reynolds (1723–92), painter

'Most people would sooner die than think; in fact, they do so.'
  Bertrand Russell (1872–1970), mathematician and philosopher

'However much thou art read in theory, if thou hast no practice thou art ignorant.'
  Sa'di (1184–1291), Persian poet

'Theory helps us to bear our ignorance of facts.'
  George Santayana (1863–1952), philosophical Spaniard

'Few people think more than two or three times a year. I have made an international reputation for myself by thinking once or twice a week.'
  George Bernard Shaw (1856–1950), dramatist

'It is better to emit a scream in the shape of a theory than to be entirely insensible to the jars and incongruities of life and take everything as it comes in a forlorn stupidity.'
  Robert Louis Stevenson (1850–94), novelist

'Thinking is work. In the early stages of a man's career it is very hard work. When a difficult decision or problem arises, how easy it is, after looking at it superficially, to give up thinking about it. It is easy to put it from one's mind. It is easy to decide that it is insoluble, or that something will turn up to help us. The more one does it the more one is unfitted to think a problem though to a proper conclusion.'
  Lord Thomson of Fleet (1894–1976), Canadian entrepreneur and publisher

'If one wants to be successful, one must think; one must think until it hurts. One must worry a problem in one's mind until it seems there cannot be another aspect of it that hasn't been considered.'
   Lord Thomson of Fleet

'He who loves practice without theory is like the sailor who boards ship without a rudder and compass and never knows where he may cast.'
   Leonardo da Vinci (1452–1519), Renaissance man

'The real contribution of improved machines and methods is to relieve thinkers from routine operations, giving them more time to think.'
   Thomas Watson, Sr. (1874–1956), IBM founder

'Most managers get into trouble because they forget to think in circles.'
   Karl Weick, cryptic academic

TIME MANAGEMENT

> Managers are great enthusiasts about managing their time well. They buy diaries with intricate breakdowns of every minute of the day. They buy personal organizers and color-coded wall charts which give a breakdown of how much time they spend on different aspects of their job. And then, having assembled this array of gimmicks (and attended a course on the subject), they continue to fill their days with needless meetings.

'I love deadlines. I like the whooshing sound they make as they fly by.'
Douglas Adams (b. 1952), writer and producer

'If you don't have time to do it right you must have time to do it over.'
Anon

'When you have a number of disagreeable duties to perform, always do the most disagreeable first.'
Anon

> *'If it weren't for the last minute, nothing would get done.'*
> ***Anon***

'To choose time is to save time.'
Francis Bacon (1561–1626), Elizabethan writer and thinker

'I believe the twenty-four hour day has come to stay.'
Max Beerbohm (1872–1956), essayist and caricaturist

'The ruins of Time build mansions in Eternity.'
William Blake (1757–1827), poet and artist

'You have to pick the things you can influence, and get out of the way for the rest.'
Larry Bossidy (b. 1935), Allied Signal boss

'Never do today what you can put off till tomorrow. Delay may give clearer light as to what is best to be done.'
   Aaron Burr (1756–1836), politician

'Don't be afraid to give your best to what seemingly are small jobs. Every time you conquer one it makes you that much stronger. If you do the little jobs well, the big ones will tend to take care of themselves.'
   Dale Carnegie (1888–1955), self-improvement author

'There is time enough for everything in the course of the day if you do but one thing at once; but there is not time enough in the year if you will do two things at a time.'
   Lord Chesterfield (1694–1773), statesman

'Know the true value of time; snatch, seize, and enjoy every moment of it. No idleness; no laziness; no procrastination: Never put off till tomorrow what you can do today.'
   Lord Chesterfield

'One never notices what has been done; one can only see what remains to be done.'
   Marie Curie (1867–1934), Polish-born chemist

'What is the major problem? It is fundamentally the confusion between effectiveness and efficiency that stands between doing the right things and doing things right. There is surely nothing quite so useless as doing with great efficiency what should not be done at all.'
   Peter Drucker (b. 1909), management theorist and writer

'Time waste differs from material waste in that there can be no salvage.'
   Henry Ford (1863–1947), automobile manufacturer

'Remember that time is money.'
   Benjamin Franklin (1706–90), statesman, inventor and writer

'Who begins too much accomplishes little.'
   German proverb

'If you want work done well, select a busy man – the other kind has no time.'
Elbert Hubbard (1856–1915), American author

'Time flies like an arrow, fruit flies like a banana.'
Groucho Marx (1890–1977), comedian

'For tribal man space was the uncontrollable mystery. For technological man it is time that occupies the same role.'
Marshall McLuhan (1911–80), Canadian critic and commentator

'Work expands so as to fill the time available for its completion.'
C. Northcote Parkinson (1909–93), academic and author

'We're in such a hurry most of the time we never get a chance to talk. The result is a kind of endless day-to-day shallowness, a monotony that leaves a person wondering years later where all the time went and sorry that it's all gone.'
Robert M. Pirsig (b. 1928), novelist and philosopher

'So little done, so much to do.'
Cecil Rhodes (1853–1902), statesman

'Both in thought and in feeling, even though time be real, to realize the unimportance of time is the gate of wisdom.'
Bertrand Russell (1872–1970), mathematician and philosopher

'To do two things at once is to do neither.'
Publilius Syrus (42 BC), Latin writer

'Hardly a competent workman can be found who does not devote a considerable amount of time to studying just how slowly he can work and still convince his employer that he is going at a good pace.'
Frederick W. Taylor (1856–1917), creator of Scientific Management

'Our costliest expenditure is time.'
Theophrastus (370–287 BC), Greek writer and philosopher

'Time moves slowly, but passes quickly.'
Alice Walker (b. 1944), author of *The Color Purple*

'Punctuality is the virtue of the bored.'
Evelyn Waugh (1903–66), writer

'Anywhere is walking distance, if you've got the time.'
Steven Wright, comedian

'A composer's job involves the decoration of fragments of time. Without music to decorate it, time is just a bunch of boring production deadlines or dates by which bills must be paid.'
Frank Zappa (1940–93), musician

TOUGH TALKING

Talking tough comes naturally to some, especially when they reach the negotiating table. 'Here's the rule for bargains: do other men, for they would do you. That's the true business precept,' says Dickens' Jonas Chuzzlewit. Around the negotiation table bargains are often thin on the ground. In the tactical to and fro of offer and counter offer, any weakness is pounced upon, any shift is analyzed. When the talking gets tough, the tough probably aren't talking at all.

'Compromise is never anything but an ignoble truce between the duty of a man and the terror of a coward.'
   Anon

'Compromise is but the sacrifice of one right or good in the hope of retaining another – too often ending in the loss of both.'
   Anon

'What are facts but compromises? A fact merely marks the point where we have agreed to let investigation cease.'
   Anon

'We know what happens to people who stay in the middle of the road. They get run over.'
   Aneurin Bevan (1897–1960), legendary Labour politician

'Compromise. Such an adjustment of conflicting interests as gives each adversary the satisfaction of thinking he has got what he ought not to have, and is deprived of nothing except what was justly his due.'
   Ambrose Bierce (1842–1914), journalist and writer

'The concessions of the weak are the concessions of fear.'
   Edmund Burke (1729–97), statesman and writer

'Concentration is my motto – first honesty, then industry, then concentration.'

Andrew Carnegie (1835–1919), industrialist

'Compromise used to mean that half a loaf was better than no bread. Among modern statesmen it really seems to mean that half a loaf is better than a whole loaf.'

GK Chesterton (1874–1936), writer

'An appeaser is one who feeds a crocodile – hoping it will eat him last.'

Sir Winston Churchill (1874–1965), statesman and purveyor of quotes

'The English never draw a line without blurring it.'
Sir Winston Churchill

'Never hold discussions with the monkey when the organ grinder is in the room.'

Sir Winston Churchill

'Jaw-jaw is better than war-war.'

Sir Winston Churchill

'If you are not very clever, you should be conciliatory.'

Benjamin Disraeli (1804–81), statesman and writer

'If you never budge, don't expect a push.'

Malcolm S. Forbes (1919–90), publisher

'Necessity never made a good bargain.'

Benjamin Franklin (1706–90), writer, statesman, inventor and more

'It is the weak man who urges compromise – never the strong man.'

Elbert Hubbard (1856–1915), American author who sank with the Lusitania

'Let us never negotiate out of fear, but let us never fear to negotiate.'

John F. Kennedy (1917–63), 35th American President

'If one cannot catch a bird of paradise, better take a wet hen.'
Nikita Khrushchev (1894–1971), Russian politician

'A bluff taken seriously is more useful than a serious threat interpreted as a bluff.'
Henry Kissinger (b. 1923), politician

'Compromise makes a good umbrella but a poor roof.'
James Russell Lowell (1819–91), writer

'Only free men can negotiate. Prisoners cannot enter into contracts.'
Nelson Mandela (b. 1918), South African President

'Better bend than break.'
Scottish proverb

'The timid man yearns for full value and demands a tenth. The bold man strikes for double value and compromises on par.'
Mark Twain (1835–1910), novelist

'When money is at stake, never be the first to mention sums.'
Sheikh Ahmed Yamani (b. 1930), oil minister

TRUTH AND LIES

> The honor involved in business has always been of a somewhat murky sort. When does a subtle misrepresentation of the facts become an outright lie? When are the sales figures true and untrue? Is the advertising campaign fraudulent if it fails to tell the whole truth? Around such truths and lies, the manager tiptoes and dashes every day of his working life.

'One falsehood spoils a thousand truths.'
Ashanti proverb

'A truth that's told with bad intent beats all the lies you can invent.'
William Blake (1757–1827), poet and artist

'The opposite of a correct statement is a false statement. But the opposite of a profound truth may well be another profound truth.'
Niels Bohrs (1885–1962), physicist

'Men occasionally stumble over the truth, but most of them pick themselves up and hurry off as if nothing had happened.'
Sir Winston Churchill (1874–1965), statesman

'Falsehood is the jockey of misfortune.'
Jean Giraudoux (1882–1944), French writer and diplomat

'I don't want yes-men around me. I want everybody to tell me the truth even if it costs them their jobs.'
Samuel Goldwyn (1882–1974), filmmaker

'Let's start with the truth and work back.'
Gerry Griffin (b. 1966), communications director

'It is always the best policy to tell the truth, unless, of course, you are an exceptionally good liar.'
Jerome K. Jerome (1859–1927), Thames-inspired writer

'In order that all men may be taught to speak truth, it is necessary that all likewise should learn to hear it.'
  Dr. Samuel Johnson (1709–84), man of his words

'If you don't tell the truth you can end up with a pile of bodies in a sea of blood.'
  Alexander Lebed, Russian politican

'It is hard to believe that a man is telling the truth when you know that you would lie if you were in his place.'
  HL Mencken (1880–1956), journalist and writer

'Truth does not lead to fortune.'
  Jean-Jacques Rousseau (1712–78), philosopher

'Of course, it's the same old story. Truth usually is the same old story.'
  Margaret Thatcher (b. 1925), politician

'It takes two to speak the truth – one to speak, and another to hear.'
  Henry David Thoreau (1817–62), naturalist and writer

'Tell the truth and so puzzle and confound your adversaries.'
  Sir Henry Wootton (1568–1639), poet and diplomat

VISION

The vision thing has haunted managers as well as George Bush, who searched elusively for it. The cliché is that great leaders have an all-encompassing, powerful vision which motivates their followers. This image is colorful and attractive, but usually bears little relevance to the factory floor. More worrying is the biblical observation from the Book of Revelation that 'Where there is no vision, the people perish.'

'I may not have gone where I intended to go, but I think I have ended up where I intended to be.'
Douglas Adams (b. 1952), writer and producer

'The whole world steps aside for the man who knows where he is going.'
Anon

'Everyone takes the limits of his own vision for the limits of the world.'
Anon

'You got to be careful if you don't know where you're going, because you might not get there.'
Yogi Berra (b. 1925), baseball player, coach and manager

'Aim for the highest.'
Andrew Carnegie (1835–1919), industrialist

'The farther back you can look, the farther forward you are likely to see.'
Sir Winston Churchill (1874–1965), statesman

'The best vision is insight.'
__Malcolm S. Forbes (1919–90), publisher__

'Vision is free. And it's therefore not a competitive advantage any way, shape or form.'
Bill Gates (b. 1955), computer buff

'The last thing IBM needs now is a vision.'
   Lou Gerstner (b. 1942), IBM chief, as he takes over

'We need a fresh vision of business enterprise. In a society that has become predominantly urban and suburban we need a form of work organization and a work ethic, that offers men and women a certain scope, a certain dignity and freedom, and not just an existence.'
   George Godyer, British executive

'One never goes so far as when one doesn't know where one is going.'
   Johann Wolfgang von Goethe (1749–1832), German writer

'The last little secret of vision is that ultimately it's in the eye of the beholder, and almost always after the fact...we rarely recognise a leader as having a vision until it has been proven true.'
   Walter Kiechel III, editor of *Fortune*

'A vision goes beyond the numbers that are typically found in five-year plans...It says something that helps clarify the direction in which an organization needs to move.'
   John Kotter (b. 1947), Harvard Business School guru

'The trouble with our age is that it is all signpost and no destination.'
   Louis Kronenberger (b. 1904), writer and educator

'Many of the great strategies are simply great visions. And great visions can be a lot more inspirational and effective than the most carefully constructed plan. Only when we recognize our fantasies can we begin to appreciate the wonders of reality.'
   Henry Mintzberg (b. 1939), Canadian academic and author

'A man to carry on a successful business must have imagination. He must see things in a vision, a dream of the whole thing.'
   Charles M. Schwab (1862–1939), American steel magnate, first president of U.S. Steel

'Vision is the art of seeing things invisible.'
   Jonathan Swift (1667–1745), writer

'Good business leaders create a vision, articulate the vision, passionately own the vision, and relentlessly drive it to completion.'
Jack Welch (b. 1935), General Electric chief

'No man that does not see visions will ever realize any high hope or undertake any high enterprise.'
Woodrow Wilson (1856–1924), 28th American President

WINNING AND LOSING

> Successful businesspeople enjoy winning. Indeed, some are obsessed with winning. They are unable to come to terms with defeat no matter where it may occur. Losing a set at tennis is regarded as a deadly assault; a game of backgammon is played with the same intensity as one of Russian roulette; a casual kick around becomes the cup final. It is highly pleasurable to beat such people. But, in enjoying their abject misery, you are simply proving that you need to win a much as they do.

'Always imitate the behavior of winners when you lose.'
   Anon

'In a game, just losing is almost as satisfying as just winning ... In life the loser's score is always zero.'
   WH Auden (1907–73), British poet

'It is not products, but the processes that create products that bring companies long-term success. Good products don't make winners; winners make good products.'
   James Champy and Michael Hammer (b. 1948), consultants and authors

'Think win–win.'
   Stephen Covey (b. 1932), Mormon man with a managerial mission

'What we need to do is learn to work in the system, by which I mean that everybody, every team, every platform, every division, every component is there not for individual competitive profit or recognition, but for contribution to the system as a whole on a win-win basis.'
   W. Edwards Deming (1900–93), American-born quality guru celebrated in Japan

'Contrary to the cliché, genuinely nice guys often finish first or very near it.'
Malcolm S. Forbes (1919–90), publisher

'He may well win the race that runs by himself.'
Benjamin Franklin (1706–90), American inventor, writer and statesman

'Only one firm can be the industry leader, only one country top economically, there are always richer or more successful neighbors to compare ourselves with. Competition is healthy, maybe even essential, but there has to be more to life than winning or we should nearly all be losers.'
Charles Handy (b. 1932), best-selling author

'Sure the game is rigged, but if you don't play you can't win.'
Robert Heinlein (1907–88), American writer

'There's nothing to winning, really. That is, if you happen to be blessed with a keen eye, an agile mind and no scruples whatsoever.'
Alfred Hitchcock (1899–1980), filmmaker

'You're never as good as everyone tells you when you win, and you're never as bad as they say when you lose.'
Lou Holtz (b. 1937), American football coach

'The will to win is not nearly as important as the will to prepare to win.'
Bobby Knight (b. 1940), basketball coach

'Pick battles big enough to matter, small enough to win.'
Jonathan Kozol (b. 1936), American author

'You must be present to win.'
Las Vegas casino sign

'It's easy to have faith in yourself and have discipline when you're a winner, when you're number one. What you've got to have is faith and discipline when you're not a winner.'
Vince Lombardi (1913–70), legendary American football coach

'If winning isn't everything, why do they keep the score?'
Vince Lombardi

'Winning isn't everything – it's the only thing.'
Vince Lombardi

'Winning is not everything – but making the effort to win is.'
Vince Lombardi

'The probability of winning is inversely proportional to the amount of the wager.'
McGoon's Law

'If you don't try to win you might as well hold the Olympics in somebody's back yard.'
Jesse Owens (1913–80), athlete

'There are two sorts of losers – the good loser, and the other one who can't act.'
Laurence J. Peter (1919–90), creator of the Peter Principle

'First we will be best, and then we will be first.'
Grant Tinker (b. 1926), U.S. television executive

'Most of us miss out on life's big prizes. The Pulitzer. The Nobel. Oscars. Tonys. Emmys. But we're all eligible for life's small pleasures. A pat on the back. A kiss behind the ear. A four-pound bass. A full moon. An empty parking space. A crackling fire. A great meal. A glorious sunset. Hot soup. Cold beer. Don't fret about copping life's grand awards. Enjoy its tiny delights. There are plenty for all of us.'
United Technologies Corporation advertisement

'*Next to* I win, I told you so *are the sweetest words.*'
Gore Vidal (b. 1929), novelist

'No man can lose what he never had.'
Izaak Walton (1593–1683), author of *The Compleat Angler*

*W*OMEN AND MEN

'Behind every successful man stands a surprised woman,' said Maryon Pearson, wife of the Canadian Prime Minister. But, behind every successful woman stands an extremely surprised man. Despite initiatives of various sorts, the number of female senior executives remains minuscule.

'We still think of a powerful man as a born leader and a powerful woman as an anomaly.'
Margaret Atwood (b. 1939), novelist

'Male: *n.* A member of the unconsidered, or negligible sex. The male of the human race is commonly known (to the female) as Mere Man. The genus has two varieties: good providers and bad providers.'
Ambrose Bierce (1842–1914), journalist and writer

'The economic victims of the era are men who know someone has made off with their future – and they suspect the thief is a woman.'
Anon

'Women who seek to be equal with men lack ambition.'
Timothy Leary (1920–97), psychologist

'Men are made to be managed and women are born managers.'
George Meredith (1828–1909), poet

'If women didn't exist, all the money in the world would have no meaning.'
Aristotle Onassis (1906–75), Greek shipping tycoon

'A man who has no office to go to – I don't care who he is – is a trial of which you can have no conception.'
George Bernard Shaw (1856–1950), Irish-born dramatist

'It is not the glass ceiling that holds women back from rising high, it is the children hanging on to their hems.'
Polly Toynbee (b. 1946), British journalist

WORK

Hard work brings prosperity, playing around brings poverty, notes the Bible. This, for the most part, is the final word on work. Work is good. You may not enjoy it. You may not find it spiritually uplifting. But, it brings in the money and without that, well …

'Work is a four letter word.'
   Anon

'Don't condescend to unskilled labor. Try it for a half a day first.'
   Anon

'All paid jobs absorb and degrade the mind.'
   Aristotle (384–322 BC), Greek philosopher

'In order that people may be happy in their work, these three things are needed: They must be fit for it; they must not do too much of it; and they must have a sense of success in it – not a doubtful sense, such as needs some testimony of others for its confirmation, but a sure sense, rather knowledge that so much work has been done well and fruitfully done, whatever the world may say or think about it.'
   WH Auden (1907–73), British poet

'I am afraid that the pleasantness of an employment does not always evince its propriety.'
   Jane Austen (1775–1817), novelist

'It is not real work unless you would rather be doing something else.'
   Sir James Barrie (1860–1937), dramatist and novelist

'It is necessary to work, if not from inclination, at least from despair. Everything considered, work is less boring than amusing oneself.'
   Charles Baudelaire (1821–67), poet

'Work would be terribly boring if one did not play the game all out, passionately.'
Simone de Beauvoir (1908–86), writer and feminist

'Work is not the curse, but drudgery is.'
Henry Ward Beecher (1813–87), clergyman and abolitionist

'A man's work is rather the needful supplement to himself than the outcome of it.'
Max Beerbohm (1872–1956), cartoonist and essayist

'No fine work can be done without concentration and self-sacrifice and toil and doubt.'
Max Beerbohm, essayist and caricaturist

'Anyone can do any amount of work provided it isn't the work he is supposed to be doing.'
Robert Benchley (1889–1945), humorist, actor and scriptwriter

'After all, it is hard to master both life and work equally well. So if you are bound to fake one of them, it had better be life.'
Joseph Brodsky (1940–96), Russian-born poet

'If you want a place in the sun you've got to put up with a few blisters.'
Abigail van Buren (b. 1918), American writer

'A man willing to work, and unable for find work, is perhaps the saddest sight that fortune's inequality exhibits under this sun.'
Thomas Carlyle (1795–1881), essayist

'A man is a worker. If he is not that he is nothing.'
__Joseph Conrad (1857–1924), novelist__

'All growth depends upon activity. There is no development physically or intellectually without effort and effort means work.'
Calvin Coolidge (1872–1933), 30th President

'People might not get all they work for in this world, but they must certainly work for all they get.'
Frederick Douglass (1817–95), American journalist and campaigner

'Work is victory.'
Ralph Waldo Emerson (1803–82), poet

'Toil, says the proverb, is the sire of fame.'
__Euripides (484–406 BC), Greek tragedian__

'It's a shame that the only thing a man can do for eight hours a day is work. He can't eat for eight hours; he can't drink for eight hours; he can't make love for eight hours. The only thing a man can do for eight hours is work.'
William Faulkner (1897–1962), novelist

'Work is the meat of life, pleasure the dessert.'
BC Forbes (1880–1954), publisher

'There is joy in work. There is no happiness except in the realization that we have accomplished something.'
Henry Ford (1863–1947), auto manufacturer

'He that hath a trade hath an estate; he that hath a calling hath an office of profit and honor.'
Benjamin Franklin (1706–90), statesman and writer

'It is the working man who is the happy man. It is the idle man who is the miserable man.'
Benjamin Franklin

'The world is filled with willing people; some willing to work, the rest willing to let them.'
Robert Frost (1874–1963), poet

'Work is love made visible.'
Kahlil Gibran (1883–1931), Syrian-born poet and artist

'All work is empty save when there is love.'
Kahlil Gibran

'When work is a pleasure, life is a joy! When work is a duty, life is slavery.'
Maxim Gorky (1868–1936), Russian writer

'Unless the concepts of work and play and reward for work change absolutely, women must continue to provide cheap labor, and even more, free labor exacted of right by an employer possessed of a contract for life, made out in his favor.'
Germaine Greer (b. 1939), feminist writer

'Work is more than a job. In the past, business was the employer of all those who wanted to work. In the future there will be lots of customers, but not lots of jobs.'
Charles Handy (b. 1932), British management thinker

'Some have work and money but too little time, while others have all the time but no work and no money. Those with the privilege of idleness see it as a curse because they tend to be at the bottom, not the top, of the heap. We seem to have made work into a god and then made it difficult for many to worship.'
Charles Handy

'Work is society's chosen way of distributing income.'
Charles Handy

'I like work; it fascinates me. I can sit and look at it for hours. I love to keep it by me. The idea of getting rid of it nearly breaks my heart.'
Jerome K. Jerome (1859–1927), idler

'I think that we have to appreciate that we're alive for only a limited period of time, and we'll spend most of our lives working. That being the case, I believe one of the most important priorities is to do whatever we do as well as we can. We should take pride in that.'
Victor Kiam (b. 1926), businessman

'While you're negotiating for a 35 hour week, remember they have only just got 66 hours in Taiwan, and you're competing with Taiwan.'
Victor Kiam

'Why should I let the toad work squat on my life?
Can't I use my wit as a pitchfork
And drive the brute off?'
Philip Larkin (1922–85), British poet

'Work is life, you know, and without it there's nothing but fear and insecurity.'
John Lennon (1940–80), Beatle

'My father taught me to work; he did not teach me to love it.'
Abraham Lincoln (1809–65), American President

'To work – to work! It is such infinite delight to know that we still have the best things to do.'
Katherine Mansfield (1888–1923), New Zealand-born writer

'We do what we are and we are what we do.'
Abraham Maslow (1908–70), motivational theorist

'One still works because work is a form of entertainment. But one is careful lest the entertainment be too harrowing.'
Friedrich Nietzsche (1844–1900), philosopher

'Hard work never killed a man. Men die of boredom, psychological conflict and disease. Indeed the harder your people work, the happier and healthier they will be.'
David Ogilvy (b. 1911), founder of Ogilvy & Mather advertising agency

'Work expands so as to fill the time available for its completion. General recognition of this fact is shown in the proverbial phrase *It is the busiest man who has time to spare.*'
C. Northcote Parkinson (1909–93), academic and author

'A pint of sweat saves a gallon of blood.'
General George S. Patton (1885–1945), soldier

'Far and away the best prize that life has to offer is the chance to work hard at work worth doing.'
Theodore Roosevelt (1858–1919), American President

'It is too difficult to think nobly when one thinks only of earning a living.'
Jean-Jacques Rousseau (1712–78), French philosopher

'The highest reward for a man's toil is not what he gets for it, but what he becomes.'
John Ruskin (1819–1900), critic and writer

'Work is of two kinds: first, altering the position of matter at or near the earth's surface relative to other such matter; second, telling other people to do so. The first kind is unpleasant and ill-paid; the second is pleasant and highly paid.'
Bertrand Russell (1872–1970), philosopher and mathematician

'The man who does not work for the love of work but only for money is not likely to make money nor find much fun in life.'
Charles M. Schwab (1862–1939), first President of U.S. Steel

'I do not like work even when someone else does it.'
Mark Twain (1835–1910), novelist

'Intellectual work is misnamed; it is a pleasure, a dissipation, and is its own highest reward.'
Mark Twain

'Work spares us from three great evils: boredom, vice, and need.'
Voltaire (1694–1778), French philosopher and writer

'I suppose I have a really loose interpretation of *work* because I think that just being alive is so much work at something you don't always want to do.'
Andy Warhol (1928–87), pop artist

'Work is the curse of the drinking classes.'
Oscar Wilde (1854–1900), hardworking playwright

THE ENDS ... AND MEANS

'When we deliberate it is about means and not ends.'
   Aristotle

'The first sign of corruption in a society that is still alive is that the end justifies the means.'
   Georges Bernanos

'Wealth is the means, and people are the ends.
All our material riches will avail us little if
we do not use them to expand the opportunities of our people.'
   John F. Kennedy

'Modern man – whether in the womb of the masses, or with his workmates, or with his family, or alone – can never for one moment forget that he is living in a world in which he is a means and whose end is not his business.'
   Alberto Moravia

'To say that profit is a mean to other ends and not an end in itself is not a semantic quibble, it is a serious moral point. A requirement is not a purpose. In everyday life those who make the means into ends are usually called neurotic or obsessive.'
   Charles Handy

'What is there more of in the world than anything else? Ends.'
   Carl Sandburg

INDEX OF CONTRIBUTORS